CELEBRITY

CRITICAL CULTURAL COMMUNICATION

General Editors: Jonathan Gray, Aswin Punathambekar, Adrienne Shaw
Founding Editors: Sarah Banet-Weiser and Kent A. Ono

Celebrity

A History of Fame

Susan J. Douglas *and* Andrea McDonnell

NEW YORK UNIVERSITY PRESS

New York

NEW YORK UNIVERSITY PRESS
New York
www.nyupress.org

References to Internet websites (URLs) were accurate at the time of writing. Neither the author nor New York University Press is responsible for URLs that may have expired or changed since the manuscript was prepared.

Library of Congress Cataloging-in-Publication Data
Names: Douglas, Susan J. (Susan Jeanne), 1950– author. | McDonnell, Andrea M., author.
Title: Celebrity : a history of fame / Susan J. Douglas and Andrea McDonnell.
Description: New York : New York University Press, [2019] |
Includes bibliographical references and index.
Identifiers: LCCN 2018030568| ISBN 9781479852437 (cl : alk. paper) |
ISBN 9781479862030 (pb : alk. paper)
Subjects: LCSH: Celebrities. | Fame. | Social influence. | Social status. |
Mass media—Social aspects. | Popular culture.
Classification: LCC HM1176 .D68 2019 | DDC 302/.13—dc23
LC record available at https://lccn.loc.gov/2018030568

New York University Press books are printed on acid-free paper, and their binding materials are chosen for strength and durability. We strive to use environmentally responsible suppliers and materials to the greatest extent possible in publishing our books.

Manufactured in the United States of America

10 9 8 7 6 5 4 3 2 1

Also available as an ebook

For Paddy Scannell, teacher, scholar, mentor, friend

CONTENTS

Introduction

In the twenty-first century, celebrity culture and celebrity journalism are everywhere: they are inescapable fixtures in our media landscape and our everyday lives. Celebrity culture has become a central, dominant, and structuring force in American life, leading some to note that our society has become "celebritized" or "celebrified."[1] Whether you're standing in the checkout line at the supermarket or drugstore, checking your Facebook, Instagram, Snapchat, or Twitter feed, or, of course, simply turning on your TV, celebrities—the stories they tell, the stories about them—bombard us from every media outlet. The famous face is ubiquitous, it seems to spring up in every direction, an undeniable presence that surrounds and consumes us, as we consume it. While this is a revolution especially of the past twenty-five years, its origins go much farther back. This book provides an overview of that revolution, its repressed history, the underestimated cultural work it has done, its consequences, and especially the role that new communications technologies have played in enabling it.

Yes, of course, from Mary Pickford to Bette Davis to Marilyn Monroe, stars claimed the center stage of American life in the twentieth century. But in 1980, only 19.9 percent of homes had cable TV (and most cable companies only offered up to twelve channels), the celebrity magazines had not yet gone through their rapid, multiple mitoses, there was no reality TV that instantly manufactured stars, there were not yet celebrity chefs and celebrity chief executive officers, and there was no Internet or social media. Now we have all these. Thus, the status of celebrity culture and gossip has changed dramatically, especially since the early twenty-first century. Celebrity culture and gossip, except for truly major, high-profile romances or divorces (like those between superstars Elizabeth Taylor and Richard Burton in the 1960s and '70s), were seen as down-market, trashy, irrelevant fare that educated or respectable middle-class people should avoid. But today these are impossible to avoid and, more importantly, knowing about celebrities—at least some of them anyway—is now an often necessary part of one's cultural arsenal of knowledge. The tone has changed as well, especially with the multiplication of gossip magazines, blogs, and social media in the twenty-first century and their delight in scandal and often the derision of celebrities as well as the opportunity for us to feel closer to and even interact with those who are well known. What is the significance of all this, for us, and our society?

Celebrity culture today consists of four major building blocks: the celebrity, of course, the media, the public, and the celebrity production industry, which consists of managers, agents, promoters, and some elements of the media, from gossip magazines to Instagram. Celebrity itself has typically involved four elements: a person, some kind of achievement, subsequent publicity, and then what posterity has thought about them ever since.[2] Thus celebrity can be, of course, fleeting and banal: today's star could easily be tomorrow's has-been. But the *fact* of celebrity culture, its permanence and growth, the industry that supports it, the huge profits it generates, the distractions it provides—and promotes—these are no longer trivial. Celebrity gossip and culture used to be confined to fan magazines, a few tabloids, and certain TV talk shows. Now, celebrities and stories about them are everywhere, in the nightly news and in politics, on the covers of women's and public affairs magazines, on reality TV shows and multiple, proliferating TV talk shows, and especially on our smartphones. Indeed, the country's forty-fifth president was a former reality TV show star, who converted his status as a celebrity into political power. When what used to be more on the margins of the media becomes absolutely central to it, and thus to our culture, we need to understand how and why, and what the implications are for our society and for us as individuals.

What, then, do we mean when we speak of a celebrity and why they can matter so powerfully to so many people? *Celebrity* derives from the Latin root *celebrem*, which suggests that one is celebrated, but also *thronged*, flocked by a crowd.[3] Indeed, celebrities are persons who live their lives in the public eye; by definition, they are highly visible, known to many. Such mass visibility relies on and is made possible by the media; thus some have argued that celebrity is "essentially a media production."[4] More to the point, celebrity gives one a kind of capital, which accrues from "accumulated media visibility that results from re-current media representations."[5] Celebrities are enviable because they are given greater presence, a wider scope of agency and activity in the world; they are allowed to move on the public stage while others watch.[6] Celebrities are deferred to as unique, entitled individuals: they go to the head of the line, or don't have to stand in one at all; they rise above the herd. They gain additional economic power by endorsing products and brands, and they are invited into expanded social networks, where they get to meet other powerful or famous people. Celebrity status confers upon a person not only economic power but also a certain discursive power. Celebrities have a voice above others—a voice that is legitimately significant. If an ordinary person seeks to bring attention to a national or international problem, few listen. When Oprah or George Clooney or Selena Gomez do or say something, they get a national and even inter-national platform, and so the celebrity capital they possess can be con-verted into other kinds of capital—political, philanthropic, and the like.[7] As the Harvey Weinstein scandals and #metoo movement dramatized, celebrity voices can bring attention to problems that have vexed every-day people for decades, in this case sexual harassment and misconduct.

What is the difference between fame and celebrity? Being a celebrity today of course means being well known. But in ancient and medieval times, one could indeed be famous—as a king, queen, or emperor, as a successful military leader—but not necessarily constantly visible. When identities and social roles were quite fixed by birth and social position, and demarcated, between peasants, artisans, the aristocracy, and then royalty, there was a line of authority from top to bottom, with those at the bottom rarely seeing those at the top. Fame was reserved for those rare people who were known because of their hereditary positions or extraordinary achievements; there was an aura around them; they were remote and inaccessible. As the historian Neal Gabler has noted, "In-deed, fame was less likely to be sought than imposed as a consequence of accomplishment or office. In effect, it was a mantle one wore, not something one chased."[8] So fame rested on distance, deference to great-ness (whether achieved or inherited), and often adoration. Compared to today there were very few outlets for widespread visibility. The prolifera-tion of media and communications technologies beginning in the nine-teenth century, especially those involving the mechanical reproduction of images like photography and film, changed all that and enabled the democratization of fame. The big change, as Gabler noted, is that now the whole point of being famous is visibility: "being seen on the right pages and at the right places with the right people. To hold yourself aloof seems pathological."

Today, some twenty-first-century celebrities, it is said, are famous simply for being famous. Scholars such as Leo Lowenthal argued that there exist different types of celebrities—some who are known for their hard work, talents, and achievements, and others who are infamous for their sensational lifestyles, scandals, and pure entertainment value.[9] Chris Rojek divided celebrity status into three categories: ascribed, meaning you were born into fame, like a member of a royal family or child of a celebrity; achieved, meaning you earned it through admired accomplishments; and attributed, which is a media-generated fame, such as a reality TV star or someone involved in a scandal.[10] Thus, while we may tend to think of celebrities as models of excellence—the smartest, fastest, and most beautiful, the most talented—they may also be models of scorn—the notorious, the wasteful, the failed. Still others consider them as mere irritants, purposeless chimeras.

Celebrity culture is not only about the hallowed few who find the spotlight—it is also, perhaps especially, about the fans who consume it and the pleasures we find in that consumption. We relish the escape, the fantasies of wealth, beauty, and deference, and the ability to feel superior to people who may have (or once had) "it all," but now have gained weight, married poorly, or truly embarrassed themselves in public. And the "behind-the-scenes" blogs and Twitter wars, with the supposed real dirt that exposes publicists' spin or gives a sense of being in the know, convey a sense of being able to rip open the curtains hiding the great and powerful Oz.

Celebrities are the conduits for our dreams—if they can do it, I can do it; I want to do what they get to do. Whatever the category of celebrity, these individuals offer up visions of potential; they serve as avatars who perform our dreams, and sometimes our nightmares. They warn us of what could be if we choose the wrong path. By publicly performing their own scandals and controversies, they serve as glitzy stand-ins for everyday issues of deep concern to people, from infidelity and divorce, to financial ruin, to illness and aging, and to broader social issues, like sexism, racism, and homophobia. Celebrity culture polices the boundaries of everyday behavior: what celebrities are praised for, we should emulate; what they are reviled for, we should spurn. They may give us hope for the future, warn us of what could be if we choose the wrong path, and even make us feel thankful for the ordinariness of our own lives. "Stars matter," as Richard Dyer writes, "because they act out aspects of life that matter to us."[11]

For these reasons, various scholars have argued that celebrities—and the industries that produce and maintain them—reinforce, or at times challenge, certain dominant cultural ideologies. Of course they embody standards of beauty, handsomeness, and an idealized body. They also help to create and sustain our dreams of upward mobility, especially in an era of increased inequality between the rich and everyone else. In this way, they can also even work to justify economic and social hierarchies. Some, like James Dean in the 1950s or Tom Cruise in the 1980s, functioned as models of male youthful rebellion or bravado, while Madonna in the 1980s and 1990s and Beyoncé in the 2010s were models of female strength, agency, and defiance of traditional constraints placed on women. In this way, celebrities and the narratives that circulate around them serve as "vessels," which perform and, in doing so, reveal the hopes and anxieties of the cultural moment in which they exist.[12]

But celebrities do not only reflect—or even come to alter—our cultural values; they also speak to our ideas about ourselves. The nature of celebrity, which claims to offer us public visions of private persons, may have a deep impact on the way in which we think and feel about our bodies, our relationships, and our very identities. Indeed, contemporary celebrity journalism obsessively tracks the personal, "private" lives of famous figures, chronicling (and critiquing) the minutiae of their lives, while inviting audiences to do the same. Twenty-first-century celebrity, therefore, combined with the explosion of social media, have been criticized for allegedly helping to foster a generation of narcissists, obsessed with publicly performing their lives (usually online) and willing to adopt for themselves the relentless judgment that accompanies such performances.[13]

With these critiques in mind, it may be easy to dismiss celebrities as consumerist booby traps, meant to suck us into purchasing the latest designer bag, fad diet, or ridiculously expensive pair of jeans. Or as mere distractions, simply deflecting attention away from current events and the depressing stream of stories that dominate the evening news. Or as trivialities, social climbers grasping for Andy Warhol's infamous fifteen minutes of fame, perhaps snagging only six or seven in today's frantic media economy. You would not, of course, be wrong. Yet these are some of the very reasons that celebrities deserve our attention. The story of celebrity is the story of our cultural experience, particularly in our contemporary society where they dominate our popular culture. The mechanisms by which individuals become famous, the ideological visions that celebrities represent and communicate, the reasons why "ordinary" people are attracted to stars, and the influence that this cycle of production and consumption has on our culture is profound, growing, and worthy of our attention.

That celebrity is often trivialized and marginalized in journalistic, academic, and political discourse, despite being intensely popular and generating billions of dollars, makes the study of fame all the more important. We should not be pooh-poohed into thinking that celebrity culture is *merely entertainment*. Because that dismissal urges us to ignore an industry that promotes certain kinds of values and attitudes, about gender, sexuality, success, class, race, relationships, and happiness, while utterly minimizing others. These values also affirm which kinds of people deserve admiration, comfort, and success and which kinds do not. In the pages that follow, we will critically examine the evolution of celebrity in an effort to develop our understanding of the relationship between famous figures, media technologies, and audiences. By attending to the history and evolution of these relationships, we can better understand the ways in which media systems and the famous figures they produce reflect our pleasures, values, and aspirations back to us in their glittering images. We can also appreciate that many aspects of celebrity culture actually have a long history, and that once electronic media technologies developed in the nineteenth century and beyond, significant precedents were set about celebrity production and consumption that are still with us today.

Fame is not an immutable phenomenon, but rather one that has emerged, proliferated, persisted, and changed thanks to evolving technological, cultural, and ideological mechanisms. Contemporary media modalities, including the Internet and social media, mobile technologies, and an ever-growing array of digital platforms, have created a boon in the celebrity industry, spawning a vast cohort of stars and an equally impressive bevy of news programs, blogs, and magazines that endlessly clamor for new personas to attract our attention, and our dollars. With social media in particular, the barriers to becoming well known have been crumbling. So celebrity should not be seen as a static, fixed state, but an ongoing process requiring the constant renewal of media visibility; otherwise, your celebrity capital declines. After all, celebrity is a disposable commodity (the "has-been")—in the media today, gone tomorrow. Thus, there is constant competition to stay in the media spotlight and garner that increasingly scarce and overburdened resource, audience attention. Today, with so many competing 24/7 platforms for individual promotion, with celebrity status more attainable for many yet also more fleeting, celebrity has become "status on speed."[14]

But in order to understand the explosion of twenty-first-century celebrification and the ways it functions in an urbanized, globalized, and hyperlinked culture, we need to look back, before the advent of the smartphone and Facebook, to the relationship between mass communication technologies and the evolution of celebrity in our history. Emphasizing this link, between the particular affordances of different media, both traditional and digital, and the nature and proliferation of celebrity culture, is one of our central points. As Richard Schickel argues in his study of fame, "The history of celebrity and the history of communications technology over the last century are very closely linked."[15] Yet while Schickel suggests that celebrity is a phenomenon that only truly begins in the twentieth century, we look further back in time, especially to the nineteenth century when modes of mass communication and forms of mass entertainments proliferated, in an effort to trace the production, evolution, and uses of celebrity and its effects on the everyday lives of ordinary people.

Media technologies have, during different eras, enabled individuals to broadcast themselves—their ideas and images—to a large-scale audience. In this way, mediated representation allows the individual to become known by the many. The media, therefore, whether magazines, radio, the Internet, or Twitter, have been central to the production and maintenance of celebrity. Each media technology critically shapes and refines the way in which we come to know, perceive, and interpret the ideas and images it presents. As David Schmid writes, "The introduction of each new media technology represents a decisive shift in both the types of fame available in a culture and the ability of that culture to disseminate fame."[16] Indeed, contemporary media technologies, in which multidirectional interaction and response have supplanted the broadcast model, continue to redefine our relationship with famous figures. Because the television interview and on-camera close-ups simulate face-to-face interaction, and because interviewers have become more prying and more unctuous, audiences can establish (and imagine) a new form of intimacy with stars that did not previously exist. And now, with celebrity Facebook pages and Twitter, Instagram, and Snapchat accounts, fans can feel an even greater familiarity and intimacy with totally unknown and unknowable people. While this is a pseudointimacy, intimacy at a distance, an intimacy that is not reciprocated, there is certainly a great pleasure for fans here—they can feel they are in the know, in an inner circle. Yet, at the same time, we can now eavesdrop on celebrities, put the stars under surveillance, without having to respond, be clever, or expose ourselves to them.

Who becomes a celebrity and why? What is our role in celebrity production, in who gets to stay in the spotlight and who doesn't? The book begins by reviewing the various theoretical approaches that have sought to explain the power and significance of celebrity culture, the ideological work it does, and the relationship between stars and audiences. Why do we even have celebrities, and why do they matter to us as individuals and as a society? In tracing the evolution of academic thought on the subject of fame and fandom, we may better appreciate not only the power of the stars themselves but also the scope and potential of the relationship between ordinary people and celebrities.

Fame and the Quest for Immortality

What is the allure, the pull, of fame? Why do some people actively seek it and others—many of us—fantasize about it? In the twenty-first century, being a celebrity seems to bring so much: wealth, of course, being known in a way others are not, being envied, being deferred to, having other famous friends who, presumably, are exciting and fun.

The desire for fame is nothing new; it has existed for millennia. It springs from another deep human fantasy, a longing: the desire for immortality. Fame seems to promise an escape from one of the basic inevitabilities of life—death. For certain celebrities, even years after they die, their presence continues to exist, living on in the images and recordings that made them famous. Posters of Marilyn Monroe and Audrey Hepburn still grace people's walls, and images of celebrities as diverse as Elvis Presley, Johnny Cash, and Lucille Ball and Desi Arnaz are "managed" by rights companies so that, decades after their deaths, they can still be used to sell products. They are gone, but still with us, in an uncanny mode of eternal life through media imagery. Like secular gods, the famous defy the rules of human existence while also providing us with aspirational models to worship. They continue to live on after their death through us, their fans. It is we who make the stars immortal as we worship and deify our favorite actors or musicians. Elvis's Graceland has become a sacred site for his fans where people still leave flowers on his grave (some even believing he's still alive). Fans collect autographs or pictures, or even possessions of their idols, documenting the existence of stars and possessing some modicum of their being, creating their own celebrity reliquaries.

Thousands of years ago, this quest for immortality, to be remembered by posterity, was restricted to a very privileged few. In ancient times, as Leo Braudy notes in his history of fame, with kings, like the pharaohs, also seen as gods, "fame meant a grandeur almost totally separate from ordinary human nature." There was an "extraordinary exaltation of a single man" through art, his headgear and clothing, palaces, and through monumental tombs like the pyramids, all testifying to and asserting his power and immortality. The tombs of the Chinese emperors, Mayan rulers, and Egyptian pharaohs contained inscriptions, amulets, and objects that proclaimed the deceased's singularity and influence. These relics showed the powerful individual imbued with godlike powers, their persona linked to mythic narratives and imagery through carvings, paintings, and decorations of the body.[17]

For the ancient Greeks, it was heroism, the "pursuit of honor," achieved primarily through war and conquest, that allowed men— through the legends about them—to live beyond death. Epics such as the *Iliad* and the *Odyssey* immortalized heroic achievements and inspired the person Leo Braudy calls the "first famous person," Alexander the Great (356–323 BC). Alexander did win fame through his wide-ranging conquests, but, as Braudy notes, "Nothing was ever enough for him."[18] He sought fame not through some predetermined, ascribed status, like being the son of a king or emperor, but through his achievements. He was determined to have these achievements, and his image, widely known and preserved for posterity. As Karsten Dahmen notes, "Much of Alexander's importance lies in his posthumous fame."[19]

Today, we may not think that we are participating in the reproduction of fame when digging around in our pockets for spare change, but in ancient societies coins played an important role in self-promotion. They were one of the earliest mass-produced technologies for circulating fame, and set the precedent for presidents and kings to have their faces on coins and later on bills. Alexander the Great imprinted his likeness on coins in order to make his image and authority known to his subjects, although it was after his death that Greek and Roman rulers promulgated most of the coins bearing his likeness in an effort to be allied with his empire-building.[20] Widely circulated and able to withstand time and touch, coins allowed for the spread of the ruler's face across wide swaths of territory. The power of the coin lay not only in its ability to provide a visual representation of a leader whom most subjects would never see, but also to couple that image with phrases and iconography that conveyed a sense of authority and gravitas. When new coins appeared, the person on the street knew there was a new government and a new leader. Alexander minted coins as he conquered, circulating his likeness to current and future subjects. In his monetary renderings, his features were blended with those of Greek gods and icons of mythology like Hercules. In this way, Alexander's coins not only captured his likeness but also linked him with recognizable qualities and themes with which he wished to be associated.[21] While Alexander died at the age of thirty-three, his fame lived on through the continued circulation of these coins.[22]

There were other representations of Alexander: paintings and mosaics (he had himself depicted "clad in panther skin," which was normally associated with the gods),[23] portrait heads and busts, and statues in stone and bronze.[24] Sculpture also allowed for the public display of one's face and body. The human figure carved in stone provided a lasting depiction of the subject's entire body, and then positioned that body in the public space, for all to see. Imposing and grand, statues confronted the viewer with the presence of their subjects, a moment of poise, or of active heroism, frozen in time and publicly memorialized; the person had to be approached as a monument.[25] The longevity and expense of the materials used to construct such works—bronze, marble, granite— suggest that its subject's influence will extend well into the future, impervious to the changes of time.

With the spread of Christianity, especially after the fall of the Roman Empire, sculpture went into decline because of the belief that statuary verged on idolatry.[26] One replacement was portraiture, which served to bring together the king's "two bodies"—the mortal body that aged and died, and the symbolic body of the monarch. A tradition of deifying portraiture in order to establish and enhance a ruler's fame and prestige dates back at least to medieval and early Renaissance artists who made similar connections by painting rulers in Christ-like poses.[27]

Kings and queens especially grasped the value of the portrait in affirming their importance, and thus a new profession arose, the "court painter" retained by royal or noble families. They often managed a group of assistants or apprentices, all of whom produced various forms of imagery—portrait miniatures, illuminated manuscripts, heraldic seals—to circulate and affirm the royals' authority and fame. There was especial emphasis on the royals' face. By the late 1500s and early 1600s, in England, for example, portraits of rulers from William the Conqueror to Henry VIII would be displayed, often in chronological sequence, in the grand homes of the aristocracy but also in civic buildings and educational establishments. These paintings could be inexpensively reproduced based on previous portraits and copied by artists.[28] And they cemented and circulated the royals' historic significance long after their deaths.

Until the Renaissance period and the emergence of early capitalism in the 1500s, fame had been restricted primarily to royal and religious leaders. But with the growth in trade and the rise of a moneyed merchant class, portrait painting emerged as a more portable, more accessible means of recording and displaying one's individual likeness and his or her success. "Portraiture," as Shearer West writes about the history of the genre, was "very important to celebrity, as the cultivation of celebrity depends to an extent upon the familiarity and dissemination of likeness."[29] As the number of public professions increased, those aspiring to importance realized how portraits could make them seem more symbolically valuable, more powerful.[30] As Braudy notes, "Everyone who made a career in public—and the number of public professions was speedily increasing—was being made to realize how both art and printing could make him more symbolic, more essential, and more powerful."[31] In turn, as the demand for portraits grew, artists who benefitted from the patronage of the rich also became famous. Those who became famous—and remain so today—because of their work for rich patrons include Leonardo Da Vinci (1452–1519), Michelangelo (1475–1564), Raphael (1483–1520) and Botticelli (1445–1510). The result, notes Braudy, "was an unprecedented propaganda of images for both patron and artist to trumpet their importance."[32] The prevalence of the painted portrait, and later printed, photographic, and digitally reproduced versions, helped to establish visual self-representation as a critical mode for communicating one's public value and identity.

Portraits served as status symbols, affirming the power of those represented, even depicting them as having historical importance; in Italian Renaissance painting, lords and ladies might be painted within notable scenes, or alongside famous figures. The characteristics of the portrait—the posed subject, carefully selected background setting, and efforts to represent the subject's internal character in addition to his or her physical appearance and possessions—are tropes that have shaped the nature of self-representation through to the present day. Specific (and often idealized) postures, expressions, and gestures were depicted alongside props and other items signifying particular elements of the subject's identity, class, or station. Some of these portraits, like photographs of celebrities today, provided models for how to dress, how to hold one's body, and what were the most elegant gestures and poses.

With the invention of the printing press in the late 1400s, and the more widespread use of engraving in the next century, portraits could proliferate and circulate in even greater detail. We think of competition over publicity as being relatively recent, but, as Braudy notes, the "competition of images we blindly associate with the present had already by the sixteenth century begun in earnest. It was a new world of fame in which visible and theatrical fame would become the standard, and public prominence a continual theme."[33] Certain rulers, notably England's Elizabeth I and France's Louis XIV, appreciated the power of printing and engraving to spread their fame and authority over great distances. Both of them directed their scribes and artists to create written and visual materials in the service of self-promotion. Elizabeth I's persona was carefully crafted to embody a unified, imperial England, a "combined cult of herself and her country." Louis XIV, who launched a premeditated program to have himself celebrated as the Sun King, was described by one aristocrat this way: "If he was not the greatest king, he was the best actor of majesty at least that ever filled a throne." The king told his official historians that "the most precious things in the world to me" was "my glory."[34] By the late eighteenth century, with the conversion of the Louvre palace into a museum, and then the establishment of national portrait collections, such as the English National Portrait Gallery in 1856, there were now even more monumental yet accessible public spaces for the archive and display of influential individuals.

Over time, the practice of sitting for one's portrait became commonplace even outside of elite circles. Throughout the eighteenth and nineteenth century, to have one's portrait made was a sign of bourgeois success; it became possible for the middle class to emulate the stoic, reverent postures of high society. The portrait also worked to highlight the unique qualities of esteemed and respected individuals who had made discoveries or contributed to culture. Portraits of scholars, authors, inventors, composers, and political thinkers celebrated the unique quality of the individual, elevating these often middle-class persons, who also gained celebrity thanks to their efforts and talents. Meanwhile, some royals and institutional leaders began to present themselves more casually and portraits evolved from the formal and staged to the personal and domestic, complete with pets and familiar possessions. Some eighteenth-century portraits of Marie Antoinette, for instance, emphasized her role as mother, picturing her in a relaxed, domestic setting, accompanied by her children.[35] While the common folk used portraits to emulate the elite, some royals presented themselves as important, yet approachable, a critical suggestion for rulers like Antoinette, who was largely viewed as extravagant and unsympathetic. Her efforts at image management especially backfired when she dressed up as a shepherdess or milkmaid at her simulated farm on the opulent Palace Versailles, an extravagantly wealthy royal playing at and seeming to mock the poor.

By the late seventeenth and early eighteenth centuries, the growth of a nonaristocratic and increasingly influential bourgeoisie whose economic and political fortunes were affected by royal policies began to be less deferential to and more critical of that power. And just as the new technologies of printing could be used to bolster royal authority, these new media could also be used to criticize and even undermine that power.

Indeed, this can be seen as the beginning of celebrity gossip. In France, by the mid-1700s, "a vast underground literature attacking the prerogatives and pretensions of monarchs, aristocrats, and the church had emerged" that was circulated by an increasingly assertive bourgeoisie and written in a style that "anticipated the gossip columnists of the yellow press." One such exposé was *The Private Life of Louis XV*, a *chroniques scandaleuse*, a diatribe against the corruption and decadent behavior of the nobility.[36] By the late 1700s, such printed gossip challenging the authority and the personas of elites had spread to England, other European counties, and the American colonies.

Jürgen Habermas famously theorized this period as a critical moment in cultural history, in which society shifts from a top-down representational culture, where influence based on edicts and imagery was hierarchically disseminated from the elite few to the masses, to a critical, participatory culture in which ordinary citizens could be informed about, and participate in, discussions regarding matters of public concern.[37] Here, we see that it is not the official histories, the gilded Bibles, or even the elite newspapers of the day that were most influential, but rather the cheap broadside posters, pamphlets, and street literature— what Leslie Shepard calls "the ephemera of the masses"—that transformed social relations by widening the scope of public discourse.[38] With the spread of print, and the rising literacy rates that followed, Habermas saw the emergence of the "bourgeois public sphere," a realm apart from the state that thrived in coffeehouses, taverns, and salons, where individuals—at this time primarily propertied, educated men— could debate issues of public concern and challenge state authority. Thus certain individuals were transformed from a position of passive deference to the social order into active participants in public culture. As Habermas argues, the idea of the democratic society rests on the model of the political public sphere. The public sphere in turn is dependent on the *fourth estate*, the press that acts as a watchdog, fostering an informed and empowered public. It is the informed public that is thereby able to hold those in power accountable.

Of course there was never just one public sphere, but various counterpublics that especially grew in size and influence in the eighteenth and nineteenth centuries. The rise of these public spheres, especially in cities, and sustained by the explosive growth of newspapers in the 1700s and 1800s, had a powerful effect on how traditional elites were regarded. And it was especially in the nineteenth century in the United States that we see how this historic shift, and the rise of an increasingly commercialized and consumer culture, that enabled nonelites to gain visibility, furthered the shift from fame to celebrity. Increasingly public figures "owed more to their visibility and ability to attract publicity than to their achievements or pedigree."[39]

From tombs and coins to statues and portraits, all of these monuments and objects preserved one's image, and in some cases their fame, long after they had died. One classic example of how fame can span millennia is the notoriety of King Tutankhamun, the boy pharaoh of the eighteenth dynasty of ancient Egypt, born around 1341 BC. King Tut, as he came to be known, became pharaoh at the age of eight after the disastrous rule of his predecessor Akhenaten. Akhenaten had violated various rituals and practices sacred to the Egyptians, and Tut, relying on excellent advisors, restored the previous practices and became a symbol of this restoration to "the proper order of things."[40] Beyond this, his reign was not particularly notable.[41] When he died at the age of eighteen, he was buried in the Valley of the Kings, his tomb filled with murals depicting his journey to the afterworld and various artifacts, including precious jewelry, statues, and toys from his childhood.

In the nineteenth century, wealthy Europeans began to explore and excavate various ancient sites, hoping to find artifacts for their homes or to place in museums. One aristocrat, Lord Carnarvon, fascinated by Egyptology, funded the work of the archeologist Howard Carter who was looking for tombs of the royals and upper classes. Just as Carnarvon—who had been funding Carter since 1907—was about to pull the plug, Carter and his workmen, in November 1922, discovered an opening to a descending stairway leading to an underground tomb. They eventually got to a door with Tutankhamun's name on it and broke through it.

There they were stunned to find a nearly perfectly intact tomb, which included almost 5,400 objects the pharaoh might need in the next life, from perfumes and oils to sandals and linen underwear to his solid gold coffin.[42]

The discovery of an untouched 3,000-year-old-tomb was an international sensation that sparked further fascination with ancient Egypt; it took Carter ten years to catalog all the treasures, which eventually went to the Egyptian Museum of Cairo. It also inspired what came to be called a wave of "Tut-mania," with newspapers vying for stories and scoops about Tut, the tomb, and, especially, the alleged "Pharaoh's Curse," meaning death for anyone who invaded or disturbed a pharaoh's tomb.[43] Egyptian motifs became popular on clothes, jewelry, and in Art Deco architecture; a fruit company featured King Tut brand lemons; President Herbert Hoover named his dog King Tut. Carter and Carnarvon (along with Tut) became instant celebrities; the American magician Charles Carter rebranded himself as Carter the Great. A 1923 record, "Old King Tut," became a hit.[44]

Fifty years later, in 1976, the blockbuster museum exhibit *The Treasures of Tutankhamun* became an American obsession, touring the country for three years; it was the most popular museum show in U.S. history.[45] As the Associated Press reported, "People waited in lines for nine hours to see it during its first stop two years ago in Washington. In Chicago, crowds gathered at 10 the night before the show opened." The *Los Angeles Times* called the phenomenon a "King Tut binge" and said museum attendees were like "a human tidal wave."[46] The *New York Times* estimated that at least 400 manufacturers were producing Tut-inspired products, including whiskey bottles in the shape of Tut's death mask.[47] By April 1978, the comedian Steve Martin appeared on *Saturday Night Live* in a pharaoh's costume singing his instantly hilarious and famous song "King Tut," which contained the lyrics "Now when he was a young man / He never thought he'd see / People stand in line to see the boy king" and "Now, if I'd known / They'd line up just to see you / I'd trade in all my money / And bought me a museum." He ended with "He gave his life for tourism."

Why this fascination with a pharaoh from over 3,000 years ago? Why did he become an unwitting celebrity? Because so many tombs of the pharaohs had been looted, to find one so complete and untouched was unique and thrilling. And, in part, it was all of the surviving possessions, the gold, the jewels, the statues, as opposed to any singular accomplishments in his life, which made him a twentieth-century star. But the tomb was also a window into what was believed to be the first great civilization, and it was the use of mummification and the myth of the pharaoh's curse that tied Tut and ancient Egypt to the supernatural, the occult. His tomb, with all of the clothing, food, and the like that were to accompany him into a fervently believed in afterlife, tap into our fascination with and fears about death and fantasies of immortality. All this physical evidence of a faith in an afterlife, and then everyday people seeing someone who died 3,000 years before but is now newly known, did mean Tut now mattered to posterity, was not fully gone at all. As humans grapple with the meaning of life, with the "why are we here" question, seeing evidence of those who came before us, what they made, how they lived and what they believed connects us to a sense of origins. Tut and ancient Egypt were, to twentieth-century Brits and Americans, exotic, different. Yet he was an emblem of the persistence of human striving, and of the faith in eternal life.

Do our lives matter? Does what we do matter after we're gone? By the twentieth century, the rise of secularization and a waning belief, for some, in an afterlife, "bred a twin obsession with posterity and death."[48] Celebrity—to be known by millions, to be mourned when you go, to live on in the hearts and minds of people—tied the new mechanisms and technologies of fame production with that age-old longing for everlasting life.

Celebrity and Aura

If remote, unknowable, but famous royalty had an aura about them that stemmed in fact from their being so rare, so distinctive, so elevated from everyday people, what has omnipresent, intensified visibility done to the aura of the famous? In the mid-1930s, the social critic Walter Benjamin wrote an essay entitled "The Work of Art in the Age of Mechanical Reproduction," in which he argued that technological innovation, especially with the rise of "mass culture," led to a shift in the nature and value of art, and his argument applies to how mass-produced visuality may have affected the shift from fame to celebrity. Early art, he argued, was one of a kind, embedded in specific locations and rituals, and because a painting or sculpting was not identically reproducible, it had an aura. Think, for example, of the aura surrounding the *Mona Lisa*. Part of the aura, embedded in it, was knowledge of the artwork's particular historical uses and its ownership over time. This aura imbues the work with authenticity; the one-of-a-kind painting, for example, was distinguished by its uniqueness and its remoteness from daily life. Benjamin contended that the *aura* of the art object has been destroyed by widespread reproduction—we can all get prints of the Mona Lisa if we want—in that the process of duplicating an artwork effaces the uniqueness of the object and its distance from the viewer.

In a museum, for instance, works are presented as individual, distinctive, and therefore special; they are secured within the halls of the institution, sometimes even behind glass, and we can't own or even touch them. Elevated as singular works of inaccessible beauty that we are meant to admire, even worship, they retain their aura. Benjamin argues that new technologies, including lithography and print, but especially photography, allow artworks to be widely copied and distributed, thus shattering the aura, challenging the notion of the one-of-a-kind and authentic work, and shifting focus away from the object's symbolic value by reinstituting the work back into everyday life, where it can be acquired and used by anyone and thus brought closer to the masses. The process of reproduction, then, results in the democratization of art, an effect that Benjamin sees as politically useful, even progressive. Thus, as media scholar Paddy Scannell notes, "New forms of mass communication may transform consumers into active participants and therein lays a new relationship between producers, products, and audiences. Not the worship of the author (as genius) or of the work (as truth and beauty) by an adoring audience, but a more equal and collaborative relationship in which the author aligns himself with the audience (the masses), takes their point of view, and gives it expression in his work."[49]

In the decades that accompanied and followed the Industrial Revolution, rapidly changing technologies meant that artistic modes of self-representation were quickly expanding. Advances in printing, etching, and, later, photography allowed anyone with a relatively small amount of money to record and distribute a likeness. As a result, a greater number of people could become recognizable, their images and stories disbursed, which meant that it was no longer only the wealthy and powerful who could hope for attention or renown. At the same time, photographic reproductions allowed the public access to the images of the elite and influential, thus erasing the feeling of distance between the famous "them" and the rest of us. So while Benjamin argued that technological advancements allowed for the democratization of art, these developments also shaped the nature of fame. As self-representation became less dependent on large and expensive artistic processes like sculpture and oil painting, the aura of the famous figure—his or her uniqueness as a public person at a distance or remove from the rest of society—was thereby diminished. Fame, and the famous, appeared more accessible. Meanwhile, newspapers and photography gave the public a greater sense of access to, and influence over, well-known figures. It is this evolution that we trace in the pages ahead.

Overview of the Book

Celebrity thus provides an overview account of the history of stardom, its dynamic relationship with technologies of mass communication, and the academic theories that have emerged to help explain the production, circulation, and effects of celebrity culture. We offer a brief history of fame, and the historical modes of celebrity production, and how they have changed (and persisted) over time. We cannot possibly discuss everyone who became a celebrity since the nineteenth century, so we have sought to focus on certain exemplars of different types of fame and stardom. A central aspect of the history of fame is, in Braudy's words, the "changing ways by which individuals have sought to bring themselves to the attention of others and, not incidentally, have thereby gained power over them." From the beginning, "fame has required publicity,"[50] the forms of which have also both persisted and evolved. Within this narrative, we uncover the relationship between fame, politics, fandom, and economic and discursive power.

The exponential speed in which technologies have developed throughout the twentieth and twenty-first centuries has prompted significant changes in the role celebrities play in society, and in the ways audiences engage and interact with them. It is through our interaction with famous figures via these mediated encounters that they come to hold meaning and value, for us and for our culture. We will emphasize the central role of the media and communications technologies and their particular affordances, to the manufacture, proliferation, and democratization of fame and celebrity. So we take a closer look at the development of media technologies, from newspapers, photography, and early fan magazines through to radio and television and including contemporary digital platforms such as Twitter, Instagram, and YouTube, in order to understand how each new advance in media molds the meaning of celebrity within popular culture at that particular historical moment. We will also consider how these evolving technologies interact with, shape, and are shaped by the changing industrial conditions around the production of fame.

While many elements of celebrity—who becomes one and why, how it is produced—have remained surprisingly constant over the years, it is also crucial to pay attention to how historical context shapes visibility and stardom. Evolving attitudes about race, gender, appropriate public behavior, sex and sexuality, and about authority and power all contribute to who does and does not gain celebrity status in different historical eras. What has been condemned as celebrity behavior in one era—say, having a child out of wedlock—barely raises an eyebrow in another.

Celebrity culture is a huge and profitable industry in the United States. It also plays a major role in constituting who we are, and what we hope for and dream about. And celebrity culture has a history. However evanescent and trivial particular celebrities and their triumphs and tragedies may be over the years, this media juggernaut, and what lies in its wake, is not immaterial. We need to appreciate its evolution, its industrial production, and its multiple effects, especially now, when celebrity culture has its grip on nearly every aspect of American life.

1

Theories of Celebrity

Why, exactly, do we have celebrities and, now, so many of them? What needs do they fulfill, in our culture and our economy, even in our politics? But, also, what needs do they fill in us? Why do we as individuals pay attention to them, talk about them, adulate them, or, alternatively, hate them? What pleasures do they offer us and how has that contributed to the sheer numbers of celebrities, including "everyday people," who have become famous, especially in the twenty-first century? How are we to think about and make sense of this phenomenon? Here we address these questions, examining the work of scholars who have considered both the broader sociological and historical explanations for the rise of celebrity and the more individual and psychological analyses of our engagement with people we will never meet or know. And it is important to emphasize that many of these theories are not mutually exclusive, but can work together to help us appreciate why this has become such a salient feature of modern life.

The Importance of the Audience

As previously noted, the rise of celebrity is made possible through the individual's relationship to a mass audience, a public. The role of the audience is, therefore, crucial in the production and maintenance of fame. Indeed, as P. David Marshall argues, it is the public, the celebrity's "followers," who empower the construction of celebrity itself.[1] "The historical emergence of the celebrity sign," Marshall points out, "coincides and correlates with the rise of the audience as a social category," adding that "Celebrity is an acknowledgement of the public's power."[2] It is the attention of the public, our fascination and adulation, which make celebrity as a phenomenon possible. So at the heart of celebrity culture was, and is, a contradiction. Celebrities are seen as unique and elevated people, above the masses, yet are absolutely dependent on the good will and admiration of those masses for ongoing recognition and success. Thus, the twin pulls on our desire that celebrities be special and transcendent yet also regular people and "just like us."

Francesco Alberoni offers similar observations about the power of the audience, suggesting that stars, despite their influence and success, are in fact powerless, at the mercy of the public. It is the public's judgment of the famous that allows the elite to maintain their position. One of the ways in which this judgment functions is through the public's perpetual affirmation and reaffirmation of social codes vis-à-vis celebrity actors. Celebrities, Alberoni notes, play a critical role in maintaining social standards and cohesion in large-scale society. As regularly (sometimes constantly) "observable" and "knowable" individuals, celebrities are available to be evaluated, loved, or criticized by their audience.[3] The lives of celebrities, Alberoni writes, especially their social relationships, can be "a benchmark for positive or negative evaluation" by us, and a source both of identification and a projection of the needs of a mass audience. They are also "a living testimony to the possibility of achieving a rise in personal status."[4]

Celebrities and Presentation of Self

The connection between celebrity and fan is a symbiotic relationship, fulfilling mutual needs and offering benefits to both. It builds on a deep and fundamental aspect of everyday interaction between people: when we engage with others, especially in public, it is a performance. We don't often think of our interactions this way, as we like to think of ourselves as genuine, as not faking it or putting on a role. But in each culture there are rules about how to perform—in the classroom, at work, in a restaurant, even bumping into a friend on the street—that we learn in unspoken ways starting in childhood. And since most of us want to be liked, to be thought of as an admirable and attractive person, we try to conform to these rules and not violate them.

These rules form the foundation, the building blocks, of successful celebrity. So to understand what makes some stars admirable and others not, what makes some seem genuine and others fake and manufactured, we need to first review how performance in everyday life affects who we like, respect, even love, and who we don't.

We all know that feeling of sitting in a restaurant or bar, say, and the person at the next table is talking too loud, bragging, acting like a know-it-all, and being obnoxious to the wait staff: we think right away, "what a jerk" (or something more unprintable). The person has transgressed the taken-for-granted mode of performance we have come to see as acceptable; the impression he gives off undermines the impression he is *seeking* to give. Anyone who has worked in retail, or a restaurant, knows there are often very specific rules about how to perform—what to say, how to say it—with the customers. Even walking across, say a campus, there are different modes of greeting for those you know only slightly versus those with whom you are very close, and if you mix them up, your performance seems odd.

So like us, but even more so, stars and their handlers need to devise and preserve a public persona that seems authentic and likeable. The increasing emphasis in our media-saturated culture and digital environments for all of us to craft effective, convincing performances, while stars seek to seem genuine and not manufactured, has led scholars analyzing celebrity culture to turn to the groundbreaking work of the sociologist Erving Goffman in his 1959 book *The Presentation of Self in Everyday Life*.[5] Unpacking and revealing these often unspoken yet precise rules of how we present ourselves to others was at the core of his book. Goffman examined the sociology of how people present themselves, and the nature of interpersonal interaction and influence.[6] This work has become foundational to our understanding of celebrity performance and culture.

To conduct his study, Goffman traveled to a most unlikely research locale, the remote Shetland Islands off the northeast coast of Scotland, and observed, often in minute detail, the face-to-face interactions of the people there. His major insight was to view human interactions in theatrical terms, through a dramaturgical lens, noting how all people must perform in everyday life, to present a convincing, idealized image of ourselves. People can either perform their identity sincerely or with cynicism (not truly meaning what we say), or flip back and forth between the two. And a person tends to "conceal or underplay those activities, facts, and motives which are incompatible with an idealized version of [self]."[7]

In one example, Goffman describes someone walking up to a friend's house for a visit. Approaching the house, the person may be expressionless or even scowling, lost in thought. But as soon as she knocks on the door and hears the friend approaching, she will put on a big smile and become animated as she attempts to control the impression she is making. Of course, the person answering the door now must perform as well, as the two participate in what Goffman called the "definition of the situation," the agreed upon roles they should each play given the nature of the interaction. Each one is an actor, even though they are friends, each managing the impression they give.

Various crucial rules operate in most interactions—meetings, dinner parties, job interviews. Goffman noted that there is the impression that we give (the one we seek to control) and the impression we give off (the one we might not control so well), and they might be quite different. Some of the worst things that can happen during an interaction are what Goffman called unintended, ungovernable acts, behaviors that can disrupt our performance and that we must control, like yawning, rolling our eyes, looking past the person you're talking to (to someone else) at a party or conference, burping, sweating, or having your voice crack. We can't lose muscular or facial control, or belch, trip, stutter, appear nervous, gulp, forget what we were saying, or, god forbid, fart. These can be especially disastrous for celebrities. Actors "lose face" when they fail to perform their roles in a way that meets social expectations.

Thus, the "front stage" self, the version of our identity that we perform for others and allow people to see, may conceal the work that we do "back stage," behind the scenes, in order to maintain the version of self that we present to the world. This is true for private individuals, but especially salient for public persons, who may perform cynically, not meaning what they say or concealing certain facts in order to enhance their status, present a glorified version of self, or win admiration or sympathy. We are often especially suspicious of these "front stage" presentations of politicians.

Because we know that most people—and especially those in the public eye—seek to present themselves in the most favorable light, we often "use what are considered to be the ungovernable aspects" of a person's expressive behavior "as a check upon the validity of what is conveyed by the governable aspects."[8] If a candidate for a job expresses enthusiasm for the position but then yawns during the interview, the ungovernable act will betray what the candidate is trying to convey. It is these unguarded actions or gestures, as opposed to the performance the person presents, that we feel are the true indices of what a person is really like.

We—and the paparazzi, gossip magazines, and bloggers—use similar observational strategies when watching celebrities to determine how genuine and likeable they are. In interviews, do their facial expressions, body language, and gestures match what they are saying? When they are out in public, can they be caught doing something they have failed to control or govern, something that suggests their public image is a lie? Hugh Grant, the charming, clean-cut, British boy-next-door actor who had shot to fame for his performance as a diffident and lovelorn patrician in *Four Weddings and a Funeral*, had his image seriously tarnished when, in 1995, he was caught in his car having sex with a prostitute: the opposite of clean cut. "When we discover that someone with whom we have dealings is an impostor and out-and-out fraud," Goffman observed, "we are discovering that he did not have the right to play the part he played, that he was not an accredited incumbent of the relevant status."[9] It's these unintentional moments, the impressions we give off, as opposed to the impression we deliberately seek to give, that seem to convey the true essence of who the person is.

Because we are performers and have to cultivate dramaturgical skill, we have what Goffman famously identified as a front region or front stage and a back region or back stage. These are often marked by physical and aural boundaries and blockades between us and our audience: the back stage of a kitchen in a restaurant versus the front stage of the dining area, for example. In the front region, we need to appear to believe in the part we're playing, to appear sincere, and the setting, our appearance, and manner should all cohere. In a classroom, for example, the successful professor will appear to be enthusiastic about her topic, dedicated to student learning and in command of the class. She should also be dressed like "a professor" and not, say, like a nightclub performer. But students have to inhabit a front stage here too: whether they like the class or not, the successful students will take notes, appear respectful, not talk to others, text throughout the lecture, or fall asleep in class. The front must have "dramatic realization" and should display what Goffman called "sacred compatibility": that there are ideal motives for acquiring the role we inhabit. The teacher does so because he loves to teach, the doctor chose her profession because she wants to save lives, or the actor chose her profession because she has loved acting since the age of three, for example. We as performers in life must constantly adjust to new settings—the workplace, a friend's party, an interview—and modulate our performances accordingly to remain liked and even admired.

These regions don't just involve individuals, they include "teams," groups of people who must collude in a performance, like the wait staff in a restaurant who seek to make you feel welcome and important. In the dining room they must be solicitous, friendly, helpful, and agreeable; "I'm Jan and I'll be taking care of you today." But in the kitchen, the façade can come down, especially if they find a customer to be overly demanding or entitled. So teams decide how they will treat the audience to its face, but behind the audience's back can derogate and even mock them. They just can't get caught doing so. Thus, teams, as well as individuals, must also work to avoid embarrassment. When such back-stage derision of the audience is exposed it can be very damaging. That's why when a waiter surreptitiously recorded Mitt Romney at a private fundraiser during the 2012 campaign saying that 47 percent of Americans are "dependent on the government, believe they are victims . . . [and] pay no income tax," so Romney's job "is not to worry about those people," it collided with his front-stage image as running for president of everyone and did significant damage to his candidacy.

Goffman's schema helps us unpack and appreciate a successful or unsuccessful celebrity performance and what the celebrity must do to convey sincerity. Celebrities who, in interviews, seem too scripted, evade questions, or give obviously clichéd or pandering answers come across as phony or as hiding something. Those who are overeager with the interviewer or don't govern their behaviors—as when Tom Cruise in 2005 famously jumped up and down on Oprah Winfrey's couch proclaiming his love for Katie Holmes—can seem not in control of their performances and even unhinged. (And the thought that Cruise actually might have *planned* such a stunt was an equally troubling view into his back region.) That episode seriously damaged Cruise's public image. When back-stage episodes become public, like Mel Gibson's anti-Semitic rant in 2006 against a police officer who stopped him for drunk driving, they can ruin a star's career, as this episode did for Gibson, because it suggested that his true, unscripted self was a hate-filled bigot. But celebrities are members of teams, too, who work to maintain their successful performances. An allegedly happily married celebrity couple, for example, should not be seen fighting in a restaurant or bar. If one of them says in an interview how happy they are, the other one better say so too. And when a celebrity grants an interview, he or she will work hard to enlist the journalist as a team member as well, striving to have the interviewer convey the best possible image of the star.

Most celebrities, of course, seek to protect their back stages, to maintain some privacy, and not to have back-stage comments or behaviors cross the boundary into the front region. But at the same time, many celebrities understand that their fans want access to the back stage, and this has become more true and more possible with the explosive increase in the number of paparazzi in the early twenty-first century and the rise of social media. So increasingly stars, or more usually someone on their staff, use Facebook and especially Instagram, Snapchat, and Twitter to present a managed view of what seems to be the back stage. In addition, social media have provided easy-to-access technological platforms that allow initially nonfamous people to create a marketable persona—a self to present to a broader, unknown public—that has led to a rise of various social-media-based celebrities.

Celebrities and the Emergence of the Mass Audience

While there have been, for millennia, people who rose to fame, the production and proliferation of celebrities in the United States really takes off in the mid-nineteenth and early twentieth centuries as a result of several intertwined phenomena: the increased democratization of society, the evolution of the United States into a much larger and more impersonal society, the rapid growth of national markets and cultures, the rise of an emerging middle class and urban, white-collar workers, the spread of popular entertainments, and the gradual rise of bureaucracies to manage businesses and the government. Increased urbanization, fueled in part by rising immigration, meant there were growing and concentrated audiences for popular culture fare. The success of the "penny press" in the 1830s and beyond, geared to everyday people and not just elites, provided venues for advertising concerts, performances, and other events. A new kind of public sphere was emerging as well, one that was more participatory and less governed primarily by white, property-owning men.

It was in the nineteenth century that the term "celebrity" emerged.[10] Unlike the top-down fame of kings, queens, or prominent religious leaders, celebrities and their creators and managers needed fans. And the rapid growth of the population and profound changes in the way people lived created them. In 1790, 95 percent of Americans lived in rural areas; only 5 percent lived in cities, and only a few, like New York and Boston, had more than 15,000 people. By 1890, industrialization and the rise of the factory system had led to a major growth in the number and size of cities, with now 35 percent of Americans living in urban areas. Between 1870 and 1920, the number of Americans living in cities grew from ten million to fifty-four million. And immigrants and their children were the major source of this growth. Between 1880 and 1920, more than twenty million people migrated to the United States, most of them moving to cities. By the 1920s, more people lived in cities than in the country, a major shift in American life.[11] The increase in the number of jobs, improvements in transportation, and, of course, the lure of public entertainments all made the city magnetic.

The rise in leisure time was also crucial to growth in public entertainments and the stars featured in them. Some estimate that in the early to mid-1800s, many people worked seventy hours or more a week. In manufacturing jobs in the 1870s and 1880s, a sixty-hour workweek was typical, and workers began organizing in the 1870s for an eight-hour workday.[12] By the turn of the century, various industries had gone to an eight-hour day, freeing many people up to attend vaudeville shows and go to the movies and amusement parks. By the 1840s, cities like New York, despite religious and moral opposition among the educated elite to the potential corruptions of theatergoing, had a robust theater culture with known actors. Thousands of new theaters, especially in cities, were built between 1850 and 1900.[13] By the 1880s, vaudeville was the most popular form of commercial entertainment, featuring anywhere between twenty and thirty acts, each performing for about fifteen minutes; an estimated 15 percent of all city dwellers attended a show at least once a week.[14]

During this approximately eighty-year period, between 1840 and 1920, the phenomenon of the celebrity begins to take hold. And, since then, the role and impact has only increased. Why? Of course there was simply the increased ability to produce them, through the building of "museums" and theaters in cities and towns, and the development of promotional apparatuses through newspapers, broadsides, and later magazines. An increase in economic wealth in the United States, and the gradual expansion of leisure time, fought for primarily by unions, helped enlarge an audience for entertainment and its stars, as did rapid technological change—the invention of the camera, phonograph, motion pictures, and then radio.

One obvious reason for the rise of celebrities during this era comes from the production side: as owners and producers of urban-based entertainments like the theater and vaudeville sought to maximize profits, they used the expanding press and techniques of modern advertising to create known name performers—stars—to attract an audience. But other explanations for the rise of celebrities come from the consumer side of the phenomenon. Of course people wanted diversion, escape, and entertainment, but there was, and is, more to it.

Celebrity Culture as a Response to the Rise of Bureaucracies

This period saw the rise of bureaucracies, especially in the post–Civil War period, to manage large-scale organizations like governments or businesses. These were characterized by their hierarchical structures, impersonal rules, emphasis on rational principles of organization, and the specific allocation of duties to specific job descriptions, which typically involved delimited tasks and spheres of influence in the workplace. As the sociologist Max Weber noted, while bureaucracies were in many ways an excellent and highly functional form of administration, they depersonalized both those who worked in them and those they served. Individual cases or exceptions that don't conform to the rules, individual ideas or initiatives not in your job description, just can't be accommodated. Just think of how we feel waiting for our number to be called at the Division of Motor Vehicles or trying to reach an actual human via a voicemail menu. Those waiting in lines to be called or served, those sitting at their desks doing their same routine jobs over and over, can feel their individuality thwarted, that they are just part of an undifferentiated herd.

Celebrities offer a fantasy of escape from this dehumanization. They don't wait in line, they can bend the rules and be treated as special individuals, they possess a singularity denied by large-scale bureaucratic enterprises. Most of us have to go to nine-to-five jobs where we are told what to do; we have to watch what we spend; we don't get to marry and divorce beautiful new people every three years; we are not supposed to be "difficult" or "high maintenance." Celebrities don't have to play by any of these rules. They get a pass. They don't have to rein in their various appetites (except, for women, hunger). For the most part, they get to escape from these confines.

Many celebrities in the late nineteenth and early twentieth centuries were self-made individuals—inventors, singers, actors, industrialists—who achieved their wealth and fame not by being born into them, but through their talents and hard work. Thus they provided living testimony to the possibility of upward mobility. They also held out the fantasy of one day breaking free oneself, of being seen as a distinct, special individual who merits recognition and admiration. Celebrities then and now embody "self-expression over conformity" and "hedonism above responsibility."[15] They are heightened examples of individual achievement, which transform and challenge the rigidity of class-based societies, representing the potential for everyone to transcend them.[16] By the 1920s, with the Hollywood star system firmly in place, celebrity stories in the new fan magazines emphasized the glories of the stars' wealth and fame, which, if handled properly, ensured even further elevation from the tedium and indignities of the bureaucratized life. During the Great Depression, as Karen Sternheimer reports in *Celebrity Culture and the American Dream*, gossip pages and the number of photos expanded in fan magazines, which served both as "a distraction from the faltering economic system" and as reassurance "that it was still possible to become rich in America, even during the Depression."[17]

There is a paradox at the core of this, because celebrities are often seen has having "charisma"—exceptional, unique, and magnetic qualities that set them apart from others—yet somehow lure us ordinary, possibly noncharismatic spectators into the reverie that we can break out from the pack as well.

Celebrity Culture as a Form of Religion

Another explanation for the purchase that celebrity culture has gained in our society is that it is similar to religion, and even a substitute for it. As Chris Rojek notes in his book *Celebrity*, in increasingly modernized, consumerist societies, where the acquisition of goods and status are emphasized and the centrality of religious institutions to everyday life wanes, people still need and look for some meaning, bigger than themselves, to admire and aspire to. Celebrity culture fills that need by providing, in a kind of macroreligious manner, a "cluster of human relationships in which mutual passion typically operates without physical interaction."[18] Appearing on elevated stages or large movie screens, beautifully lit or photographed, stars can seem like deities, bigger than we, above us. The celebrity becomes "the precious other."[19] In the magical world of celebrities, everything seems possible. By publicly defying the boundaries of ordinary human life, "celebrities take themselves and their fans higher," notes Rojek, "They are the ambassadors of the celestial sphere."[20] As with gods, we can project intensely positive, even worshipful feelings onto celebrities, and this connection can "compensate for feelings of invalidation and incompleteness elsewhere in their lives" and provide a path "into genuinely meaningful experience."[21]

According to this argument, religions have rituals, sacred sites, saints, gods or martyrs to deify and worship, and reliquaries—repositories for or relics from saints like a shock of their hair or things they possessed—and that celebrity culture has all these as well. People do worship actors or musicians; red carpet events and awards shows are annual rituals where the deities are venerated; the faithful flock to the Hollywood Walk of Fame to place their hands beside the imprints of those of the stars', forever cast in stone. Fans have collected celebrities' autographs or pictures, and those with money have sought to acquire their possessions, creating their own celebrity reliquaries, which help bring them closer to the stars and validate a connection to them.[22] In the magical world of celebrities, everything seems possible—death and rebirth, when an actor who was a "has-been" makes a comeback—and even immortality—a star like Marilyn Monroe will live forever in her movies, or photographs or recordings.

There are, as in many religions, ceremonies of ascent and descent. The new star is discovered and rises up, through performances, appearances on talk shows and red carpet events, magazine profiles and reviews. But then some stumble—they get too fat or too thin, are caught getting drunk or abusing drugs or cheating on their partners, or are involved in other scandals—and descend into the hell of public humiliation, excoriation, rejection, and even personal disappearance.[23] Yet those who have stumbled in this way can also be redeemed and work their way back into the hearts of their fans. They are resurrected.

Celebrity Culture and Capitalism

Some theorists have maintained that celebrity culture has become an essential feature of capitalism—an often efficient and successful economic system—whose biggest failure, nonetheless, is its inability to distribute its blessings fairly: it produces societies that allow for great wealth but also permit abject poverty. In the late nineteenth and early twentieth centuries, unions, activists, journalists, reformers, and some politicians exposed, especially through large-circulation newspapers and magazines, the growing disparity between rich and poor and the negative consequences of monopoly control, in so many industries, for workers and consumers. These exposés and the reform movements they prompted occurred just as celebrity culture was consolidating and expanding even further.

Thus, the argument here is that elites need everyday people to be distracted from the persistence of structural inequality in the United States. In addition, celebrity culture serves to legitimate disparities in wealth and fame—it makes hierarchies thrilling—while also affirming often elusive, but system-sustaining, myths, like the bromide that anyone can make it to the top if she or he has talent, determination, and grit. Often mixed into this argument is that people have become narcotized dupes, preoccupied and seduced by celebrity culture: they have been trained to and want to be distracted from the realities of inequality as well.

In their famous and scathing 1944 essay on "The Culture Industries," the German intellectual émigrés Theodor Adorno and Max Horkheimer were especially critical of popular culture and its potential influence. They argued that the media relay stories and interpretative frameworks consonant with the interests of the ruling classes and that their mission is to secure "obedience to the social hierarchy." Media audiences "fall helpless victims of what is offered them," which results in the "stunting of the mass-media consumer's powers of imagination and spontaneity."[24] While movie stars, for example, and the movies they're in might seem distinctive on the surface, they were simply part of Hollywood's mass production process, which cranked out a standardization of media forms and audience tastes, through patterned, predigested, and endlessly recycled cultural entities. This they called "pseudo-individuation," in which "every tenor voice comes to sound like a Caruso record, and the 'natural faces' of Texas girls are like the successful models by whom Hollywood has typecast them."[25] Such "worn grooves" in the production of stars and media fare is so numbing that in the end it thwarts people's ability to imagine anything different, in art or indeed in political and economic relations. This, they argued, was extremely helpful to the powers that be, who relied on a docile, distracted, and nonquestioning public to preserve an unequal status quo.

The Rise and Functions of Celebrity Profiles

The rapid urbanization and industrialization in the United States in the early twentieth century and the increased geographical and social mobility they produced meant that growing numbers of people lost their moorings from their families and the communities they grew up with and knew. The "first impression," touted as crucial in self-help books and in countless ads especially for personal care products, now mattered enormously for many trying to get a job, locate housing, make friends, and find love. Celebrities—how they looked, dressed, and behaved, as presented in their own performances and articles about them—provided the scripts to follow, the looks to try to imitate, for impression management and the presentation of self in everyday life.[26]

In a famous essay from 1944, "Biographies in Popular Magazines," which analyzed magazine profiles of famous people between 1901 and 1941, Leo Lowenthal argued that what he labeled "idols of production"— self-made men, captains of industry, political leaders—had after World War I given way to "idols of consumption"—primarily entertainers and sports heroes who were often elevated by "lucky breaks." The former were active agents, doers, while he saw the latter—at least as profiled in popular magazines—as passive; things happened *to* them. The article was noteworthy because it laid out an important turning point in unpacking the depiction of celebrities as both just like us yet not like us at all, a framework still very much with us.

Lowenthal's main question asked about the reason for this turn, noting that "there must be a social need seeking gratification by this type of literature."[27] He concluded several things. Celebrity biographies provide "unbroken confidence in the opportunities open to every individual," with the life stories of others serving as "educational models" one can envy, but also try to emulate.[28] Yet with the idols of consumption, the reader enters a "dream world" that focuses on the private lives, behaviors, and personal preferences of the hero (as opposed to what actually got them to the top) and provides instruction on consumption and how to spend one's leisure time, but not necessarily on how to actually succeed in life.[29]

The profiles let us into stars' personal spheres; we learn who likes to be "the life of the party," who drinks and who doesn't, who likes "Brazilian cigars," who likes to cook "Viennese dishes."[30] They urge us to judge celebrities according to their behaviors toward their tasks—if they work hard and are energetic and capable—and their behavior toward others. Are they generous, friendly, and cooperative? Do they moderate their own emotions—are they restrained, or have they succumbed to being thin skinned, irritable, or humorless? The behavioral judgments meted out provide normative codes about how we ourselves should act with others.

Yet in all of this Lowenthal emphasized the persistence of passivity in the heroes of consumption and found an odd brew of luck mixed with predetermination as explanations for their success. On the one hand, the profiles emphasized the stars' parentage and background: for example, Clark Gable's "stubborn determination" was derived from his "Pennsylvania Dutch ancestors," as if Gable himself bears little responsibility for his character traits; he simply inherited them. "The individual himself appears as a mere product of his past."[31] As children they were "midget editions" of their future selves, because they were just born with talent or predilections and always knew what they wanted to do. An athlete is described as having "been born with a love of the game"; a businessman has "an instinct" for promotion; a movie star knew she wanted to be an actress "from the time she could walk," and so they were "rubber stamped" from birth for their future careers.[32] Thus, while there was, in these biographies, an emphasis on early travails, hard work, and coming up "the hard way," there was almost always the "lucky break" of being discovered, so these celebrities were not really responsible for their own success except for how their instincts or personalities helped them. Success "merely happens," usually by chance, so it is "an accidental and irrational event."[33] There is a fatalism here, where some people become rich and famous because it was meant to be, and the rest of us don't. But we can vicariously enjoy their success through reading about them and trying to emulate how they behave and what they consume. By consuming like they do, we can become a little like them.

Industrial Production of Celebrities

As celebrity culture has continued to metastasize in the late twentieth and early twenty-first centuries, some scholars have turned their attention to the even more intensified, amped up production of celebrities, while others have explored the more individual, psychological explanations for the enormous appeal of celebrity culture. As Josh Gamson and Paul McDonald have emphasized, celebrity production is an industry—in fact, a quite elaborated one that can often look like mass production—that has relied increasingly on a growing cadre of workers: managers, talent agents, press agents, publicists, personal stylists, trainers, and the like. Both scholars see contradictory explanations for celebrity. On the one hand, it cannot be totally manufactured—its potential in a person can be spotted and nurtured, based on hard work, talent, and charisma, but not just anyone can become a star. On the other hand, fame is obviously manufactured, the stars' images tightly controlled, and, as we have learned through reality TV, almost anyone can indeed become famous. In fact, these are the two stories about fame today, that it is earned and related to achievement and talent and yet that it is cynically produced through public relations and publicity that churn out the worthy and unworthy alike.[34] Of course, there is truth to both of these stories.

Both Gamson and McDonald trace this escalated production of celebrities to the collapse of the Hollywood studio system in the 1950s when television made significant inroads into movie attendance. In Hollywood during the 1930s and 1940s, most stars were bound to one of the five major studios, which, for the most part, produced and owned the stars. With the erosion of the studios' power, stars had to become "'proprietors of their own image,'" which meant, in part, mastering the image of being unique and apart from the crowd while also, of course, being "just like us."[35] Thus, the need in the 1950s, and beyond, for agents, managers, publicists, and the like to manage image control, with celebrity production becoming an increasingly elaborated and extensive business.

In the 1970s, with the success of *People* magazine and its imitators, and a growing number of television shows profiling famous people, especially movie, television, and singing stars, the industrial production of celebrities ramped up even further. By September 1981, the first movie actor to become president would be shot by John Hinckley Jr., who was bizarrely trying to impress another celebrity, Jodie Foster, while a new, syndicated TV show *Entertainment Tonight* premiered. Americans began to get a sense that celebrity culture was assuming a much more commanding role in their culture. By the late 1980s, when Dan Rather included accounts of problems in the marriage of Robin Givens and boxer Mike Tyson on *CBS Nightly News*, we knew we had come a long way from Walter Cronkite, the "most trusted man in America" who had steered the country through the John F. Kennedy assassination, the civil rights movement, and the Vietnam War. When Britney Spears shaved her head in February 2007 it was a lead story for two days on CNN, "the most trusted name in news."

New networks and cable channels were emerging to challenge the big three—ABC, NBC and CBS—on TV. As the "national market" gave way to market segmentation and niche marketing, competition for viewers increased. Channels needed to "brand" themselves, and to produce shows that would attract specific demographic niches of interest to advertisers. Cooking channels produced "celebrity chefs," while channels on finance and investing produced celebrity financial advisers and celebrity CEOs. And with the rise of twenty-four-hour cable news channels and their ever-needy news holes to fill, celebrity scandals, crimes and trials, or crimes and trials that turned unknowns into celebrities, further broke down what was once a solid wall between "the news" and entertainment. Because the problem now was there weren't enough celebrities—true "A-list" actors or rock stars and the like to fill the need for all this programming. Reality TV, which had the advantage of being very cheap to produce compared to scripted programming, could get and hold an audience and produce its own celebrities.

The radiation of the tentacles of celebrity culture has been driven further by the media consolidation of the 1980s and beyond, as the octopi conglomerates have bought up publishing houses, news outlets, movie theaters, production studios, amusement parks, record companies, television stations, cable systems, and the like and insisted on "synergy" and maximum profits from them all. And twenty-four-hour cable television, with all its competing, insatiable programs, needs to be constantly fed; celebrities are the fodder. New profit-maximizing alliances within these media behemoths mean that all kinds of cross-promotions can be launched that seem utterly natural or spontaneous when they are anything but. Thus, the winner of CBS's *Survivor* was immediately booked on CBS's *Late Night* with David Letterman, those "fired" by Donald Trump on NBC's *The Apprentice* ended up on *The Today Show*, and so forth. A story in Time-Warner's *People* can also serve as a story or interview on Time-Warner's CNN. When *The Bachelor* was launched on ABC in 2002, the network's parent company Disney also had a 50 percent stake in *Us Weekly*. Thus, the magazine played a central role in promoting the show, its contestants, and the drama among them, turning many of them into celebrities, however briefly. (Wenner media, which also publishes *Rolling Stone*, bought back Disney's stake in 2006.) Each media mastodon has multiple ways—and a pressing need—to promote its own celebrities, adding to the glut. Of paramount importance is ratings, sales, buzz, profits. Celebrities, whether adored or reviled, triumphant or mired in the tar pits of scandal, deliver these.

Thus we began to get what Gamson has called "industrialized celebrity production." Along with it, there has been a kind of democratization of fame. And what comes with such proliferating opportunities is an increased desire among many to gain the spotlight, however briefly. With this kind of fame, merit and talent no longer mattered particularly. People, as the cliché goes, became famous for being famous. As David Schmid has noted, there has been something of a collapse of the difference between fame and notoriety. "Recognition and self-exposure," he rightly observed, "are now believed to be absolute goods in themselves."[36] Ironically, while "it has never seemed easier to be famous just for being you, and possibly get rich in the process," as Karen Sternheimer writes, "the gap between the wealthiest 1 percent and the rest of Americans has widened and wages remain stagnant."[37] So the desire to get on a reality TV show, or to promote yourself as a YouTube star or Instagram influencer, may be even more intensified in such an unequal economy.

Celebrity culture is then, in the twenty-first century, the result of an intricate, interconnected, and many-faceted industry targeted especially, although hardly exclusively, to younger people, especially women age 18–34.[38] Celebrities are, or become, commodities used to attract us—consumers—to TV shows, movies, concerts, magazines, and the like. So they—their very identities—have to be marketed and have to fill certain market niches. They thus "operate as sources of capital" for various branches of the entertainment industry, as Paul McDonald notes, and "form a point of intersection between meaning and money."[39] Through various attention-getting devices—a breakout performance or outrageous behavior, backstories about adversity and crisis—the star first has to gain symbolic value as someone who appeals to people. Here they need to seem above us, yet we also need to identify with them, and they need to be seen as distinct, branded personalities—Sandra Bullock needs to be seen as different from Reese Witherspoon, for example. These specific traits—hair color and facial features, but also speech patterns, modes of behavior, how they present themselves, and stories about their rise to the top—if appealing to enough people combine to create their symbolic value as admirable individuals. As that symbolic value increases through publicity and marketing, the celebrity begins to gain economic value, which is the real mark of success.[40] And, of course, when their symbolic value declines—the "has-been," the "where-are-they-now" former celebrities, those who are caught in scandals or do or say offensive things, as Mel Gibson did—so does their economic value.

While certain celebrities remain stars for much of their lives, mostly because of their talent and achievements, but also because of very shrewd marketing and PR decisions, many others are "one-hit wonders," or flash-in-the-pan child or reality TV stars, or were stars of formerly very popular television shows that have long been off the air. Thus, there is a pressing industrial need, especially in our overheated and highly competitive media market, to constantly find and produce new celebrities. Indeed, our contemporary media economy seems increasingly fixated on creating, promoting, and capitalizing on famous figures who, in turn, give audiences cause to turn on, tune in, and link up with a rapidly expanding array of media technologies.

Celebrity Culture and Neoliberalism

Yet another important explanation for the explosive rise in celebrity culture over the past several decades is the establishment in the 1980s and beyond of what scholars call "neoliberalism," but might just as well be termed neoconservatism or small-government market fundamentalism. Advanced especially by the Ronald Reagan and Margaret Thatcher administrations, and fervently embraced by the Trump administration, this was a new common sense about limiting the role of government and the absolute centrality of individual responsibility to personal success. Neoliberalism attacked the general acceptance, which emerged during the Great Depression and was cemented in the post–World War II period, that the state has a responsibility to mitigate inequality, to provide basic services, and—through a combination of monetary and fiscal means—to even out capitalism's boom-bust cycle.

Prior to the New Deal in the 1930s, there was barely any governmental safety net that protected those who had lost their jobs, were unemployed widows with children, or older people who could no longer work. The Great Depression, with a 25 percent unemployment rate in 1933 alone, drove home how brutal and untenable this laissez-faire approach was.[41] With the New Deal, it now became a given that the state should focus on full employment, economic growth, and the welfare of its citizens, and that "state power should be freely deployed" alongside of or even intervening in market processes to achieve these ends. Thus, over a thirty-year period, we got Social Security, unemployment benefits, pension funds, and Medicare and Medicaid.

But in the wake of the various economic problems of the 1970s— "stagflation" (high inflation plus high unemployment), the OPEC oil embargo that limited oil and gas imports into the United States, soaring interest rates—and the election of Reagan here and Thatcher in England, market fundamentalism became the new gospel. This religion consists of the following core tenets: a belief in what was called "trickle down" economics (cutting taxes on corporations and the wealthy will allegedly prompt them to produce more jobs, so that benefits "trickle down" to everyone) and efforts to limit or eliminate the government's role in redistributing wealth, which rests on cutting taxes, especially for the wealthy.

There is a complete faith that the market, not the government, is the best arbiter of wealth distribution. Thus, the government should stay out of providing services, especially for the needy, the poor, or retired people, because the state is allegedly less efficient, and more corrupt than, say, Wall Street or corporate America. To justify this, neoliberalism glorifies individualism and individual responsibility. As David Harvey succinctly put it, "All forms of social solidarity were to be dissolved in favor of individualism, private property, personal responsibility and family values."[42]

How are we everyday people meant to internalize the market fundamentalism mantra? What persona must we assume here? And how is it related to celebrity culture? Neoliberalism insists upon and promotes the need for an idealized, productive citizen who must learn how to govern himself or herself. It is up to us to achieve self-mastery, and if we do we will control our own destiny and be autonomous and fulfilled. So our very selves must become an ongoing project, something we must work on, transform, and improve, so we can compete effectively and even succeed in this environment.[43] In this worldview there are no structural, institutional obstacles that might thwart such choices for some or, conversely, offer opportunities and advantages that make them possible for others.

Celebrities, whether ones with genuine admired talent or those created through reality TV or Instagram, are such people. They personify the benefits of constant self-cultivation, self-monitoring, and self-transformation. The ones who seem to work hard, take individual responsibility for their careers and behaviors, and succeed are exemplars of—and role models for—the ideal neoliberal subject. More to the point, their prominent success as distinct, self-fashioned individuals legitimates neoliberalism as a system: they supposedly did it on their own, and definitely without help from any government or social services. Conversely, those celebrities who fail to take responsibility for fashioning a productive, individually responsible self are castigated and personify the dangers and humiliations of lacking self-mastery. In celebrity culture, there are no structural impediments to success and no need for governmental safety nets: it is all about individuals and individual agency.

In addition, for everyday people, self-actualization comes through buying the right stuff: being a persistent and shrewd consumer, not just of goods but also of services, like gym memberships, financial advice, and private health care. Neoliberalism relies crucially on consumerism, and vice versa. The media—whether *The Oprah Winfrey Show, Judge Judy,* or *Keeping Up with the Kardashians*—have been full of advice about how to govern, discipline, and reinvent oneself, and provide a road map for how to be a successful subject of the market fundamentalism ethos.[44] And celebrity gossip magazines, with their features on how you can get the same look, go on the same diet, get the same furniture, buy the same baby clothes, all drive home that copying celebrities' consumer choices can be a central component of your own success when, indeed, it's all up to you.

At the same time, most celebrities who gain a certain level of visibility and respect feel they need to be involved in at least one charitable organization. Some, like Elton John or Annie Lenox or Ellen DeGeneres, have donated to over forty organizations.[45] Although many celebrities are genuine about and often deeply invested in their concerns—Michael J. Fox and his Foundation for Parkinson's Research, for example— they also understand that not being philanthropic, especially given the amounts of money some of them make, will hurt their image. But widespread celebrity support of charities as diverse as the Breast Cancer Research Foundation or Feeding America or Make Poverty History—all completely noble causes—also emphasize the necessity of private funding to combat social problems in the face of government inaction. If we have so many celebrities giving to or championing private foundations or nongovernmental organizations, do we really need government programs to support the sick and the needy?

Fandom and the Pleasures of Celebrity Culture

While scholars like Josh Gamson, Paul McDonald, and others have emphasized that we have such an overblown celebrity culture because it is a huge business with a constant need for new raw material, they and others have also explored the consumption side of the equation. Why do we as individuals pay attention to them, even need them? Being a fan of one celebrity or another has become an utterly routine part of everyday life now. We use their biographies (however invented) as guideposts for our own lives: By what age did they do such-and-so, and can I do that too? We want their relics—the towel they used, the glove they wore, the pen they held—to somehow shorten the distance between us and them.

Early writing about fans—drawing from the word "fanatic"—mostly dismissed them as "obsessed individuals" or members of a "hysterical crowd" (think images of young women in the 1960s gripped by Beatlemania). This drew, in part, from late nineteenth and early twentieth century anxieties—based on large-scale immigration, rapid urbanization, and the explosion of popular entertainments—as working-class people, having enjoyed a degree of improvement in economic, living, and labor conditions, sought opportunities to savor the newly created weekend. As new pastimes emerged and people flocked to the boardwalks, amusement parks, and movie houses, so, too, did concerns surface about the emergence of irrational and impressionable "masses."

In the 1940s, communication scholars working in the Marxist, Frankfurt school tradition, Adorno and Horkheimer, mentioned earlier, were deeply skeptical of the impact of new media—from recorded sound to film and radio programs to magazines—on fans' abilities to see the world, especially power relations and inequality, clearly and critically. They lamented mass culture's standardization and dilution of culture and argued that passive consumption of such content served as a form of ideological manipulation. Scholars such as Paul Lazarsfeld, influenced by socialism but not a Marxist, also took a paternalistic attitude toward the audience, worrying whether or not radio listeners were tuning in to "serious" broadcasts—folks of lower economic and educational achievement, it turned out, were not. Even as radio researcher Herta Herzog's study of nonelite, female radio listeners pioneered the gratifications approach—a method that emphasizes a desire to understand the rationale and meaning-making process of audiences—Herzog nevertheless argued, from a Freudian psychoanalytic position, that the uneducated listeners were primarily motivated by a compensatory desire to fulfill their own personal lack; that is to say, a sense of resentment toward those who were more educated than themselves.

Social critics saw the "masses" as passive consumers, the dupes of popular culture, feminized and highly vulnerable to its seductions. For example, when the silent movie star and matinee idol Rudolph Valentino died in 1926 at the age of thirty-one, and his hundreds of thousands of mostly female fans went into a highly emotional state of mass mourning, the phenomenon simply corroborated the notion of fandom as "excessive" and "bordering on deranged behavior."[46] In this view, fans were inept, socially isolated individuals (and typically women), and fandom served as psychological compensation for "the absence of 'authentic' relationships in their lives."[47] Yet while fandom could make up for low self-esteem, lack of friendships or community, and a dull, boring life, it was also seen as "a risky, even dangerous, compensatory mechanism."[48]

In time, scholars began to raise, in earnest, critical questions about the nature of fandom and the desires and motivations of audience members. A notable shift occurred in the 1980s in media studies, when various scholars, while not denying the power of the mass media or celebrity culture, began to take issue with the image of media audiences as passive dupes, accepting whatever was presented to them. Stuart Hall, one of the field's most eminent media studies scholars, and director of the Centre for Contemporary Cultural Studies in the United Kingdom, proposed a model for how audience members might make meaning from the media they consume. His famous and highly influential "encoding-decoding" schema argued that some people do, indeed, take the dominant or preferred meaning of a media text at pretty much face value. Others, however—people who think all the news is biased, or hate television on basic principle—typically engage in "oppositional" readings of media texts, rejecting their premises, values, and storylines. Most people, however, engage in "negotiated" readings; they bring to bear their own knowledge and experiences when watching television or a film or reading a magazine, and accept some elements of the text while questioning or rejecting others.[49]

Other scholars began both testing and extending Hall's work, and this applied to conceptions of fandom as well. In his book *Claims to Fame*, Josh Gamson interviewed fans themselves, as well as analyzing the celebrity production system, and developed a detailed typology of fan types. He laid out the three broad interpretive strategies that celebrity watching audiences use, depending on how aware they are of the production process, how much they believe in the veracity of the celebrity text, and how much they engage with celebrity culture. On one end of the spectrum are "Traditionals" who see fame as a recognition of internal gifts, believe most of what they read and hear, and have minimal knowledge of the actual apparatus of celebrity production; this is the stereotypical, gullible fan. "Second-order traditionals," in the middle of the spectrum, appreciate a more complex narrative about the star in which publicity mechanisms play a role in producing his or her fame, but this knowledge does not undermine the fan's esteem. This kind of fan is not ignorant of the publicity system but takes it into account.

On the opposite end of the spectrum is what Gamson labeled "postmodernist/antibelievers," the total skeptics. They are interested in the techniques of artifice in and of themselves; they know about celebrity manufacture and seek out its evidence and its details, rejecting the story of the naturally rising celebrity as naïve and false. Their belief in celebrity gossip (and in the legitimacy or authenticity of celebrities) is minimal, and their awareness of and cynicism about the production process is high. This is a form of engaged disbelief, and the revelations of the celebrity-production techniques feeds rather than undermines their interest. For example, when Jake Gyllenhaal began dating the pop star Taylor Swift and then quickly broke up with her, a skeptic might wonder whether he and his publicists were trying to keep him in the headlines to help promote his latest film *Southpaw*.

This shift in thinking about the way audiences actively use media provided for additionally nuanced understandings of fandom. Rather than think of fans as passive consumers whose lack of taste drives their choices, John Fiske argues that fandom is denigrated precisely because it is typically linked with the consumption and enjoyment of "cultural forms that the dominant value system denigrates."[50] If fandom had become, as Fiske noted, "a common feature of popular culture in industrialized societies,"[51] then we should rethink its functions and, yes, its pleasures. While knowledge and consumption of official or what used to be called "high" culture (opera, fine wine, art) enhances our cultural capital, knowledge about celebrity culture has come to do that too. Fiske noted how fandom can fill a cultural lack by providing a community, and one based on having a specialized knowledge of and relationship to the star that enhances social prestige and self-esteem.

Fandom serves as a tie to others with the same passions, tastes, and affinities, and Fiske especially wanted to emphasize how fans work to produce meanings about celebrities through different modes of "productivity," and thus elaborate on and produce our own extended meanings from the offerings of the culture industries. "Semiotic" productivity involves the ways in which fans use the stars they admire as resources to construct their own identities, often more empowered, often in opposition to prevailing expectations about appropriate behaviors. One example was when many Madonna fans in the 1980s drew from her defiance of norms around female sexuality to embrace their own desires for sexual agency as girls and women.

"Enunciative" productivity is one we all know: it is shared commentary, sometimes praiseworthy, sometimes condemnatory, between us and others, about a celebrity (or a performance he or she is in) that relates them and their behaviors to our everyday lives. Indeed, as Fiske notes, "much of the pleasure of fandom lies in the fan talk that it produces."[52] At the height of MTV's *Jersey Shore* phenomenon, for example, people loved watching the show together and (typically) expressing shock or outrage over the latest excesses of the show's stars. Viewers of *The Bachelor* (and *The Bachelorette*) often text or tweet with others while the show is on to comment, often derisively, about the comments and behaviors of those on the screen. Such enunciative productivity affirms a group's core values, what it admires and disdains, and what values binds it together. "Textual productivity" is when fans create and circulate texts based on celebrities, TV shows, and movies, typically online, and often extend or utterly alter the characters and meanings of the original production to suit their own needs and desires. All of these forms of productivity rest, in part, on the notion that "stars are constructed by their fans and owe their stardom entirely to them" and serve central functions in constructing individual and group identities.[53] Fiske's work helps to outline how active fandoms, expressed both individually and in concert with other fans, allow audiences to benefit emotionally and socially while enhancing our cultural capital within the fan community.[54] In a large-scale society, the enunciative productivity that Fiske outlines is made possible thanks to our collective access to a common cohort of actors whom we know and about whom we can engage in sociable conversation. Studies show that gossip, despite its trivial reputation and negative connotations, actually serves important social functions, such as encouraging bonding and camaraderie among friends and family members. It can also allow us to release stress, share ideas, and strengthen friendships.[55]

Indeed, scholars like Joke Hermes have noted how celebrity culture— and especially gossip about celebrities—serves as a kind of social glue within large-scale societies. In her study of gossip magazine readers, Hermes identified a series of pleasures associated with celebrity gossip, from the vicarious enjoyment of a world of wealth and glamour to the feeling that celebrities are a part of our own inner circles, a kind of extended family.[56]

Gossip has been typically associated with women, taken to refer to malicious talk about people not present and to reinforce a form of informal control over others. But the explosion in celebrity gossip has shown that it can also be highly pleasurable, and hardly only a female practice or domain. Nor is such gossip always mean-spirited; it can be admiring and friendly. Gossip about celebrities—their achievements, their marriages and divorces, their cheating scandals, their trips to rehab—draws people together to evaluate behaviors and to construe standards of shared morality, about what is and is not acceptable behavior. It serves to create in-groups and out-groups. So it helps establish solidarity, a sense of community, including a moral community that identifies and locates what we feel to be ethical, behavioral certainties. Unlike discussing politics or current affairs, for example, which can be contentious, or involve grasping esoteric policy problems, celebrity gossip allows us to make judgments without having to think too hard. Thus it provides a form of confident self-expression about famous, rich, and often powerful others. It is, for the most part, safe and easy commentary and can protect us from more serious engagement with each other.[57]

Hermes identified a series of other pleasures we get from celebrity gossip. It can enlarge the reader's private world, where we can enjoy a vicarious world of glamour and can feel involved with celebrities who are richer and more famous than we are; they are brought into our circle of family and friends. Through what she calls the "extended family repertoire," which relies on a highly personal mode of address to the reader, we can develop a strong emotional connection to the stars. We can gain what can seem like "secret" knowledge about them and their lives that may "confer an imaginary sense of power over the rich and powerful," but also over others because you're in the know and they are not.[58]

Some of these are emotional pleasures, but Hermes notes there are cognitive ones as well. When we read about a rumor or speculation about a celebrity, especially because we know some of this gossip is false or exaggerated, we engage in puzzle solving, trying to ascertain what we think is true and what isn't. There is a pleasure here, the fun of speculation in trying to "ferret out" the truth, because most of us have our doubts about the truthfulness of gossip magazines. Today, we can often fact check stories, compare sources, and even troll celebs' social media accounts to learn the "truth." We are ever more aware of the ways that celebrities "fake it"—from Photoshop to plastic surgery to strategically placed paparazzi and leaked tidbits. Such reading may involve the intellectual activity of hypothesizing about relationships, where we rely on our intuition and previous experiences with similar stories.[59]

Another pleasure of course is schadenfreude, relishing the misfortunes of others. With celebrities, we often love judging them, denouncing them, and ridiculing them as much as we love admiring them.[60] And when they fail or are exposed as phony or superficial, it can be consoling to those of us who never made it into the spotlight.[61] Kathie Lee Gifford, as the cohost of the highly popular *Live with Regis & Kathie Lee* in the 1990s, constantly bragged about her fantastic marriage and that her husband, Frank, was a "human love machine." Then in 1997, Frank was caught having extramarital trysts with a female flight attendant at New York's Regency Hotel. To those irritated by Kathie Lee's superior, smug, self-satisfied presentation of her allegedly perfect marriage, there was great satisfaction here in her humiliation. More recently, in 2013, when nineteen-year-old Justin Bieber was arrested for speeding through a Miami neighborhood, driving under the influence, and resisting arrest, and later egging his neighbor's home, those who envied his massive success at the young age of fifteen took great delight in this tarnishing of his image. A massive—and to some deeply satisfying—fall from power was the disgrace of Harvey Weinstein, who not only had reportedly harassed and assaulted women for years, but had verbally and publically humiliated men as well.

But are we all, then, just nasty people? Why do we find glee in this kind of schadenfreude? The pleasure we find in celebrities' pain is actually quite rational. First, when stars fail, their failure reinforces our own, perhaps preexisting, sense that the standards of beauty, wealth, and success that the celebrity industries embody are unrealistic, even for those who appear to have "made it." Second, when we judge celebrities and find fault in their actions, we have the opportunity to affirm our own moral codes, or punish deviance, thus creating and reinforcing boundaries around our own moral frameworks.[62]

While we may criticize stars in ways that bolster normative values (e.g., oh, she got too heavy, he is a cheating dog), we may also actively disagree with those moral codes, standards of conduct, and rigid demands of physical perfection. Indeed, much of the pleasure of celebrity gossip may actually lie in subverting these codes. When we tell a friend how Bono spent nearly two grand to have his favorite hat flown to him or how P. Diddy bought his son a $340,000 car for his sixteenth birthday, we take pleasure in the raised eyebrows and scornful looks that we share.[63] These moments let us know "we are the same, we are normal. These people are not." In these moments, we reaffirm our own values and beliefs, often in rejection of those that celebrity culture deems ideal.[64]

Gossip that is critical, or that rejects the codes of the celebrity universe, may be seen as an expression of what Alison Jaggar calls *outlaw emotions*. Jaggar argues that subordinated individuals may pay a higher price for disagreeing with the status quo and therefore become frustrated, fearful, or even angry when faced with so-called norms. Rejections of socially sanctioned identities and behaviors, in this theory, may serve as a mode of resistance.[65] Young women, for instance, who have been told that they have to be supergirls in order to "have it all," may take pleasure in scoffing at the impossible, paradoxical standards that make it compulsory to be white and heterosexual, standards that remain dominant across much of celebrity media. Gossip that seems catty may actually be a rational response to the claim that, for women, independence and success *are* possible, but totally tenuous, at risk of being ripped away at any moment due to some minor perceived inadequacy or failure to measure up.[66] Talking back may be a way of rejecting conformity to the standard conventions of successful femininity. Expressing these types of outlaw emotions, especially in concert with other like-minded people, can be deeply satisfying.

It is a kind of pleasurable subversion. We enjoy the opportunity to engage in a form of confident self-expression about famous, rich, and often powerful others. We flex the public's ideological muscles, as if to say, "You may be wealthy, gorgeous, and all the rest, but we still get the final say." While these moments can be mean-spirited, they are more centrally about our ability to affirm social norms in concert with other like-minded people. We judge celebrities not only to make ourselves feel better about our own place in the social landscape but also as a means of picking and choosing which values we adhere to and which we reject.

Because celebrities' lives are publicly enacted, through what Hermes calls the "repertoire of melodrama," which rests on sentimental and sensational language and narratives, their miseries, dramas, and feuds also become our own. We use celebrity life as a way of considering our own experiences, and stories about the private lives of the rich and famous reaffirm a sense of basic human equality.[67] But as we also wallow in the misery of the privileged few, we may feel somehow righteous; we can imagine a cosmic (if not a political or structural) justice being exacted. We learn the price paid for daring to rise above others (the shame) or for squandering fame through ego or excess or overindulgence. These narratives remind us that even wealth and success do not free us from sorrow, and such tales of stars' suffering can impart a sense that in the end we're all equal with our crosses to bear, despite disparities in wealth and fame. Grief is democratized. Joys and sorrows are common.

Obviously many of us do not read celebrity gossip "straight," taking it at face value. We know that celebrity gossip is trashy, and to appear sucked in by it makes us look like gullible dupes of the media, so by indulging in it while, at the same time, distancing ourselves from it, we can assume an ironic stance toward it, laugh at it, and make it clear that we know how bad it is. We can even boast of reading the *Enquirer* or clicking through *TMZ* as a way of being campy and immersing ourselves in low taste. Celebrity texts now anticipate our critical gaze, presenting content with a wink and a sly nod to our own skepticism so that even the most jaded can enjoy. That way we can enact (through enunciative productivity) that we are inoculated against it.

The Psychology of Fandom

A number of theories have emerged to explain the psychology of fandom and our relationships to celebrities. Today, we take for granted that the media and the celebrity culture it sustains have created new forms of publicness, through which we might have intimate relationships with people we have never met. As Richard Schickel wrote in *Intimate Strangers: The Culture of Celebrity*, one of the first, key books written about the cultural study of fame, thanks to media technologies we are brought ever "closer" to the famous, allowing us to enjoy an illusion of intimacy with them. "To a greater or lesser degree," we have internalized celebrities, "unconsciously made them a part of our consciousness, just as if they were, in fact, friends."[68] He continued that celebrities take up "permanent residence" in our inner lives as well, becoming central to our "reveries and fantasies, guides to action, to sexuality, to ambition." Now, indeed, celebrity culture can be "permanently insinuated" into our sensibilities, as many of us carry them, their traits, and our relationships with them around as part of our "mental luggage."[69]

Media representations, including those of celebrities, can foster in us a sense that we actually know and may understand famous figures as though they were a part of our everyday lives, like friends or family members. When we experience these feelings toward a media figure, this is called a "parasocial relationship." Such relationships, in turn, produce "parasocial interactions" (PSI), which occur when audience members respond to media figures as if we were with them in a face-to-face social relationship, talking to or feeling empathy for that individual as though he or she were a personal acquaintance.[70] Examples include when we might yell at a newscaster, or someone featured in a news story on TV, as if they could hear us, or when we know a character is about to walk into a dangerous situation and yell "Don't do it!"

Initially, as with early thoughts about fandom, some scholars saw parasocial relationships as a form of mental lack, a compensation for loneliness or deficiencies in one's social life. As David Giles has noted, "The implication that PSI is 'imaginary,' or 'pseudo-social,' pathologizes viewers who form strong parasocial attachments."[71] Other work has disputed these claims, and examined the affective functions of this phenomenon. For example, our one-sided interactions with media figures (real or fictional) allow us to use and assess their behaviors and attitudes as ways of understanding and measuring our own lives, and this may be especially true for adolescents as they seek to use celebrities as role models for their own identity formation. In these ways, PSI can be seen as "an extension of normal social cognition."[72] Research has shown that PSI can be especially robust if our attraction to the media figure is strong and the program or film in question is especially realistic. Indeed, perceived similarity between the media figure and the audience member, otherwise known as identification, can be a very important factor in the strength of the parasocial relationship. Physical similarities, taste in dress, or shared hobbies and passions can make audiences feel that famous figures really are "like us." And for parasocial relationships to be sustained, we need to believe that the celebrity is not so very different from people in our own social circles.[73]

Giles sought to identify different types of relationships we might form with famous unknown others, which can help us understand why we might connect to some celebrities and not others, and to connect with them in different ways. First there is identification, when we recognize some characteristics in the media figure that we feel we share. Yet while we might identify with a star, we may or may not engage in PSI with him or her. There is also wishful identification, where we desire to emulate the figure with whom we identify, and affinity, where we like the media figure without necessarily identifying with him or her.

But the kind of media figure the celebrity is, and how we are addressed, can shape our levels of parasocial interaction. Direct address to us—by talk show hosts, comedians, newscasters—can especially evoke strong PSI. The mode of address in celebrity gossip magazines is also intimate and direct: the magazine is your best friend with the latest insider, confidential info, talking to *you*, with headlines like "The Joan Rivers You Didn't Know" seeking to lure us in. Unlike the *New York Times*, which would not have headlines like "What Was Andrew Wiener Thinking? His Secrets Inside!," the questioning titles seek to engage you and immediately turn you from a passive recipient of information into an active adjudicator of the moral issues involved. And with each question, betrayal, triumph, or crisis, a judgment is required; it is a given that you are an authority on such matters and will bring your own social knowledge and moral compass to bear on the topic at hand. You are hailed as having every right to evaluate these rich and famous people, and to speculate about their futures.[74]

Jackie Stacey interviewed female fans and she too found that they had various, often powerful, relationships with movie stars, from worshipping and adoring them to identifying with them. Some identified with stars with whom they felt some similarity, either in appearance, values, or behavior, and some used the stars—how they looked, dressed, and behaved—as resources for their own behavior, as a way to transform themselves, to play with identity, or to craft for themselves a mode of successful femininity. Others, however, loved losing themselves when watching a film as they imagined themselves taking on the role and identity of the star in the movie. There was a pleasure here for viewers in this "temporary loss of self" and of "sharing emotional intensity with the star."[75] Stars "serve a normative function," providing "ideals of feminine attractiveness" but also ideals around self-confidence, self-assurance, strength, and sophistication that some viewers sought to emulate.[76]

Melanie Green and her colleagues have called this type of escape "transportation." Green et al. conceptualize transportation as a distinct mental process that melds our attention, media imagery, and feelings. Their concept, known as "transportation theory," seeks to specify how it is that audiences take pleasure in the feeling of escape and loss of self that media texts may provide and the ways in which those texts facilitate transportive experiences.[77] Their work on the mechanisms of media enjoyment also helps explain why celebrity culture and gossip can be so absorbing. Transportation is, they argue, a desired state; we want to be taken into alternative universes (we all know that feeling of disappointment when we can't "get into" a book or TV show). We enjoy the feeling of being taken away from our mundane reality into a story world. Many audience members are eager to escape from their everyday lives into another realm, in part to leave our worries, stresses, and self-consciousness behind. We connect with media characters, and through transportation may temporarily inhabit or even adopt their thoughts, goals, emotions, and behaviors, developing an illusion of intimacy with them.

Transportation expands our horizons, opens up new information, and provides us with opportunities for identity play. We can try on different personas, attitudes, and behaviors, and explore other possible selves with minimal real world costs. So we can use characters' situations and experiences to understand our own lives and, at the same time, use criteria we typically apply in our own lives to evaluate characters' actions and behaviors. Transportation is not always pleasurable in obvious ways; when we watch horror movies, or action films where the hero nearly dies multiple times, or desperate tearjerkers, transportation can be extremely scary or deeply upsetting. Yet these media experiences allow us to explore our ability to tolerate unpleasant emotions such as rage, fear, and sadness, and we may even seek out transportive opportunities to engage such emotions. In this way, there is "enjoyment from traveling to the

Dark Side." The delight in immersing ourselves in such narratives is their relative safety—by contrast, our real world is safe and nonthreatening, and if the hero survives the risks, so do we. "These safety modalities," the authors argue, "interlock to banish the terror of death or failure."[78]

While Green et al. focused primarily on fictional narratives like novels or films and that feeling of being "lost" in a story, we can be transported into nonfictional narratives as well, and it is that powerful sense of being transported that enables us to identify so powerfully with certain celebrities. Transportation via years-long narratives—starting in 2005, for example, the ongoing "Brangelina" love triangle and divorce saga, later the endless Kardashian dramas—allow us to "get to know" and develop a sense of intimacy with their famous protagonists through our narrative immersion. So when we open a celebrity magazine, with shots of stars in sunny Southern California in features about them being "just like us," we can be transported, however fleetingly, into this balmy and privileged world ourselves. And just as we enjoy the highs, we also can take pleasure in the lows; when we read an in-depth profile of a celebrity, particularly one who has been through a recent triumph or tragedy, we can inhabit their feelings and relate their experiences to our own, creating a sense of pathos and shared experience.

Celebrity and Identity

Our ability to relate to and identify with celebrities also allows us to use stars as a way of considering our own identities, values, and beliefs. In our media-saturated world, being a fan is often integral to our own self-formation. Teens, in particular, may be fascinated by stars, as they manage their own ideas and expectations of self and adulthood, a connection that may help to explain why young adults are major fans and followers of celebrity culture, pop music, and individual idols.[79] Indeed, we all have to develop a story about who we are, what we care about and stand for, what we hope to do with our lives, and what we do *not* want to be like. The vast arsenal of celebrity profiles, successes, and disasters provides raw material, resources we can try on, weave in, or reject as we construct our self-identity.[80]

But the lessons that celebrity narratives teach us about which personal characteristics and values are celebrated, and which are punished, are often problematic, especially when it comes to issues of gender, race, and sexuality. Stories about celebrities have, since the nineteenth century, shaped notions of admirable, even enviable identities and warned us about those to be avoided. Today, in the United States and Britain, celebrity narratives continue to emphasize stars who are white, heterosexual, and female, despite the fact that fans identify across lines of gender, race, and sexuality. In addition, young women continue to be the main subject of celebrity gossip, and its target audience.

Nonetheless, there are major pleasures for female consumers of celebrity gossip. As Andrea McDonnell has argued in *Reading Celebrity Gossip Magazines*, here "women take center stage"—especially women between the ages of eighteen and thirty-four, with the magazines investigating and celebrating "women's triumphs and challenges, all narrated from a female point of view."[81] Unlike the mostly male political public sphere, where government policies and current events are debated, this female-centered intimate public sphere foregrounds what is marginalized as unimportant elsewhere in the news: marriage, relationships, childbirth, motherhood, divorce.[82] Celebrity culture offers an alternative realm to the mostly male-dominated news in the mainstream press. Women and girls are absolutely central to this world— they matter symbolically and economically. Women—which ones are to be admired and which ones loathed—are the drivers of celebrity journalism. They are the ones who propel the magazines off the racks. Corporate profits rest on them. Take the Kardashians: they challenge the patriarchal family; it's the mother and the sisters who run the show and keep the dollars flowing in. Unlike schoolteachers, daycare workers, or secretaries, these women are not paid less than they're worth, but *more* than they're worth. And unlike in the precincts of Congress, families and children are of utmost importance. Women in this realm work long hours and are still able to have families because they have the support to do so.[83]

For young women in the early twenty-first century who have been told that they have to be supergirls, celebrity gossip magazines and sites serve as important primers. How to be sexy but not overtly sexual? How to have a career and a family? How to have success and male approval? In an age of collapsed courtship rules and "hooking up," how to find a guy and have a long-term relationship? These are the questions about combining femininity and success that, week in and week out, celebrity gossip dramatizes. And who else to provide the right answers than female stars who seem to have cracked the code?[84]

But these pleasures come at a price. Because from the blogs and vlogs (video logs) to fashion and gossip magazines, the primary focus of these is not the famous female's latest professional accomplishment, but rather her personal life, her appearance, emotions, and relationships: her life events. The central beat of celebrity journalism is emotion: love, hate, heartbreak, despair, joy. As McDonnell found in her analysis of celebrity magazines, the top five cover story topics, in order, were relationship troubles or breakups; pregnancy; stories about celebrities' weight, bodies, or plastic surgery; weddings or engagements; and dating and romances.[85]

Celebrity magazines and their TV and online counterparts serve as persistent primers on what constitutes successful femininity, and what does not. Female celebrities are under relentless, withering, microscopic scrutiny. And their faces and bodies, as opposed to their talents, their smarts, and their inner lives, are where their true "selves" are located. Su Holmes and Diane Negra argue that when it comes to celebrity scandals, the media treat women differently and more critically than they do men. They see a persistent framework in which female celebrities are somehow poised between emotional and relational chaos and happiness, serenity, and control over their lives. Will this relationship, this marriage, this friendship work out this time or lead yet again to betrayal and heartbreak? "[We] are invited to play a 'waiting game' to see when their hard-won achievements will collapse under the simultaneous weight of relationships, family and career."[86] In this way, they personify most women's struggles for work-life balance, especially when it comes to juggling having a job with raising a family. More to the point, when female celebrities fail, it legitimates the notion that, for women, achieving such a balance is in fact not possible. We see this push and pull activated in three main narratives that swirl around famous women: the quest for physical perfection, the adherence to norms of decorum and social acceptability, and the maintenance of idealized domesticity in the form of a heterosexual marriage plot and the attainment of selfless motherhood. If they don't conform to—and bolster— the standard conventions of successful femininity, they will pay. They are the "train wrecks," out-of-control women who fail to uphold, and even rebel against, traditional, even retrograde, gender norms.

As public figures, the bodies of famous women are constantly on display, extolled as the height of physical beauty and success. "Hot bodies" are a form of cultural capital that allow famous women to secure movie roles, magazine covers, and the attention and adoration of the public. Bodies that do not conform are singled out for ridicule. Women are supposed to be extremely thin and fit. With a few exceptions, being overweight is cause for derision. One magazine told Kate Moss (!) to "tone up her midsection," while the *National Enquirer* sniped that "Rosanna Arquette has a beach ball for a belly," and that "Queen Latifah doesn't deprive herself—and it shows!" Reese Witherspoon, at the beach with her kids, was pictured with a yellow circle drawn around her stomach and a caption that tells her "it's time to hit the gym!"

Being too thin is also bad, but a cause for shock and concern instead of ridicule. "Shocking Trend: Stars Flaunt Their Stick Figures" blares *In Touch*, with yellow circles drawn over the offending parts like "twig shoulders," "bony back," and protruding "ribs." "Stars used to show off their cleavage," complained the magazine. "Now they show off collarbones."[87] "SKINNY S.O.S!" brays the cover of the *Star*; "Star's Scary New Affliction—Foodophobia and It's Contagious!" "BARES BONES!," the magazine screams, pointing out celebs whose "collarbones are more concave" and "stomach skin hangs looser."[88]

Famous women also come under scrutiny for their actions, and no social taboo is too minor for ridicule or condemnation. Nothing is more important than self-regulation and serious self-monitoring—of your figure, face, hair, outfits, behavior, sexuality, and maternal practices. You also need to manage your career well, but that seems secondary to everything else. Ideal women here are both independent—they have their own professions, money, and sources of success—and yet completely reliant on the love and approval of men. And they get that approval because their economic independence is tempered by their hyperfemininity.[89] So you better be a good judge of character, in potential boyfriends or husbands, and in friends, who are also crucial to success and happiness. If you chose wrong, you could end up with one of those numerous celebrity husbands who is discovered to be screwing your nanny on the side.

Proper consumption is of the utmost importance. Celebrity gossip magazines glorify consumerism and have become a showcase for various products, nearly all of them pitched to women. Product placement is ubiquitous and we learn which lipstick, workout clothes, low calorie snacks, nail polish, handbags, headphones, lamps, basinets, vacation resorts, and the like various celebrities swear by. Stars who know exactly which outfit to wear, which restaurant to patronize, and which smoothie to sip gain cultural capital and enhance their influence as marketers. Gossip narratives often revolve around products, presented as a solution to every possible woe. Social media stars, minor and A-list alike, make a living peddling everything from gadgets to sneakers to cosmetics. By purchasing what they love and recommend, you can be a little like them too. Ad pages seek to mimic such features, with banner headlines like "Hollywood Summer Trends" or "Fun in the Sun Celebrity Favorites" introducing readers to perfume, "high fashion" backpacks, and "interactive jewelry."[90]

Some of these stories are geared at teaching middle-class people how to consume like the stars, but at a fraction of the cost, thus gaining access to the good life. Others, like *Life & Style*'s "Money I$ No Object," present the good life as totally inaccessible, showing "diva" Mariah Carey sporting $1,500 Tom Ford sandals, a $5,600 minidress, and a thirty-five-carat diamond engagement ring estimated at $10 million.[91] While these stories revel in conspicuous consumption and make hierarchies based on wealth seem perfectly legitimate, even exciting and deeply enviable, they also stoke our resentments about income inequality. Especially galling are the features about how much celebrities spend on clothes and jewelry for their infants and toddlers, who in a few months will completely outgrow their little Gucci leather jackets or Prada dresses. To avoid any potentially negative blowback from the trappings of wealth, famous women must also be polite, deferential, and friendly. Stars who are deemed "high maintenance" are condemned, for narcissism is a big sin; *Life & Style* regularly asks readers if stars are behaving like a "Diva or Down-to-Earth," pitting celebs who pick up their own takeout against glamazons who won't lift a finger to open a car door.

But celebrity narratives insist that the most important goal for famous women, no matter how wealthy, independent, or successful in their careers, is to find a loving, heterosexual relationship (ideally, with a "soul mate") in order to be truly happy. Women *must* be in a romantic relationship, and these are always "blissful" and "perfect" until the nasty breakup.

Here's where the men come in. The ideal catch is financially successful, caring, faithful, attractive, fun-loving, and supportive: an independent yet domesticated man. Cheating, drinking too much, or drug abuse are signs that the man is unable to restrain his appetites or control his emotions and behaviors. Depending on women for money is also a sign of weakness and failure. It was bad enough that former basketball star, and husband of Khloe Kardashian, Lamar Odom, nearly overdosed in a brothel. But that he "squandered large sums [of money] on booze, drugs and hookers" meant he would be "still going after Khloe's money."[92] The worst crime, however, is domestic abuse. In this world men must protect their women.

A typically laudatory story noted that Romain Dauriac, husband of Scarlett Johansson, who was "exhausting herself" on the set of her latest movie, "[came] to the rescue" by renting a nearby house "so he could help care for her and their daughter [Rose, twenty-one months]."[93] In a fake "world exclusive" cover story, *Life & Style* announced "A Baby for George!" (Clooney), implying that his wife Amal was pregnant. Inside, however, we learn they are supposedly planning to have a child in the next year or so because "Amal is ready to be a mom, and George is doing everything to make her dream come true." But he was also "born to be a dad," is "truly great" with children, and "he'll make an incredible father." In a sidebar (and in contrast to the ageism directed at women), we meet "famous dads" who "welcomed newborns at age 55—and older!"[94] In *Life & Style*'s "Boyfriend Report Card," swimmer Michael Phelps comes in for a world of hurt, earning a C–, because he's been "slacking a bit on daddy duty" by not changing enough diapers.[95] Kourtney Kardashian's on-again, off-again boyfriend and party animal Scott Disick (and father of her three children) is regularly chastised for "dating a new girl every week," for drinking too much and falling off the wagon, and for needing to get a job.[96] The "runt of the Kardashian litter [and] f*ckup father of Kourtney's three children," a man "without any skills," sniped *GQ* online, makes his money for doing nothing: appearing at clubs and agreeing to stay for one hour. For this and his other failings, he is "routinely mocked on national television."[97]

While men's appearance does not come under near the scrutiny that women's do, these magazines have also started trashing men's bodies, jeering at those with "man boobs" or who are "man blobs" or "beached males." Rob Kardashian reportedly wanted his "moobs" (man boobs) reduced after losing fifty pounds so he doesn't "have to run from the cameras" during his new reality TV show.[98] Jack Nicholson has "flabby pecs," Simon Cowell has "perky moobs," and even former body builder Arnold Schwarzenegger was ridiculed by *TV Guide* for now having "boobs" and that his days of having a "rock hard body" are "long gone."[99]

The culmination of the romantic relationship is inevitably the birth of a baby. So quickly do the stories jump from love to babies that coverage of celebrity weddings often promise pregnancy before the rings have even been exchanged. Thus, losing your man is a big tragedy, but remaining childless is even bigger. Two-inch headlines like "BABY NEWS" and "HOLLYWOOD'S BABY BOOM" are constantly recycled. Motherhood has now become nearly compulsory for female stars: they must have a baby to fulfill what is allegedly every woman's innate dream to become a mother. Babies are cast as bundles of joy and life-changing blessings, never stressful. Julia Roberts was constantly hounded about having kids until her twins arrived. George Clooney, by contrast, was not badgered about when he would reproduce (although his wife Amal was).[100] Women who opt out of motherhood are portrayed as tragic. Poor Jennifer Aniston has been prodded for over a decade because she did not have any children and supposedly was pining for them. Time and time again, the stories that heralded her alleged pregnancies turned out to be false.

This hypernatalism of celebrity journalism has led to a feature we never used to see, the rise of the invasive "bump patrol." Ever since a nude and fully pregnant Demi Moore graced the cover of *Vanity Fair* in 1991, display of one's belly has become less embarrassing and even glamorous. So telephoto lenses now zoom in on the midsections of scores of female celebrities accompanied by speculation about whether she's pregnant or simply ate too much for lunch. The *Star* has featured its "Bump Brigade" and "How to Dress a Bump (and Not!)" that showcase stylish maternity clothes that are "HOT!" The bump patrol works to further police famous women's bodies and sexualities. Through these narratives and images, the public is offered access to the most intimate details of a woman's personal bodily changes and choices. Gossip magazines draw giant circles around stars' stomachs, encouraging readers to comment and judge. Doting moms are celebrated while "bad" moms—think Britney Spears driving with her baby on her lap—are failures, not only as parents, but as women.[101]

With standards set so impossibly high, it is perhaps unsurprising that, in this world, successful women can't get along with each other. Instead, they "clash," "butt heads," and "fight," particularly over scarce resources: attention and decent men. The real or alleged feuds between celebrity women ask you to take sides, and usually the woman who lost her man to someone else is cast as more sympathetic than the one who stole him away. These are high school sensibilities at their finest. This was true in 1959 when Elizabeth Taylor "stole" Eddie Fisher from America's sweetheart, Debbie Reynolds, and was clearly cast as the evil one, a story revived in the never-ending Jen-Brangelina saga, in which all-American Aniston was typically the victim, Jolie the vixen. Male relationships, when they are featured, are not cast in this catty light—they betray women, not each other. For women, sisterhood is not powerful; it is impossible.

When not fighting over men, women are battling over every detail of their appearance. Indeed, what is especially striking is the constant pitting of gorgeous women against each other. Gossip magazines and talk shows routinely provide visual lineups based primarily on red carpet photos, of women wearing the same or similar outfits and then judging who looked the best, typically based on the minutest details. *In Touch* and *OK!* feature "Who Wore It Better?," *US Weekly* has "Who Wore It Best?," and *Life & Style* "Who Wears It Best?" in which two celebs are juxtaposed against each other in the same dress or outfit. One gets a circle with a checkmark titled "she did," the other a circle with an X, crossing out her efforts. The loser has worn shoes that are "too heavy (and just don't match)" or her bust is "bursting out of the dress."[102]

In "Red Carpet Ready?," celebrities are actually made to compete against *themselves*. The same woman is seen in two different outfits at different events and in one she is labeled "ready" and the other "not ready." Celebrity commentator Perez Hilton compares women's current and previous hairdos; either the woman's current self loses to her past self, or vice versa.[103] The *Enquirer* has its weekly "fashion hits & misses" in which some women are exhorted to "Trash Your Stylist," because the fashion blunders are deemed so egregious. *Life & Style* asks "Who's Got the Best . . ." and focuses on women's lipstick choices and hairstyles. Here we have women who on the one hand seem strong and independent, yet on the other hand are constantly shown to be inadequate in some way or another.[104]

Thus, celebrity narratives teach powerful lessons about the featured stars, who are primarily young, white, and heterosexual, and what constitutes success for such women. And given both the target market for such magazines, TV shows, and websites, and the notorious ageism of Hollywood, especially when it comes to women, older women are rarely seen in these precincts. There are three major exceptions: the star who has gained too much weight or is a victim of bad plastic surgery; the "tragic" allegedly sick or dying star, almost always cast as forgotten, possibly broke, and alone; and, even more rarely, the "hot" exception, like Helen Mirren. As Holmes and Negra point out, the "markers of ageing are relentlessly scrutinized and judged, with women variously castigated for the 'sin' of 'letting themselves go,' or mocked for displaying highly visible, or unattractive cosmetic surgery procedures."[105] Those who enjoyed fame in their youth are either scoffed at for not keeping up with their appearance or, like Goldie Hawn and Janice Dickinson, ridiculed for the vanity of plastic surgery.

One exemplar of these ageist beauty standards was forty-seven-year-old Susan Boyle, who became a star after belting out a killer version of "I Dreamed a Dream" from *Les Misérables* on *Britain's Got Talent*. Her instant fame was propelled by the shock, expressed by both the show's judges and the audience, that a conventionally unattractive forty-seven-year-old, slightly overweight woman with overly thick eyebrows and somewhat disheveled hair could *actually* have talent. When Boyle first introduced herself, stated her age, and said she wanted to be a singing star, the camera showed the judges smirking and audience members rolling their eyes. After the performance, the audience and the judges alike gave her a rousing standing ovation. Judge Piers Morgan exclaimed, "Without a doubt, that was the biggest surprise in my three years on this show"; what he didn't say was that it was because of the contrast between her age, weight, and appearance and the stunning sound of her voice.[106]

Women of color may face less scrutiny in the world of celebrity gossip, but that's because they are rarely featured. Studies show that white women are the most popular subjects of magazines and films and few Black, Latina, Asian, and Native women occupy the top tiers of the A-list. In 2016, *Forbes* listed Jennifer Lawrence, Melissa McCarthy, and Scarlett Johansson as the top three earning female stars.[107] The only nonwhite actresses earning top dollar, Indian actress Deepika Padukone and China's Fan Bingbing, are largely unknown to the Western media market. While some celebrities of color—Beyoncé, of course, and Jay Z, Kanye West (primarily because of his marriage to Kim Kardashian), Kerry Washington, and singers like Alicia Keys—are regularly the subjects of gossip, TV shows, and websites, it takes a major scandal or event, such as Beyoncé's sister Solange attacking Jay Z in an elevator in 2014, and having it caught on surveillance tape, to have celebrities of color make it to the top headlines or magazine covers.

The same is true for LGBT stars. Much has changed since the 1990s in the acceptance and often sympathetic depiction of gay and lesbian celebrities. Think of Ellen DeGeneres, whose sitcom was cancelled in 1998, a year after she came out as gay on *The Oprah Winfrey Show*. Though *People* magazine covered Ellen's marriage to Portia de Rossi, it was not until the early 2000s that Ellen returned to television and earned national adoration with her quirky dance moves and comical antics in a daytime talk show. And while we've seen more gay characters, even TV networks and YouTube channels aimed at queer audiences, few top stars have emerged from their ranks to break into the mainstream gossip press. Gay women continue to be regarded with suspicion. Stars like Michelle Rodriguez, Kristen Stewart, and Cara Delevingne have all been scrutinized for their choice of romantic partners; the idea that an attractive woman could want to be in a relationship with another woman continues to confuse the gossip press. Meanwhile, out gay men like Neil Patrick Harris, Anderson Cooper, and Ricky Martin have become media mainstays.

More recently, transgender stars have garnered public attention on reality TV shows and in the pages of tabloids. Since former Olympic athlete and Kardashian family dad Bruce Jenner's 2015 revelation that he identified as a trans woman, changing her name and identity to Caitlyn, transgender celebrities have been the subject of fascinated and mostly supportive commentary; Jenner famously told her story in the July 2015 issue of *Vanity Fair*, where she became the first sixty-five-year-old woman to appear on the cover. The issue garnered 432,000 single copy sales, making it the highest-selling cover for *Vanity Fair* in nearly five years.[108] Nevertheless, coverage of LGBTQ stars remains limited and compulsory heterosexuality continues to be a hallmark of celebrity coverage.

Considered together, these narratives reveal a limited framework of success and happiness that privileges a narrow range of identities, bodies, behaviors, and life choices while punishing or excluding those who don't check all of the prescribed boxes, all of the time. It may be difficult to understand, then, how it is that audiences, especially those who do not fit the lauded models (i.e., 99% of us) can find pleasure in such representations. Why would I want to read about stars who seem nothing like my friends, my family, or myself?

Celebrity narratives provide us with the opportunity to consume vicariously, to indulge in a pleasurable escape to a world where money is no object. We enjoy the visual simulation of perfection and luxury that famous bodies, homes, vacations, and sports cars convey. We may temporarily forget our own financial constraints, our budgets, our rent payments. We may be seduced by the suggestion that, if we can buy some trinket that the stars love and recommend, our lives might be just a bit more glamorous. We are transported away from our workaday routines, our boring commutes, our ho-hum grocery lists, into a world of fantasy and fun.

While the pleasures of this type of transportation may be fleeting, celebrity narratives also promise us the potential for permanent escape. Stories that insist celebrities are "just like us" perpetuate the long-running tale that anyone can be famous; you, too, could live this life. Today's digital platforms, where user-creators self-promote and brand themselves in an effort to attract followers and earn capital, both cultural and monetary, amplify the sense that we are all just a few well-conceived clicks away from Instafame. This fantasy of democratic access, of meritocracy and social mobility, may be especially appealing to audiences during our contemporary era, where inequalities between rich and poor, haves and have-nots, have widened and deepened.

As previously noted, celebrity news places women and girls at the center. The top-selling and most viewed magazine covers, TV shows, and Instagram feeds belong to women. Modeling and acting remain two of the few fields where women can actually earn more than men;[109] here, the Kardashians earn millions just for Tweeting baby pics. And unlike in the precincts of Congress, where male politicians dominate and issues like women's health care and child-care access are regularly ignored or fought against, in celebrity-world, Julia Louis-Dreyfus, Alfre Woodard, Gina Davis, and Robin Wright have all occupied the Oval Office as commander in chief. For many women, lacking political power and faced with much more logistically complex, and economically tenuous, situations, these stories offer an appealing reverie.

Celebrities as models for how to look and behave, embodying fantasies of rising above the herd and being seen as a distinctive individual, celebrity gossip as emotionally and cognitively satisfying puzzles to solve and, also, as a kind of social glue, celebrities as the inevitable result of the rise of leisure in capitalist systems, the media's need for increasing numbers of celebrities to attract viewers and ad dollars, the role of celebrity culture in transporting us out of our everyday lives—all of these and more, when taken together, help explain why celebrity culture has exploded in the late twentieth and early twenty-first centuries.

2

The Rise of Mass Culture and the Production of Celebrities

It would be quite easy to see celebrity culture and celebrity journalism as fairly recent phenomena, commanding our attention primarily in the late twentieth and early twenty-first centuries. But by the early nineteenth century, celebrities—what they stood for, what fans invested in them, what behind-the-scenes or self-aggrandizing promoters sought to extract financially from them—had come to assume an unprecedented role in the cultural life of the country. And despite the absence then of electronic media, which is now so central to celebrity production, many precedents were set about how stars were created, promoted, and embraced. This trend was enabled by the rise and intersection of several key technologies—the telegraph that expedited the spread of news, the railroads that carried entertainers around the country, photography that made the famous visible more quickly and cheaply, and, most important, the explosive rise of daily newspapers and then mass-circulation magazines, nearly all supported by advertising, that made celebrity construction and maintenance possible.

The Astor Place Riots

In 1849, in what was still the early republic, a feud between two well-known actors—or, more accurately, their fans—caused a riot in New York City in which twenty-two people were killed, 150 injured, and eighty-six arrested. It was the deadliest event of its kind in the city up to that point. The melee was ostensibly about which actor was better. But conflicts about celebrities are never only about them. Ever.

Celebrities—their appearance, behaviors, their expressed attitudes, their biographies, their failings, their scandals—have, in the past and the present, served as flashpoints for clashes about larger contentious issues gripping a culture. In this case, what came to be known as the infamous Astor Place Riots was a battle about class identity, resentments over economic and cultural privilege, and about manhood and national pride. It was a battle personified by allegiances to two actors and what they stood for: the British performer William Charles Macready and the American Edwin Forrest, both celebrated Shakespearean actors.[1] Today, we associate Shakespeare with "high art" and culture, but in the nineteenth century Shakespeare was by far the most popular playwright in the United States, beloved by people across a range of socioeconomic classes. His plays were performed in venues from opulent theaters to saloons, and many knew key lines so well that they would recite them along with the actors.[2] By the 1840s cities like New York, despite religious and moral opposition among some of the educated elite to the potential corruptions of theatergoing, had a robust theater culture with known actors. Thousands of new theaters, especially in cities, were built between 1850 and 1900.[3] The theater, then, was one of the first venues for the production of entertainment celebrities in the United States.

Early nineteenth-century theaters—often very rowdy places known for their shouting, spitting, the smell of booze—contained audiences (mostly men) from all walks of life who were then spatially segregated by income, line of work, class, and race. The expensive boxes above and to the side of the stage were reserved for the wealthy. Below the boxes (what we would today call the orchestra) was "the pit," where the emerging middle class—manual laborers, sailors, mechanics, tradesmen, and, in New York, the Bowery b'hoys—sat. Known for their boisterous (often drunken) behavior, bright clothes, and love of the theater, the b'hoys were single, working-class men, mostly firemen and mechanics. Above and behind the pit were the cheap gallery seats (today's mezzanine) occupied by newsboys, apprentices, and other lower wage workers; segregated from everyone in the upper third tier were African Americans (assigned the very worst seats), and prostitutes and their clients.[4] Those in the gallery were known to pelt actors who displeased them (as well as those in the boxes) with rotten fruit, eggs, peanuts (hence the peanut gallery), and pennies. Those in each sector of the theater resented the others. As the historian David Nasaw noted, "The box holders were disgusted by the rowdiness of the pit and gallery; the pit was offended by the box holders' continuous chatter and inattention to the stage; the gallery was disgusted by the actors' fawning attention to the box holders."[5] As you can imagine, this was becoming a tinderbox of class resentment.

As a result, this segregation within theaters began to give way to seg-regation between theaters. The new, luxurious Astor Place Opera House opened late in 1847 and was meant for the rich.[6] In May 1849, William Charles Macready, known for his restrained, intellectual style, was slated to perform *Macbeth* there. Indeed, most of the big names in American theater at this time were English actors who, with their reputations as stars already established, would come to perform in the United States. At the same time, Edwin Forrest, the country's first great tragic actor,[7] a more dramatic, extravagant performer deemed to embody the "Ameri-can" style of acting, was to portray Spartacus at another theater just a few blocks away. A feud had begun between them, and Macready had already denounced Forrest's "vanity," his "deficiency in taste and judge-ment," and especially "the facetious applause of his supporters, the 'Bower lads.'"[8] Forrest—and his fans—were still smarting from Forrest having been hissed when he performed in England. In retaliation, he allegedly hissed at a performance of Macready as Hamlet,[9] and declared that Macready "should never be permitted to appear again upon the stage" in New York City.[10]

The rise of theaters coincided—and interacted with—the rise of the "penny press," which embraced and fanned such conflicts to increase circulation and sales. As their name suggests, penny papers, which began to proliferate in the 1830s, were tabloid-style newspapers pur-chased for a single penny, which traded in lurid crime, gossip, and social stories. In doing so, they prompted a reconsideration of the standards of newsworthiness—what, and who, is worthy of public discussion. Un-like their six-cent counterparts, which targeted a more affluent audience, both their content and cost were designed to reach the greatest number of possible readers, especially the emerging middle and working classes. So the penny press played an important role in the creation of the mass public and constituted a crucial communications network in the nine-teenth century. Much like the gossip magazines and websites today, the penny press also provided a new vehicle for the creation and discussion of celebrity. Theater owners used the penny press as well as playbills to promote their productions and actors, and between dueling promotions of the theatrical performances and the bad blood between the two fa-mous men, enmity was in the air. The penny press fanned, especially, the personal attacks between the actors.[11]

Hundreds of Forrest's supporters, many of them the b'hoys, bought tickets to Macready's first performance on May 8, stoked in part by broadsides that asked "Working Men, Shall Americans or English Rule in this City!" It urged them to "express their opinions" at the "English Aristocratic Opera House," which indeed they did. As Macready sought to perform, Forrest's supporters shouted him down and threw rotten eggs, potatoes, and other vegetables. He swore he would return to England, but the city's elite persuaded him to stay and continue the engagement, which he resumed on May 10.

The b'hoys were ready, and so were Macready's supporters—and the police, all 250 of them. But in addition to those in the Astor Place Opera House, an estimated 10,000 fans of both actors had gathered outside the theater. By the fourth scene, Macready could not proceed again given the hissing and booing, the hurling of more rotten vegetables, as well as a bottle containing the Indian spice asafetida, which "diffused a most repulsive stench throughout the house."[12] The police burst in to eject the culprits, and Macready rushed through the play to finish. But the b'hoys outside were not having it and began hurling bricks and paving stones at the theater. The police called in the state militia, 350 of them, the first time they had been called to disperse a crowd. Unable to calm or break up the group, some of whom were throwing bricks and paving stones at the police, the militia fired a volley over the crowd, and then one into the crowd, and then more. Many of those killed and injured were working-class people and innocent bystanders.

The next day, after the deadliest event of its kind in the country, the Astor Place Opera House gained the monikers "Massacre Opera House" and the "Disaster Place."[13] The *Courier and Enquirer* denounced Forrest as an actor who had "earned a distinction of which no predecessor will ever be likely to rob him"; he "inflicted a thorough and lasting disgrace upon the American character."[14] News of the riot quickly spread around the country via telegraph.

The *New York Tribune* expressed disbelief that so many people could be killed or injured because "two actors quarreled!"[15] But the conflict was about so much more, and what the stage stars embodied: national pride and identity, class position and resentments, and different versions of masculinity. Macready personified Britain's sense of its cultural superiority; the English novelist Frances Trollope, who had visited the

Figure 2.1. "Great riot at the Astor Place Opera House, New York on Thursday evening May 10th 1849." Lithograph, N. Currier, Library of Congress.

United States and wrote about it in her controversial and bestselling 1832 book *Domestic Manners of the Americans*, expressed shocked outrage over the spitting, tobacco chewing, drinking, and overall disorderly behavior she witnessed in American theaters. Her book made British condescension toward American culture quite clear. Macready's fans were the growing elite in New York City and embodied upper-class snobbery. The b'hoys, through their identification with Forrest, were rebelling against such cultural hierarchies, the special privileges of elites, and that they and the American culture of which they were part were somehow inferior. Through their jeers and their rotten fruit they sought to project onto Macready—and exorcise—what was a needling sense of cultural inferiority, of not having "class," and of not being the "right" kind of "cultured" men.

The Astor Place Riot was an exemplar of how popular culture is rarely "just entertainment," that battles over which entertainments and stars are worthy of admiration and which ones not are always battles about larger norms, values, and attitudes and indeed about the social order itself. And while an extreme example, the riots demonstrated that fans have been and are active and participatory meaning makers, key players in the production of celebrities and their meanings.

Minstrelsy

Race has also been central to the production of celebrity, including white celebrities. In the immediate aftermath of MTV's 2013 Video Music Awards, Miley Cyrus received a barrage of criticism for twerking and using black women as props in her performance (one of whom she slapped on her butt) as an instance of racially insensitive black cultural appropriation. This practice—of imitating or caricaturing African Americans to promote the fame of white people—goes back at least to Thomas D. "Daddy" Rice, a white man, who became a star of minstrel shows in the 1830s. Minstrel shows, which soared in popularity in the pre–Civil War years, featured white men who blackened their faces with burnt cork and impersonated their versions of black men on the stage. T. D. Rice, the "father of minstrelsy," developed his song-and-dance version of a slave called "Jim Crow" (later used to describe the severe segregationist practices in the American South). He quickly began to draw sold-out crowds who demanded numerous encores. Rice became so wealthy from his celebrity that he came to wear jackets with gold and diamond studded buttons. Wooden statues of him appeared in various locations in New York.[16]

Rice's enormous success led to the establishment of various minstrel troupes, including the Virginia Minstrels in 1843, promising "the essence of old Virginny," and Christy's Minstrels, which gave more than 2,700 performances in about a ten-year period. Minstrelsy reached its height during the 1860s, when there were 100 minstrel companies that played nothing else. What these shows did, of course, by inventing and ridiculing the stage version of the slow-witted, childlike "darky," was to cement derogatory stereotypes of African Americans as lazy, indifferent to success, terrified of ghosts, and possessing a natural aptitude for dancing and rhythmical movement.

Why did white men create such a character? According to the scholar Nathan Huggins, what he called the "Stage Negro" was the antithesis of the Protestant work ethic, with its emphasis on working hard, exercising restraint, deferring gratification, saving, and spending wisely. (One of the enduring minstrel characters, "Jim Dandy," was an inveterate gambler.) For a culture tied up in anxieties over achievement, Huggins argued, it made sense to create a persona that is completely self-indulgent and irresponsible, because the Stage Negro represented what white men feared they harbored within themselves and dreaded. So they objectified that self, put it on stage, laughed at it, exorcised it. The Stage Negro objectified and created a distance between white men's normative selves and what they feared were their natural selves. Again, stage characters and the celebrities who created them spoke to much broader and deeper cultural anxieties, in this case not only about race and justifications for slavery but also about legitimate masculinity.

P. T. Barnum and the Birth of Promotion

The theater and the penny press were two intersecting platforms producing and reinforcing fame in the mid-nineteenth century. But possibly the greatest maestro of publicity and celebrity production during this era was P. T. Barnum who possessed, according to one biographer, "an instinctive understanding of what startled, amazed, astonished, titillated, [and] thrilled."[17] He is widely regarded as the greatest showman in our history, and a pioneer of self-promotion. While the working classes typically worked six or even seven days a week, the growing middle class of retail clerks, salaried workers, and some industrial workers and their families[18] began to have more money and leisure time for entertainment, providing a new market for eye-catching and often unique acts.

Barnum both responded to and enlarged this market. In the mid-nineteenth century in New York, what were called museums were very different from those of today. They featured a combination of allegedly "scientific" and historical exhibits, "freak" acts, animal shows, and performers like magicians, mind readers, fire-eaters, and contortionists. In 1842, Barnum opened his museum in downtown Manhattan, in what is now the financial district, and used the public's fascination with the pseudoscientific, the exotic, and the curiously surreal to draw attention to his museum and traveling show. He quickly filled his museum with oddities like the infamous "Fiji mermaid," which was in reality the torso and head of a small, mummified monkey sewn onto the bottom half of a fish.

While Barnum is especially known for his promotion of hoaxes like this, he was also one of the earliest and most wildly successful creators of celebrities, who were featured in his museums, his circus, or on their own tours. Dubbed "the Shakespeare of advertising," he capitalized on print technology and the power of mass distribution, using newspaper advertisements, pamphlets, press releases, and provocative broadsides, complete with detailed illustrations of his wondrous collection, splashed across metropolitan centers to publicize his shows.[19] He was especially skilled at getting newspapers to run stories about his upcoming shows or performers and using billboards to do the same.[20] Just as the sides of many buses in cities today are emblazoned with large ads, Barnum sent horse-drawn carts around New York plastered with posters and signs promoting his museum. Barnum was also one of the first to take advantage of the new rail system, moving his circus across the country by train. In doing so, he was able to send hype men ahead of the acts, ensuring public interest before the circus—or other performers—even arrived.

One of his biggest stars was "General Tom Thumb," a two-foot-tall boy who had stopped growing at the age of six months, whom Barnum trained to sing, dance, and impersonate famous people, and who became a sensation in the United States and Europe. The promotion of Tom Thumb was so successful that he was often mobbed wherever he went and his 1863 marriage to another little person was front-page news.

Barnum also "discovered" Jenny Lind, a successful and famous Swedish opera singer unknown in the United States who then became one of the first major female celebrities in America. In order to promote her, he "launched an unprecedented press campaign" extolling her virtues as a charitable and benevolent woman who spent most of her time engaged in philanthropy; he believed that most Americans would be unfamiliar with opera music but would be charmed and attracted by her morality.[21] Indeed, Barnum understood that for certain types of people to become admired stars, they had to be connected to certain values, the right kind of values. He also billed her as "the Swedish Nightingale," and auctioned off tickets to see her. By the time she got to the United States in 1850, tens of thousands met her ship when it docked. She performed before sold-out crowds, her ninety-five concerts grossing $712,161, the equivalent of $21 million in 2016 dollars.[22] "Lindomania" resulted, with hotel maids

Figure 2.2. P. T. Barnum and Tom Thumb, c. 1850. Photograph by
Marcus Aurelius and Samuel Root, National Portrait Gallery,
Smithsonian Institution.

reportedly stealing the hair from her brushes and selling it, and a host of
products named after her, from gloves, hats, and shawls to paper dolls.[23]
This may be one of the first examples of using a star's alleged philanthropic work—a staple of contemporary celebrity culture—to elevate
her stature and increase box office sales. And though he helped shine
the spotlight on many, it is Barnum himself who is best remembered, a
testament to his savvy in creating and maintaining fame.

On the other end of the celebrity production spectrum was the lyceum movement that flourished before the Civil War and persisted af-
terwards. Designed to promote ongoing, adult education and to foster

strong intellectual and moral values in the country, the lyceum movement featured lectures, debates, and performances given by those who traveled on the lyceum circuit. Lyceum referred both to the halls erected to hold public lectures or discussions and the association that provided the entertainment. Famous speakers in the antebellum period included writers such as Ralph Waldo Emerson and Henry David Thoreau; after the war, activists and writers like Elizabeth Cady Stanton, Susan B. Anthony, and Mark Twain—who gave hundreds of performances and was one of the leading celebrities of his time—toured as well, but now lyceums also served as venues for minstrel and vaudeville shows, leaning much more toward entertainment as opposed to uplift.

By midcentury then, at the height of the age of Barnum, a major sociological change was occurring in American life, especially in the cities and larger towns, which laid the foundation for the rise of celebrity culture by the late nineteenth and early twentieth centuries. People were now learning to assume the role of a mass audience, witnessing spectacles with hundreds and even thousands of other people they did not necessarily know. They were getting accustomed to paying for entertainment and understood that it would be provided by strangers who were often professionals. They were coming to simply expect that publicity like Barnum's would promote and frame how a major event, like the Jenny Lind visit, was meant to be received. And they were appreciating that to be an informed, with-it person, there were certain experiences they really should not miss, like attending particular, well-hyped theatrical performances. Americans were picking up the new, publicity-driven language of celebrity, acquiring a new vocabulary about who and what should be celebrated and why. Thus, crucially, people were learning how to inhabit the subject position of the fan.[24]

Photography and the New Visibility

Another crucial invention in the history of celebrity production was, of course, the photograph. Photography, developed in the 1830s and 1840s, greatly expanded the technological and artistic modes through which one could record one's existence.[25] We take photography utterly for granted today, but at the time it ushered in a revolution in visibility. Now "real life" and everyday people, as well as the famous, could be immortalized.

Photography provided more accurate (and eventually more easily manipulated) images of famous people, and they were of course more lifelike
and less removed than they were in paintings or drawings. Unlike sculpture or even paintings, which were expensive, exclusive, and difficult to
disseminate, photography was relatively portable, affordable, and fast. As
such, it opened up a wide range of new opportunities for influential figures to enhance their renown. By the 1880s, led by the *New York World*,
papers began featuring line drawings of prominent local people. This led
to a several decades boom in the need for artists to supply such portraits.
But by the turn of the century, with technological improvements in the
ability to reproduce halftones—black and white images made up of tiny
dots—newspapers began to rely more and more on photography.

The popularity of formal photographic portraits gained momentum
throughout the latter half of the nineteenth century, owing in large part
to the rise of the wildly popular *carte de visite* photograph, a thin, photographic portrait mounted on a card. Developed and popularized by
André Adolphe Eugène Disdéri, who patented the process in 1854, the
carte de visite added a new dimension to the social custom of leaving
one's calling card by linking the holder's name and image.[26] Small—2 ½
by 4 inches—and inexpensive, the cards could be purchased, traded, and
reproduced with ease.

Cartes quickly became a craze—the press called it "cartomania"[27]—as
members of Victorian society collected the cards of loved ones and family
members, along with the famous, and portrait studios emerged to meet
the new demand. The first photo albums were created to hold them. As
Elizabeth Siegel writes, "By 1863 pretty much anybody who was famous
had been photographed for card pictures, and enterprising photographers
and publishers sought to record the faces of new celebrities as they were
made."[28] These images were widely purchased and collected between the
1850s until just after the turn of the century, sold in popular magazines, and
even given away in cigarette packets. Athletes, inventors, political leaders,
and performers all appeared on *cartes*—sometimes sold in celebrity *carte
de visite* albums—and their likenesses thus became known and recognized
by the public. They were also especially popular with soldiers fighting in
the Civil War who wanted to leave a photo behind to remember them by.[29]
In this way, in one's own collection, images of the famous whom one would
never meet sat side by side with those of family and friends.

Figure 2.3. Abraham Lincoln *carte de visite*, June 3, 1860. Photograph by Alexander Hesler, Library of Congress.

The savviest sitters understood that a photographic likeness was a way to mold and craft one's image, to communicate a desired message to the public. Guides provided instruction on how to capture one's best self and props were often used to highlight the sitter's achievements, skills, or personal characteristics. Subjects would often sign their *cartes*, their handwritten autograph adding an additional layer of intimacy to the exchange. Meanwhile, photographic proofs allowed sitters the opportunity to select the most flattering images and to control their self-presentation.[30]

These techniques were recognized by the famous; President Lincoln appeared frequently in *carte de visite* albums, often on the first page. One notable *carte* from 1864 showed him in an intimate pose with his son Tad, looking at a photo album, conveying his dedication as a caring father, despite the burdens of the war.[31] The British royal family's *cartes* were widely reproduced and distributed; between 1860 and 1862, three to four million *cartes* were sold of Queen Victoria alone.[32] Yet the royals were also conscious of the impact of their image on public sentiment. Queen Victoria and Prince Albert "deliberately refrained from appearing robed and bejeweled, opting instead for the increasingly ubiquitous everyday uniform of suits and crinoline."[33] In this way, the royal family worked to widely convey to its subjects an image that was at once dignified and relatable, powerful yet approachable.

The relative affordability of the cards meant that collectors could, like queens and actors and noble men and women, sit for their own portrait and share their image with friends. In this way, the photographic process democratized the act of image reproduction. And the emergence of the *carte de visite* album, a bound book with preformed slots in which one could insert the cards, allowed collectors to create a "visual genealogy" of their personal histories."[34] Owners could organize the images as they saw fit; a spouse might be placed alongside an image of the queen or a photo of one's child could appear before an image of a politician. Here, the ordinary person can taste a moment of fame, a hint of immortality, a sense that their image may live on forever.

Mass-Circulation Newspapers and Celebrity

In the post–Civil War period, the press became the most important and influential mass medium in the country. Mass urban newspapers grew especially in the 1880s, made possible by new, high-speed presses, the linotype (a typesetting machine that produced a whole line of type instead of just a character at a time), and then half-tone photo reproduction. The number of English-language daily papers increased from 480 in 1870 to 1,967 in 1900, with circulation for all daily papers jumping a staggering amount, from 2.6 million in 1870 to fifteen million in 1900.[35] Competition among them grew increasingly fierce, as much for bragging rights as for circulation figures, which affected advertising revenues. Urban papers in particular, with large working class and immigrant populations, began to undertake exposés and "crusades" on behalf of their readers. This could now make journalists stars.

One of the most famous of the era was Elizabeth Cochran, better known by her pen name Nellie Bly. Bly was outraged by the sexism of the time, as well as by the working and other institutional conditions faced by the less fortunate, and determined to expose them. In 1887, she went undercover for ten days posing as a mentally ill patient at an asylum on New York City's Blackwell Island (now Roosevelt Island). It was highly unusual at the time for a woman to take on this kind of risky assignment. Her investigative report published in Joseph Pulitzer's *New York World* revealed widespread neglect and physical abuse. It was a massive success, becoming a book, *Ten Days in a Mad-House,* later that year. The exposé also led to a full-blown investigation of the asylum and reforms in its practices. Bly was now a major celebrity and, with further support from the *World,* vowed to break the record of travel described in Jules Verne's fictional *Around the World in 80 Days.* Leaving from Hoboken, New Jersey, in November 1889, and traveling via ship, horse, burro, rickshaw, and other conveyances, Bly's progress was continuously reported in the *World* as she completed her journey in just over seventy-two days. The paper also ran a guessing contest of how far readers thought she had gotten that drew nearly one million estimates.[36] By now she was an international star, made so by the press.

Vaudeville Stardom

With increased urbanization and immigration, vaudeville became one of the premier forms of entertainment—and sites of celebrity production—in the late nineteenth century. Between 1880 and 1890, the number of towns and cities with a population of 8,000 or more doubled, and their total population jumped from eleven million to twenty-five million. Twenty-three million people emigrated to the United States between 1890 and the 1920s.[37] This coincided with—indeed, helped to drive—the rise of leisure activities, their stars, and the newspapers that advertised them all. Entertainment came to town in the form of traveling showmen, who offered a mélange of acrobatics, singing, animal acts, comedy, and clowning in addition to cabinets of curiosities and waxworks.[38] Such acts were meant to "have it all" and to provide "something for everyone."

The nature of the business meant that performers were constantly traveling from place to place as part of a troupe, and the most popular among them became big name "acts," drawing audiences and attention. These types of traveling shows were especially attractive in rural areas, where residents rarely had access to the live performances of the day. And in urban centers such as Boston and New York, the primary theatrical programming consisted of vaudeville acts and variety shows.[39]

Vaudeville began drawing larger crowds when one of its pioneers, Benjamin Franklin Keith, hit upon the idea in 1885 of "the continuous," meaning rather than having a fixed show with a start and end time, the show just kept going, with the opening act returning once the final act left the stage. "Stay as Long as You Like," read some theater marquees, with ongoing shows, costing anywhere from a nickel to a quarter, running from late morning or early afternoon until late in the evening. Keith, who began in Boston, opened similar theaters over the next few years in dozens of cities throughout the Northeast and Midwest.[40]

To attract as many customers as possible, Keith advertised regularly in the daily papers, which by the 1880s were the most important medium for information, advertising, and promotion in the country. Before motion pictures and radio, only this synergy between the rise of vaudeville and the explosive growth of newspapers could bring celebrities before the public. The rise of mass-circulation popular magazines, which also began featuring illustrated articles about leading actors, fed an increasing appetite for celebrity news and gossip. And with the rise in the 1890s of what came to be called "yellow journalism"—highly sensational, even inflammatory stories, huge, blaring headlines, more images and cartoons, as competition between papers intensified—the press became an especially hospitable platform to promote entertainment news and stars. As one journalist noted, "It is remarkable how much attention the stage and things pertaining to it are receiving nowadays from the magazines," noting that in the 1860s such stories would have been thought "indecorous" but now news about the theater "has become a topic of conversation among all classes, furnishing an endless gossip to the trivial."[41]

Increased public interest in the theater and vaudeville led to the creation of "dramatic paragraphers," reporters whose beat was to cover entertainment and produce feature stories about show business celebrities. Gradually many reviews of the shows themselves gave way to these enormously popular features, primarily profiles of stars and their lives off stage.[42] With the success of Barnum, the understanding that "ballyhoo" and hype made stars, and that in the public realm everyone was performing, how could one know who the stars *really* were? Journalists and their readers came to believe that a person's "real self" could only be ascertained in private, from their "back stage"; thus, the rise of heightened interest in the private lives of public figures. Such public figures were now "subjected to this new mode of presentation."[43] Soon features appeared in newspaper Sunday supplements to meet the public demand. And with the rise of newspaper chains in the early twentieth century, with a single owner like William Randolph Hearst owning up to twenty daily papers, entertainment-related columns could be syndicated, with stories about stars and shows spread way beyond the city in which they originated.[44]

Keith and his partner Edward Albee bought ads—double and even quadruple in size compared to those of their competitors—in every newspaper in the community where they were presenting shows, including the foreign language press. In exchange for this paid advertising, newspapers began to establish entertainment news and reviews of shows. In addition to its novelty acts, vaudeville of the late nineteenth century had its own cast of well-known acts and highly promoted "matinee idols" to get people in the door. As the historian David Nasaw notes, "By the middle of the 1890s, one could not pick up a newspaper anywhere in the country without coming across notices, ads, reviews, interviews, features and photographs of the stars and the shows that were appearing that week in the major vaudeville halls."[45] By this time a key role was played by the press agent and publicist, the men who fed the newspapers prewritten profiles of the stars, the shows, and even copy to include in the paper's reviews.[46]

Nearly all vaudeville performers were white, including white men who, continuing the legacy of minstrel shows, blackened their faces and masqueraded as black. Black performers' access to vaudeville was extremely limited, as most managers, fearful both of alienating white audiences and attracting too many African American spectators, allowed only one black performer on a bill. (In fact, there was a group of vaudevillians called the "White Rats" who opposed women and blacks from getting on stage.)[47]

Nonetheless, a few African American performers broke through and eventually became stars in their own right. Bert Williams, a successful vaudeville performer, comedian, and performing artist, would later go on to be the first black American to star in a leading role on Broadway and challenge racial stereotypes. He performed in burnt-cork blackface, along with partner George Walker, playing the formulaic "coon" stereotype, emphasizing his features by donning wigs and darkening his complexion.[48] The two billed themselves the "Two Real Coons," and while they had no choice but to inhabit the prevailing stereotypes of black men as lazy and dumb, or as slick connivers, they also subtly undermined these roles. They produced three major musical comedies, two of them set in Africa, in which American black men encountered African royalty, power, and elegance and had to confront cultural differences and misunderstandings—universal not just to black people—before finally getting out of trouble. One of these, *In Dahomey* (1903), was a major hit and the first black musical to open on Broadway. They did a command performance of the show at Buckingham Palace in 1903 and recorded songs from this and other shows. By 1904 they were the most famous black performers in the world.

Walker became ill with syphilis (for which there was then no cure) and Williams had to pursue a solo career. He is widely regarded as Broadway's first black star. He joined the all-white Ziegfeld Follies in 1910—an unprecedented offer—and remained with the show for ten years, and it was here that Williams gained his most popular acclaim.[49] Williams became a sensation, and teamed up with the white performer Leon Errol, an interracial act being another groundbreaking move. In their skits, which they cowrote, Williams delivered most of the punch lines and often got the better of Errol.[50] In the evolution of his performances, Williams both fit in with, and challenged, the blackface performance of white actors. By the early to mid-1910s, Williams was earning a whopping $62,400 a year, approximately $1.5 million in today's money. And his extremely popular records made him, by 1920, one of the three most highly paid recording artists in the world.[51] Thus, despite institutional racism and segregation, Williams helped pave the way for the beginnings of black stardom, which would expand even more with the rise of radio.

Because so many theatrical venues, like saloons and beer halls as well as those catering to working-class boys and men, were deemed inappropriate for "proper" women to enter, vaudeville entrepreneurs had to work to promote their shows as respectable for women and families.

Figure 2.4. Williams and Walker, c. 1900s. Photograph by Hall, New York Public Library.

Yet, at the same time, many of the acts, replete with ethnic and urban humor, were hardly puritanical. Indeed, as with entertainment today, the comics, singers, dancers, and the sketches often pushed the boundaries of prevailing norms around morality. Sensationalism and scandal were also crucial to drawing a crowd. But promoters had to confront moralistic concerns that popular culture was, at the same time, frivolous yet debasing and thus dangerous. To attract a larger swath of the middle class, they embarked on the "gentrification of popular culture," banning alcohol, policing behavior within vaudeville theaters, and recruiting "high class" acts to be interspersed with those doing more lowbrow fare.[52]

Celebrity Scandal

By 1906, the template for hyping celebrity scandals to promote the sales of newspapers and boost vaudeville and film attendance was in place.

There was a further rise in "the feature" story about the well-known, profiles seeking to provide accounts of what they were like in private, in their everyday lives.[53] There was also enormous competition among the mass-circulation dailies, especially in big cities, to get "scoops" on breaking, high-profile news stories. In what was a truly notorious case and breathlessly hailed, quite prematurely, as "the crime of the century," Evelyn Nesbit, probably the first mass culture sex goddess and precursor of the "supermodel," found herself at the center of a murder scandal.[54]

"Discovered" at age fourteen, the stunningly beautiful Nesbit became, first, a model for painters and sculptors and then moved on to become one of the most sought-after models for photographers and magazine illustrators working in the booming advertising industry. She was the original "Gibson Girl," the model of the new, turn-of-the-century woman popularized by the artist Charles Dana Gibson and featured in numerous ads and publications. She was the most photographed woman of her time, gracing the covers of various popular magazines, whose numbers had also skyrocketed. In 1865, the total circulation of monthly magazines was around four million; by 1905, it was sixty-four million, many of them supported primarily by advertising.[55] Her face was, by 1900, known to millions, appearing even on a host of packaged products, like novelty cards, toothpaste, chocolate, and face creams. She then became a chorus girl in the hit musical *Florodora*. By this time Nesbit was a major celebrity and appeared regularly in the gossip columns and theatrical periodicals of the day.

Stanford White, an eminent architect in his fifties whose projects included Madison Square Garden, the Washington Square Arch, and the Tiffany Building in New York City, saw her in *Florodora* and quickly became her benefactor, which included providing her with extravagant gifts, an allowance, and an apartment. He subsequently got her drunk and then raped her; by the age of sixteen she had become his mistress, until the relationship ended a year later. Pursued by Harry Thaw, son of a Pittsburgh millionaire, Nesbit eventually agreed to marry him in 1905, at the age of twenty-one. But Thaw, mentally disturbed and by most accounts a cocaine addict, was obsessed with White, whom he saw as a rival who had deflowered his wife. On June 25, 1906, at Madison Square Garden's rooftop theater, which White had designed, in the middle of

Figure 2.5. Evelyn Nesbit about 1900 at a time when
she was brought to the studio by Stanford White.
Photograph by Gertrude Käsebier, Library of
Congress.

a performance, Thaw walked up to White and shot him at point blank
range before a horrified audience.

By this time there were twenty-eight newspapers in New York, and
their legions of reporters began scavenging the city for witnesses or anyone with information about the crime, accurate or made up. All kinds
of misinformation filled the papers. The murder and subsequent trails,
the first in 1907 (hung jury) and the second a year later, were sensational,
scandal-filled, front-page news, with Thaw eventually declared insane
and White reviled as a lecherous seducer of young women (Nesbit had
not been the first or only conquest). Indeed, the Thaw family, with public relations still in its infancy, hired a publicist and Thaw apologist, who
filled the press with a lava flow of negative stories about White's woman-
izing and debauching of teenage girls and even paid people to cooperate

with this campaign. The publicist also helped mount a play depicting the crime with the identities of the protagonists barely concealed (Thaw became "Harold Daw," for example) and with the Daw character proclaiming that no jury would convict him. Meanwhile, the district attorney's office prosecuting Thaw hired its own publicity firm to smear Thaw and Nesbit. Thomas Edison's film studio rushed out a film version called the *Rooftop Murder* one week after the crime and it became a top box office hit. The Thaws also sponsored the production of a film, again putting Harry in the best possible light. With each new twist to the story, newspaper circulation soared; the scandal dominated the press for two years.[56]

Nesbit was already famous as a model and actress, but the fevered newspaper coverage of the murder and trial, filled with sex, violence, and betrayal, expanded her notoriety, with newspaper headlines reading "Woman Whose Beauty Spelled Death and Ruin."[57] Nesbit learned painfully what many other subsequent celebrities would learn, especially those involved in scandal: that the press would incessantly violate her privacy and that many negative stories about her past, her family, and her behaviors would be made up. As she wrote, "It is a frightening experience to hear a thought to which you have never given words babbled aloud in the street. . . . It sets you frantically anxious to amend, to contradict, to correct. Your little secret is everybody's secret now. It has gained in importance, has been twisted in detail until it is like nothing you ever knew."[58] She found the publicity unbearable, but also had to resume making money. Her notoriety made her a vaudeville attraction, where in 1913 she began to dance on stage on her own and then with a partner; she became the biggest draw on vaudeville and later made several silent films that mostly depicted events in her life.[59]

It was now clear that the symbiotic relationship between the increasingly powerful newspapers, especially those that trafficked in yellow journalism, and the widely popular vaudeville had become a celebrity production machine. And, as the Nesbit case illustrates, new kinds of celebrities were being created. Now violators of the law became stars, as when Lillian Graham and Ethel Conrad, who in 1911 shot and wounded the real estate magnate W. E. D. Stokes during an argument, became the vaudeville attraction "The Shooting Stars."[60] Thus, with vaudeville especially, people became famous, however fleetingly, for being famous.

Inventor-Heroes, Captains of Industry, and Public Relations

Another kind of celebrity, produced especially by the press, was the "inventor-hero," the most famous being Thomas Edison. His canny self-promotion, and the press's eagerness to report on the latest in science and technology, established this version of celebrity that would later be enjoyed by Steve Jobs, Bill Gates, and Mark Zuckerberg. The period from the 1870s to the 1920s marked a revolution in electrical and electronic based inventions—the telephone, lightbulb, motion pictures, automobiles, airplanes, radio—and those who devised them and knew how to work the press became major celebrities. Edison used his lab in Menlo Park, New Jersey, to unveil his latest inventions to reporters, as when his demonstration of the phonograph in 1877 earned him the moniker "The Wizard of Menlo Park." Two years later he staged a dramatic media event demonstrating his incandescent lightbulb. Through this combination of serial inventions and his shrewd grasp of what kind of image of the inventor the press would embrace and amplify, Edison became a national hero and a brand. Edison, for example, emphasized his tireless work in the lab, that he barely slept, and that unlike some "old German professor" who studied "the fuzz on a bee," he pursued practical inventions that would benefit millions. When Guglielmo Marconi, the half-Irish, half-Italian inventor of the wireless telegraph, the antecedent to radio, made a deal with New York's *Herald* to cover the avidly followed America's Cup yacht races in 1899 via his new device, he too became a celebrity. So did what were called "Captains of Industry," Andrew Carnegie, John D. Rockefeller, Cornelius Vanderbilt, and J. P. Morgan. And given their extraordinary wealth—remember, this was before the Sixteenth Amendment, which established the individual income tax in 1913—they could cement their fame and a sense of immortality by establishing universities, museums, concert halls, hospitals, and libraries in their name.

As the influence of journalism grew, especially with the explosive growth of mass-circulation magazines between 1885 and 1900, the famous also learned that to be widely known was not always a boon to one's fortune or reputation, especially with the rise of the Progressive movement in the early twentieth century. Muckraking journalists worked to uncover corruption and abuse in government and within the increasingly monopolistic corporations of industrial capitalism. Prominent politicians and businessmen could be leveled with a cutting story and unflattering cartoon. John D. Rockefeller, for example, the founder of Standard Oil, controlled 90 percent of the nation's refineries and pipelines by 1882, leading to concern about such monopoly control and passage of the Sherman Antitrust Act in 1890. Rockefeller's wealth and what were seen as cutthroat business practices made him a target for muckrakers. As the *New York Times* reported, Rockefeller was accused of crushing his competition, bribing men to spy on rival companies, and building up his enormous fortune at the expense and ruin of others. In 1902, the muckraking magazine *McClure's* began publishing Ida Tarbell's scathing, serialized portrait of Rockefeller in "The History of Standard Oil," which came out as a book in 1904. Tarbell portrayed him as greedy, miserly, and viciously ruthless. The book produced a public outcry over monopolistic practices and led to the breakup of Standard Oil in 1911.

Clearly there was a market for a new kind of press agent, not just the ones who promoted vaudeville acts. By the early twentieth century, the profession of public relations had sprung up to help the powerful gain support in the press and sway public sentiment in their favor. Rockefeller hired a publicist in the wake of Tarbell's exposé, but eventually replaced him with Ivy Lee, considered the founder of public relations in the United States. Rockefeller had begun to give away portions of his considerable wealth to charities and to establish new institutions, like Rockefeller University. Lee determined that he could not explain away Rockefeller's past, but could help to change his image over time through his current and future actions, which included changing the management practices of companies the Rockefeller family had interests in. Most famously, Rockefeller began the practice of giving a shiny new dime to every person, especially children, whom he met, helping to recast his image from cutthroat businessman to generous philanthropist.

The Embedding of Celebrity Culture

Between the 1850s and the 1910s, then, a new phenomenon had emerged and continued to balloon that would redefine American life:

the technologically produced manufacture of fame. Increased urban-ization, mass immigration and overall population growth, the spread of a market economy, coupled with a gradual rise in leisure time, pro-duced audiences for entertainments and readers of newspapers. But it was the cascading developments in communications technologies—the mechanization of newspaper production that allowed more papers to be produced more quickly, transportation systems that brought entertain-ers from one city to the next, and the invention of photography, and then the phonograph, and motion pictures—that enabled the burrowing of famous people into the minds and hearts of everyday people.

As Charles Ponce de Leon argues convincingly, it was magazines and mass-circulation newspapers that became the most important institu-tions for creating and sustaining celebrity culture during this period. They made public figures visible to millions who never encountered them in real life. And they did so, in part, by responding to the promo-tional gambits of entrepreneurs like Barnum, who keenly grasped the conventions of news gathering, what would fascinate people, and how to strategically craft and present personas so they would become sought after—famous.[61] So technologies of celebrity are not always machines, but also the practices used to create and perpetuate fame. Newspapers and photography shifted the nature of fame, making it accessible not only to those already possessing wealth and esteem but also to those who wished to grab the spotlight, or those who sought to grab it for them. In turn, the public was transformed from passive followers into active consumers, invited to comment on and "get to know" those in positions of power and, in doing so, to become part of celebrity produc-tion themselves. What had become entrenched now in our culture was a "staggering machine of desire" that centered on celebrity.[62]

This era saw celebrity arising both out of the intrinsic qualities a per-son had—a singing talent, singular beauty, inventive genius—and often out of "carefully mapped out plans for attracting publicity and projecting an image that will make them interesting and attractive to the media—the essential conduits through which individuals are made visible to the public."[63] And this was happening, especially between the 1880s and the 1920s, as economic inequality—despite increased social mobility—made the rich and famous objects of both envy and resentment.

Thus, many crucial precedents were established that still dominate today: the role of an increasingly intrusive and expanding news media in introducing and promoting celebrities; the skillful use of behind-the-scenes publicity and promotion to get the press to do your bidding and make someone a star; stories about famous people's alleged philanthropy to make them admirable; stars as embodiments of cultural values and national identity; people, like Nelly Bly, becoming famous for exposing scandal and others, like Evelyn Nesbit, for being ensnared in one.

A consequential change during this period, then, that intertwined with the dramatic rise of consumer culture, as well as with increased geographical and social mobility, was a shift toward a culture of personality, as opposed to character. The emphasis on character during the Victorian era, and its focus on restraint, hard work, and deferred gratification, felt increasingly constraining with the rise of leisure time, commercial entertainments, and a growing desire for self-expression.[64] Presentation of self became more important in cities where you might no longer have strong kinship or friendship ties you could rely on for support and success; the notion of "the first impression" came to grip people's sense of themselves. Personality was how people were supposed to distinguish themselves from others, from the masses. With the freedom, even the need, to fashion a winning personality, advice books emerged with titles like *Winning the Front Place* (1908), and a new ideal of "personal efficiency" took hold. Drawing in part from new forms of management, and from the escalating emphasis on the self and the body in advertising (body odor, clean teeth, lustrous hair), personal efficiency emphasized taking control of your life by cultivating various physical, mental, and personality traits that would make you more effective and admired.[65] With this shifting social and cultural order, celebrity became a measure—and a yardstick—of success.

In this burgeoning market economy and the rise of consumer culture, celebrities became products themselves, with their faces and stories becoming products to be sold. What arose during this era, and forever transformed American culture right up to the present, was the emergence of celebrity as "a new form of public visibility" made possible by the convergence of these social, technological, and economic changes. This was the beginning of what the historian Daniel Boorstin labeled the

"Graphic Revolution" in which new and multiplying visual technologies spread the images of and stories about increasing numbers of people who would become famous to those who would never meet them in the flesh.[66] And while newspapers and magazines were—and remain—foundational to this turn, few technologies would play a more central role in the mass production, elevation of, and fandom for the star than motion pictures.

3

Silver Screens and Their Stars

It's 1895 and people are seated in a darkened theater. In front of them, on the screen, there appears a large locomotive, a hulking steam train. Passengers gather on the platform awaiting its arrival. But as the train moves down the track, chugging its way into the station, it shows no sign of stopping. In fact, it seems to move dangerously closer. It looks as though it will career off the screen and into the audience. And still the train persists in its advance. No one had seen anything like it, and it was terrifying.

Of course, for today's audiences, the thought of being so shaken by a moving picture—especially one in black and white with no menacing sounds or harrowing soundtrack—seems absurd. But for audiences of early cinema, in this case French filmgoers who viewed Louis Lumière's 1895 film, *L'Arrivée d'un train en gare de la Ciotat* (The Arrival of a train at La Ciotat Station), the experience was a jarring one that shook the boundaries between fantasy and reality. In the darkened theater, as the train chugged across the screen, viewers reportedly jumped from their chairs and fled in fright.[1]

Edwin Porter's *The Great Train Robbery* (1903), a twelve-minute film based on a holdup by Butch Cassidy's "Hole in the Wall" gang, had a similar effect. In the final scene, one of the robbers faces the camera and shoots point blank at the audience to cement their identification with the victimized travelers aboard the train. The effect was shocking, and the film became one of the fledgling industry's first blockbusters.

The arrival of Lumière's locomotive and Porter's outlaw embodied the kind of surreal experience that early moving pictures offered their audiences. While the magic lantern shows of the nineteenth century captivated people with projected scenes of humorous or "supernatural" animations, the technological innovation of moving pictures offered a vision of everyday life, transformed into a fantastic viewing experience where space, time, and motion could be manipulated in entirely new ways.[2] Audiences were enthralled, and by the turn of the century, short moving pictures on film could be viewed in storefronts, vaudeville theaters, and, starting in 1905, in nickelodeons, five-cent setups constructed from converted dance halls and cigar stores, which catered to working-class patrons. On-screen, an amalgam of popular tunes, patriotic anthems, single-reel news footage, minidocumentaries, travelogues, slapstick skits, and sporting event highlights were interspersed with live acts, from trained dogs to ventriloquists.[3] By 1907, between 3,000 and 5,000 nickelodeons had been established with over two million admissions a day; three years later, conservative estimates suggested that twenty-six million Americans were attending them each week, about 20 percent of the national population. Attendance was greater in cities, where members of burgeoning immigrant and working-class communities sought refuge from the trials of tenement life.[4]

Nickelodeons were extremely controversial, derided by reformers and critics as unsanitary, foul smelling, and overcrowded, and whose darkness could put some women at risk of unwanted advances while also encouraging prostitution. Eventual regulation required provision for ventilation, fire protection, sanitation, and adequate exits.[5] As the popularity and profitability of the medium grew, producers developed new modes for lighting, projecting, recording, and editing footage. Plots grew more complex and production values more refined; soon, multireel narratives were replacing single-reel shorts. Early film studios—Vitagraph, Edison, Biograph, Keystone—vied with each other for players and audiences.

The feature film was born and with it came a new type of famous figure—the film star. Taking the moviegoing experience so much for granted as we do now, it can be hard to appreciate what a completely revolutionary sensory encounter it was. The cinematic apparatus—sitting in a darkened theater while watching illuminated bodies and faces larger than your own performing for you and engaging with you—enabled an entirely new and deeply compelling production of celebrity, especially as theaters and screens got larger. Various theorists have argued that this particular viewing experience replicated foundational psychological moments from infancy, when we both identify with and idealize the larger faces and bodies that tend to us and nurture us. When those magnified faces on the screen are more beautiful or handsome than our own, when, through close-ups they convey the basic emotions we all feel—joy, sadness and loss, fear, desire, anger—idealization and identification, so central to fandom, are enhanced as well. The darkened theater, the multiple camera moves and shots, and the manipulation of space and time also powerfully transport us into absorbing narratives where we lose ourselves and can inhabit the experiences and emotions of those on the screen, some of them pleasurable, others embarrassing or scary. Thus it is hard to overstate the transformational role that the technology of the cinema played in infusing the impact and spread of celebrity culture into the everyday life of the country. Few technologies have been more central to the penetration of celebrities into our hearts, our very consciousness, than film.

The Hollywood Studio System

The popularity of moving pictures consolidated the possibility of national fame that had begun to solidify during the vaudeville years. Players in scripted films gained national exposure, yet early knowledge of film actors was limited. Most actors of this period were bound to one of the various studios, which, for the most part, produced and owned their personas and were adamant about their desire to protect actors' public images; until 1909, the studios hesitated even to release the names of the players. Studio execs didn't want their performers associated with the tawdry playhouses, sexual scandals, and improper after-hours antics of vaudeville or bohemia.[6] Plus, studios were leery of promoting individual players for fear that they would become intractable or demand higher pay.[7] And so names and identities were kept from the public and audiences were compelled to make up nicknames when discussing their favorites; popular silent film actress Mary Pickford, identifiable primarily by her voluminous ringlets, became widely known as "the girl with the curls" before her name became famous.

Despite rigorous efforts to create an attractive, tractable workforce, the alluring, mysterious, and literally larger-than-life film actor appeared across the screens of playhouses and theaters throughout the United States; it wouldn't take long before influential players would become recognizable to audiences.[8] As demand for films grew and competition among nickelodeon exhibitors intensified, the studios, realizing that popular players could be used to promote new films, began to shift their marketing strategies. Studios started publicizing the names of the actors in their movies, and started recruiting famous theatrical performers, like the renowned actor Sarah Bernhardt, to appear in them. By 1911, Edison Studios had developed the credit system, listing the names of starring actors on its films' introductory title cards. Two years later, players' names would be paired with their photo and the name of their character in the film.[9] The practice of naming heightened fans' connections to the actors, making popular players recognizable to audiences who could now identify with, and fantasize about, their favorites.

Soon, the studios were enlisting well-known actors to make personal appearances, pose for posters, be photographed for press books, sign lobby cards, be interviewed for newspaper articles, and be featured in advertisements.[10] In this way the studios sought to use the players—their individuality, and people's admiration of or identification with them—to manage audiences' demand for films.[11] And recognizing popular players' ability to promote a film, the studios sought to identify and groom new talent. They hired scouts to track down young men and women who might be turned into profitable players. Publicity departments worked to create easily identifiable types—the ingénue, the rebel, the seductress—and built actors' brands through a carefully constructed portfolio of press appearances, styling, and narrative construction.[12]

If someone's name was too ethnic, too unpronounceable, or not glamorous enough, it was changed. Gladys Smith became Mary Pickford; Rodolfo di Valentina d'Antonguella became Rudolph Valentino; Theodosia Burr Goodman became Theda Bara. Head shots were taken, biographies were faked; if their biographies were boring (or questionable) they were changed.[13] Studios invested large sums of money in scouting, grooming, and polishing the images of new talent. The lucky few who made it on-screen were typically young, white, pretty or handsome (unless they were comics), and, perhaps most importantly, obedient.[14]

Also in the 1910s and 1920s, in an effort to attract a more "respectable," middle-class audience than those who frequented nickelodeons, exhibitors began building more opulent movie palaces with larger and more plush seating areas. The short "one-reelers" shown in nickelodeons gave way to multiple reel, feature-length films, which gave actors more opportunities to display their craft and to appear on-screen.

All the while, film as a medium was improving, providing audiences with a higher quality and a more lifelike moviegoing experience, one that seemed to bring them ever closer to their on-screen idols. While early turn-of-the century films favored long shots, which showed an actor's entire body, director D. W. Griffith soon popularized the use of the close-up, an insert shot in which the camera cut away from the main frame to focus on the actor's face, in films such as *The Avenging Conscience* (1914) and *Birth of a Nation* (1915). The close-up, often enhanced by lighting, brought the unique, subtle, and distinctive qualities of actors' faces into high relief, allowing audiences to view, memorize, and even imitate their looks and expressions. It was the close-up's ability to make recognizable the facial features of famous actors, combined with its ability to convey intense and immediate emotion, that made the technique so powerful. Close-up shots were used to intensify scenes of emotional candor, often through exaggerated expressions and the use of makeup. "The close up," as Richard Schickel writes, "invites us to read character into the face, to formulate from the lines and wrinkles therein, an impression easily mistaken for a detailed, knowledgeable portrait of the star."[15] In daily life, we only have these kinds of close encounters—up close moments with other people's faces—with those we know and love—our mothers and children, our lovers and dear friends. The close-up brought these private encounters onto the big screen, establishing the camera as a most intimate window into the stars' being.

From Picture Personality to Star

Thus, by the midteens and early 1920s, there was a new and very commanding type of celebrity: the movie star. Some of them we remember today and some we don't, and the roles they played and their on- and offscreen personas came to embody various American hopes, fears, aspirations, and desires. These "types" also set precedents for categories of celebrities still with us today. Charlie Chaplin, who by 1915 had refined his character "the Tramp" in his trademark baggy pants, bowler hat, and oversized shoes, came to represent a comedic and sympathetic version of the resilient little guy who often stood up pathetically yet heroically to overwhelming odds and usually triumphed.[16] He was bumbling and good-hearted, often thumbed his nose at authority, and, with his

Figure 3.1. Mary Pickford, with motion picture
camera on beach, c. 1916. Library of Congress.

signature cane, tried to emulate the manners and demeanor of a more
upper-class gentleman, despite his usual status as a vagrant or vagabond.
Here class tensions were addressed and sometimes finessed.

Female stars who were not comics came to personify the "virgin" or the
"whore," with Mary Pickford, one of the country's biggest box office draws
in the teens and early 1920s, representing the radiance and innocence of a
little girl. She set the precedent for a beautiful yet virginal young woman
being labeled "America's Sweetheart." On the other end of the spectrum
was the enormously popular Theda Bara who in 1915 became an overnight
sensation as a ruthless femme fatale in *A Fool Was There* and became famous as "the Vamp," short for vampire. She was one of the first fabricated
stars with publicists alleging, variously, that she was born in the Sahara
Desert, the child of either an Arab sheik, a French or Italian artist and his
French mistress, or an Arabian princess, even though she was actually the
Jewish daughter of a tailor and his wife in Cincinnati.

Bara was the screen's first sex symbol, and to add to her mystery, she was photographed with snakes and skulls and was urged to refer to the occult and mysticism in her interviews. Publicists further added that her name was an anagram for "Arab Death."[17] Bara—whose on-screen characters could "ensnare any man, exploit him, trample him, and walk away with an enormous grin on her face,"[18] tapped into American fascination with and often fear of the power of female sexuality as a potentially destructive force. In the 1920s, Clara Bow—unlike either Pickford or Bara—became the exemplar of the flapper, the bobbed-hair, self-assured, carefree, and independent modern woman. After appearing in the film *It*, she became the first "It Girl," a woman with that something extra who had a magnetic sex appeal yet was unselfconscious about it. She became a role model for millions of women in the 1920s, a time of female liberation and a sexual revolution, and in her offscreen presentation of self she was honest about her deprived childhood and background, as well as about her gambling sprees and boyfriends.[19]

During this period, actors' public personas were promoted as amalgams of those of the characters they played on-screen. In other words, the sunny American sweetheart Mary Pickford (actually born in Canada) who, as a twenty-five-year-old woman played a child in films like *Poor Little Rich Girl* and *Rebecca of Sunnybrook Farm*, was promoted as sweet and innocent in her own life, despite her proven record as a savvy businesswoman. The idea that actors' on-screen personas mirrored their real selves produced what Richard deCordova calls *picture personalities*. These *personalities*, actors known for playing different but related roles, established performers as seemingly authentic "types" while allowing the audience to "get to know" them.[20] As deCordova writes, "With the picture personality the spectator was encouraged to follow through all of the associations created with a specific actor's appearance from film to film. The more films the spectator saw, and the more she or he focused on the actors, the richer the associations would be."[21] This system benefited not only audiences, who could identify with their favorite players, but also studios, "who could count on audiences returning again and again to films featuring their favorite stars" and who could use stars to "differentiate between filmic 'products.'"[22]

But audiences' desires to know more about the performer's offscreen identity could not be held at bay indefinitely. By 1913 and 1914, as with earlier coverage of the theater and vaudeville, the focus of journalistic profiles shifted from the professional lives and characters played to the personal lives, looks, and opinions of the individuals who played them. Audiences became absorbed by previously unknown details about the players' lives, some of them sordid and titillating, others luxurious but everyday, like what they ate or what their hobbies were. Stardom, as de-Cordova writes, "emerged out of a marked expansion of what could be known about the player. . . . the question of the player's existence outside of his or her work in film became the primary focus of discourse. The private lives of the players, not unlike those of their vaudeville predecessors, were constituted as a site of knowledge and truth."[23] Audiences could now recognize their favorite players' names, faces, and life stories, which were chronicled in the burgeoning celebrity publications of the day. The public's fascination thus fueled, attendance at cinemas skyrocketed. (By 1916, there were more than 21,000 movie theaters in the United States.) These biographies, many of them carefully constructed, some of them punctured when scandal broke, came to matter enormously to everyday people, who could see in them roadmaps, as well as reassuring myths, about how to succeed in a new, modernized society. Such profiles lay out both the material rewards of success and its costs if one got too caught up in the parties, nightclubs, reckless behavior, and an overinflated sense of one's importance, known derisively as "going Hollywood."[24]

"The Unknown Hollywood I Know": Fan Magazines and Insider Knowledge

The popularization of moving pictures ushered in a new cadre of publications, including the *Motion Picture Story Magazine*, *Photoplay*, and *Silver Screen*, devoted to coverage of the stars and geared primarily to women.[25] Early features were composed primarily of posed press photos—glamorous, celestial, and dramatically lit headshots—and studio-sanctioned stories, designed to enhance the aura of the star. These types of stories emphasized the unique talents, exceptional beauty, and noteworthiness of the stars and offered readers a coveted inside glimpse at their "true selves," encouraging a sense of wistful awe.

But by the late 1910s, the studios, realizing that audience interest could generate sales, offered fan magazines extensive, though carefully monitored, access to their actors.[26] Interest quickly shifted, and fan magazines were soon catering to readers' desire for inside scoops and aspirational storytelling, offering up a blend of fantastic glamour and plain-spoken relatability. While the narratives remained aspirational, they were also built around seeking to produce a sense of identification, highlighting simple, knowable elements about the stars' appearance, hobbies, and preferences, in which readers could see themselves.

Cinema and magazines offered a relatively inexpensive, attractive escape to Hollywood-land especially during the Great Depression; by 1933, *Modern Screen, Silver Screen,* and *Photoplay* were each selling around 500,000 copies per week at newsstands.[27] Fan magazines thus presented an enticing paradox: movie stars could be distinctive and fabulous, but also ordinary people who were, perhaps, simply luckier versions of ourselves. The magazines' narratives reflected this duality. And they developed a particular style of writing—chatty, slangy, conversational—to convey a familiarity between reader and star. Double-page photo spreads revealed behind-the-scenes glimpses into lavish homes and travelogues followed stars on trips to exotic locales. Posed glamour shots were accompanied by "candid" stories and "inside scoops," gossipy behind-the-scenes takes, and casual photos of stars playing tennis or walking their dogs, providing eager readers with details about the stars' "true" lives—their hairstyles and favorite fashions, the sports and hobbies they enjoyed, even the recipes they cooked for dinner. Domestic featurettes brought readers into the stars' homes where, as Joshua Gamson writes, "we saw them at ease, with their families, doing everyday things," to convey that their pleasures and "their most basic values were virtually indistinguishable from our own."[28]

With the coverage of celebrity scandals, and the sense that many stars were successful because of their personalities, but not necessarily because of hard work or talent, a journalistic template emerged, produced by the studios, the stars, and fan magazines, about what made someone an admirable star. Many of these tropes persist today. To stay at the top, stars had to work hard, to continue refining their craft. Aspiring to grow and to seek challenging roles was especially laudable. As Joan Crawford told the *Saturday Evening Post*, "The higher you rise, the more is expected of you. Mistakes are less readily overlooked or forgiven."[29] They had to be team players, "troupers," and not be temperamental or divas.

Figure 3.2. Publicity card of Shirley Temple with doll, c. 1930s.

And they needed to express their responsibility and devotion to their fans. As Clark Gable told one reporter, "I owe so much to the people that have enjoyed what I want to give."[30] Hard-working, ambitious in all the right ways, and responsible—especially during the Depression—these were core values stars needed as part of their self-presentation.

Themes of family and intimacy were reinforced in coverage of early child stars. Shirley Temple, for instance, from 1935 through 1938 Hollywood's number-one box office star, was ardently covered and features followed her life in great detail, as she played with her siblings, rode her bicycle, and even prayed. Temple's all-American screen image was reinforced by magazine stories, which bolstered her sweet-as-pie persona that made her a national darling. She could also move merchandise. In April 1936, movie theaters and department stores across the country held events in celebration of Shirley's ninth birthday. In addition to her wildly popular dolls, merchants also sold cheaper branded trinkets such as songbooks, coloring books, soaps, paper dolls, and other small novelties so that less privileged consumers could also partake in the celebration through their purchases.

Why did this little girl become such a megastar? Of course she was extremely cute and could sing and tap dance. But, again, public embrace of particular stars at particular times also tells us about the pull of the historical context and prevailing cultural anxieties. Let's remember that the Great Depression was the biggest crisis to date for patriarchal capitalism; Wall Street, the bankers, the captains of industry, even the president, Herbert Hoover, had all failed the nation. With so many men thrown out of work, there was a massive sense of helplessness, a crisis in masculinity and male authority. Temple's movies came to be characterized by stories about lost daddies, dead daddies, or blind daddies, whom she searched for, mourned, nurtured, and whose tragedies she and they triumphed over. Having the nation's spirit embodied by an innocent, irrepressible little girl, with her shiny future before her, captured and symbolically managed the enormous anxiety about the threatened collapse of patriarchy during the Depression's darkest days. And who could be less pretentious, less spoiled by fame than this charming child?

Meanwhile, fascinated crowds flocked to "Quintland" to view the infant Dionne sisters, who became a sensation in the early '30s as the first set of quintuplets to live through infancy. The quints represented a kind of miracle, their cherub faces gracing the covers of fan magazines. In fact, all child stars seemed to possess a kind of magic, appearing as what Leo Lowenthal calls "souls without history." These child stars were not expected to grow up, but to function as "midget editions" of grown adults, "rubber stamped" with innate talent and purpose at birth.[31]

The knowability of the stars was further honed through the genre's chatty, even divulging tone, use of first-person pronouns, and direct address to readers, all of which stitch us into the gossip and make us feel as though the stars are our friends. Being "down to earth" was especially appealing. One reporter praised Theda Bara for being "absolutely unaffected and unassuming in manner" despite her on-screen "vamp" image. Profiles of the stars at home were designed to show them as "regular people," enjoying simple pleasures like listening to the radio, cooking, hosting small dinner parties, or playing parlor games with friends. One journalist, in his profile of Pickford and Douglas Fairbanks, declared that he said to them, "Why, you are just like other people—just like others, only more so! You do the ordinary things in the ordinary manner."[32]

The April 1933 issue of *Photoplay*, which takes the reader along for Clara Bow's trip to St. Moritz, provides another classic example of this construction of chatty and ordinary fan-star friendship, a studio-constructed parasocial relationship. Photos and illustrations show her testing her skis, posing on the slopes with a St. Bernard, and riding in a sleigh with friends. "Clara's European diary" is set up as just that—a diary, featuring a day-by-day, first-person account of Bow's adventures. She begins as if she's gossiping with a close friend:

> Between you and me, I bet lots of tourists . . . come back raving about things that are starred in the guide books . . . but the incidents and sights I remember most vividly aren't like that. . . . Jan. 18th. St. Moritz. Gee, what a place. Never felt more like a million dollars in my life. They've got a special brand of mountains and sun and snow and fresh air up here that makes you eat like a truck horse, and sleep like a bear, and feel so kind and good you'd like to kiss everybody you meet. It sure is swell. Jan. 20th. Had my first skiing lesson yesterday. Was it a riot? I wasn't scared, only uncomfortable with those heavy boards on my feet. They felt ten miles long.

Clara's confessional, chatty, at times even self-effacing diary entries allow readers to feel as though the star was personally divulging her inner thoughts and feelings to us while also providing access to a luxurious world that most readers would never know.

Thus, as Anthony Slide notes, "the movies presented the star to the viewer, but the fan magazine could reach beyond the visual image and examine and reveal the 'real' personality—his or her life, loves, and most intimate thoughts."[33] Such features exemplify Joke Hermes's point about how celebrity profiles allow us to vicariously enter a world of wealth and leisure while feeling like we are members of an extended family; we come to know these people, their history, their tastes, their hobbies, their likes and dislikes.

Celebrities—how they looked, dressed, and behaved—also provided fans with scripts to follow and looks to imitate for impression management and social success.[34] Star stories provided a kind of "how to" for those seeking to impress new acquaintances—the "first impression," touted as crucial in self-help books and in countless ads especially for personal care products, now mattered enormously. Fan magazines offered readers' guides for glamming themselves up, complete with suggestions for dressing and styling one's self in the image of their favorite players. Everything from makeup to clothing to china patterns was presented, fawned over, and critiqued. These were not merely fashionable items to covet, though certainly they were, but they were also critical tools, endowing their owners with the promise of social mobility in a time where opportunities were few and a glamorous, star-approved lip color or cigarette was one of few attainable luxuries.

In one such featurette showcasing dresses made to look like those appearing in upcoming films, the magazine helpfully reminded readers that the "Hollywood fashions sponsored by *Photoplay Magazine* and worn by famous stars in the latest motion pictures now may be secured for your own wardrobe from leading department and ready-to-wear stores in many localities. . . . Faithful copies of these smartly styled and moderately-priced garments, of which those shown in this issue of *Photoplay* are typical, are on display this month in stores of those representative merchants who firm names are conveniently listed on page 119."[35] As the magazines urged women to enhance their own "personal charm" and charisma, they suggested that doing so may take her one step closer to her own personal enviability.

It's during this period that we begin to see stars of screen and popular culture appearing in print advertisements, promoting everything from cosmetics, to fashion, to household goods. These kinds of ads also placed celebrities in direct conversation with the reader, a trusted source of information and influence, offering up the promise of the good life, made possible through careful consumption. Cigarette ads from the 1930s and '40s promoted both the celebrities and the smokes, with posters highlighting new films by the likes of stars from Laurel and Hardy to Bing Crosby.[36] "*You* try Luckies, too, and see," urged an ad for Lucky Strikes, which showed Spencer Tracy smoking on the set of his new film, *Test Pilot*.[37] Even popular athletes appeared in similar ads: "To all my friends

I say smoke Chesterfields," quipped a smiling Joe Lewis, also pictured in the boxing ring, while a Camel ad showed a second-by-second break-down of baseball star Joe DiMaggio's swing (he's enjoyed the brand for "8 years," by the way).[38] In these images, the product was promoted as the vehicle that brought stars and audiences closer together. Now, through our consumption of otherwise mundane items, we could vicari-ously experience a little taste of that glamorous life.

Indeed, fan magazine coverage eschewed turn of the century tales of heroic inventors and titans of industry who had earned their renown through their financial, technological, or industrial achievements in favor of stories of good fortune and lucky breaks. Lana Turner, who was discovered as a teenager by the publisher of the *Hollywood Reporter* while she sat in a café was one such example. She was signed to War-ner Brothers in 1937 and that year appeared in her first film, *They Won't Forget*. She quickly became a fixture of celebrity magazines, who spun stories of her discovery, as in an article titled "She Won in a Walk." Here, *Hollywood* magazine writer Elmer Sunfield gushes about Lana Turner's stroll down the easy street to fame:

> Most young players have to endure hardships and rebuffs at the start of a career, but there is one exception.
>
> All that pretty seventeen-year-old Lana Turner had to do to convince producer Mervyn LeRoy out of Warner Brothers Studios that she was top-notch movie star material was to "walk right in, turn around, and walk right out again."
>
> As simple as all that! . . .
>
> This lovely little youngster has acquired the luckiest habit in the world. . . . Less than seven months ago she walked out of the side door of the Hollywood High School and walked into a tiny lunchroom near Sunset Boulevard . . . a trade publisher walked in and sat down at a near-by table. . . . [H]e'd been around the film factories long enough to recognize a good bet when he saw one, and before Lana scarcely knew what it was all about, he had her walking into the office of a player's agent. . . . the next day Lana was among twenty other girls to be tested for the role of Mary Clay. As composed as a veteran trooper, Lana walked right into a fat movie contract five minutes after producer LeRoy had seen the test! As simple as all that![39]

And Lana Turner was not the only one whose career was launched in such a fateful way. Carole Lombard was discovered by director Allan Dwan at the age of twelve while playing baseball with friends. Dwan needed a tomboy for his film, *A Perfect Crime*, and offered Lombard the role.[40] Stories like these suggest that success, even fame, are matters not of deliberation or dedication, but of being in the right place at the right time, the result primarily of fate. Hollywood itself is presented as a fantastical place, a world in which anything is possible, a dream factory of endless possibilities and opportunities, ripe for the taking. Such stories repeatedly affirmed the myth that anyone can make it to the top.

Here, famous actresses were nobodies, plucked out of obscurity and thrust into the good life. Readers were made to wonder—could this happen to me, too? As Leo Lowenthal documented, biographies of famous film stars, though sometimes referencing the early travails of actors coming up "the hard way," almost always featured a "lucky break" and a moment of discovery. Success was not a personal responsibility, but something that "merely happens," usually by chance, "an accidental and irrational event."[41] In the case of child stars, fame was a result of luck and birth, rather than hard work or sacrifice. And if talent, purpose, and success were qualities preordained from birth, our own triumphs or failures were inevitable and beyond our control.

Star stories suggested that the line between stars and the rest of us was thin and crossable, but for most readers, this was simply not an accurate reflection of the economic reality of American life. Images of stars in luxurious mansions, on whirlwind vacations and tours, sailing, and biking painted a stark contrast for readers struggling just to get by; they fascinated us, but they also stoked our envy and resentment. Depression era tales of discovery, wherein ordinary people were lifted up out of obscurity to a life of instant fame and fortune, seemed hopeful, but also reinforced the notion that wealth and recognition were meant for the privileged few while the rest were out of luck.

Gossip and Celebrity Scandals

A new profession had arrived to further public interest in movie stars—the celebrity gossip columnist. The two most famous were Hedda Hopper and Louella Parsons.[42] Parsons got her start by going to the

Chicago train station, where movie stars traveling between Los Angeles and New York had a two-hour layover, and interviewing them for the city's *Record-Herald*. (Her dubious editor asked her, "Who would be interested in reading about that?"). In 1918 she moved to New York and, in her column for the *Morning-Telegraph*, began heaping praise upon the starlet Marion Davies, the newspaper magnate William Randolph Hearst's mistress. This led to her becoming the "motion picture editor" for Hearst's *New York American*. Parsons also praised a rising actress, Hedda Hopper, known especially for her legs; Hopper, in turn, began feeding Parsons gossip about actors.

The Evelyn Nesbit case, which further bloated the circulation of New York's daily papers, showed there was an enormous appetite for celebrity scandals. While the rich and famous at the turn of the century were of course envied and often admired, the rise of the Progressive movement, the battles for unions and workers' rights, and muckraking journalism exposed the ruthlessness of many in power and the consequences of inequality. High-profile corporate and governmental scandals, President Teddy Roosevelt's "trust busting," and journalistic exposés led to a backlash against "the filthy rich." Wealth still equaled a superior social position, but no longer meant moral superiority.[43] Indeed, with revelations about the often shocking immorality of those like Stanford White, everyday people came to gain great pleasure—schadenfreude—in the downfall of the rich and powerful.

Meanwhile, a renewed version of sensationalism in journalism began at the close of World War I in 1919. The ongoing fierce competition among newspapers and magazines, and the rise of tabloids and what came to be called "jazz journalism" in the 1920s, led to even more expanded and breathless coverage of entertainment, celebrities, scandals, and crime. In 1919, the *Daily News*, a paper half the size of the other "broadsheets," whose front page featured huge screaming headlines and large, sometimes full-page photographs, hit the streets of New York. By 1924, its circulation of 750,000 was the largest in the country, and it further ballooned to 1.32 million by 1929. Even more lurid imitators like the *Daily Graphic* entered the fray with headlines like "He Beat Me—I Love Him."[44]

Little was more compelling than the celebrity scandal. Stories about the dark side of fame, and the potential downfall of stars who overreach

Figure 3.3. Roscoe "Fatty" Arbuckle mug shot, 1921.

their station, stood in stark contrast to those carefully scrubbed studio press releases of the late 1910s. The papers covered every detail, true or not. Public interest swelled.

The most notorious of these involved silent film actor and hugely popular comedian Roscoe "Fatty" Arbuckle, Hollywood's first million dollar star, who went on trial three times for allegedly sexually assaulting and murdering actress Virginia Rappe (herself known for her wild behavior and fondness for liquor) at a party in 1921. Although Rappe suffered from health problems (which may have contributed to her death), tales of hotel room romps, excessive (and by then illegal) drinking, and bad behavior on the part of all involved fueled the media frenzy. The studios distanced themselves from Arbuckle, who was eventually acquitted, but not before his reputation had been irrevocably trashed by a constant barrage of press that accused him of using his 260-pound frame to pin down Rappe, overpower her, rupture her spleen, and rape her. "His weight," as Chris and Julie Ellis note in their writing on celebrity murders, "was now used against him and rather than being portrayed as a loveable, good-natured, chubby man, he was cast as a gross, overweight monster—which Virginia had seemingly no defense against."[45] The New York papers, which had become known for peddling the most outlandish and lurid tales, endlessly fanned the story and profited from Arbuckle's woes. But where the press saw opportunity, Arbuckle found ruin; despite being cleared of the charges, his career was shattered, he became an alcoholic, and died at the age of forty-six.

With the fevered coverage of the Arbuckle case, Hollywood came to been seen as a veritable den of iniquity rife with illegal drinking and wild sex. The carefully crafted images of celebrities now confronted a "jazz journalism" determined to rip the veneer off of front-stage constructions and get to the gritty back stage. Other scandals followed suit. Mabel Normand, one of the most successful comediennes of the silent era, was rumored to be a drug addict and alcoholic given her wild all-night parties. But when a director with whom she had been involved, William Desmond Taylor, was murdered, with Normand being one of the last persons to see him alive, lurid press coverage of the case questioned her role in his death, linked her to Arbuckle, and focused on her substance abuse. Then there was filmmaker Thomas Ince, known for his westerns, who attended a party aboard William Randolph Hearst's yacht, along with Charlie Chaplin and other luminaries. Ince fell ill and succumbed to heart failure several days later, but rumors persisted that Hearst had discovered his mistress Marion Davies in bed with Chaplin, went to shoot Chaplin but missed his mark and hit Ince instead.[46]

In 1926, Louella Parsons began reporting from Hollywood, and Hearst syndicated her column in his various newspapers. She became ruthless at getting scoops. One of her earliest and biggest was the divorce of Hollywood's reigning couple, Mary Pickford (who had mistakenly confided in Parsons) and Douglas Fairbanks. By 1934, Parsons had her own radio gossip show, *Hollywood Hotel*, which included "sneak previews" of movies in which actors came and read parts of their upcoming films. She now exerted enormous influence over which movies drew audiences and became hits. Meanwhile, Hopper's acting career foundered, but her access to stars did not, and in 1935 she too began a weekly column about

Hollywood. By 1937, with her reputation for getting "the lowdown on the stars," "Hedda Hopper's Hollywood" was appearing in the *Los Angeles Times* and then additional papers and radio.

Thus, a fierce competition emerged between the two women for scoops, and they could make or break stars with their columns. The studios, in the wake of the high-profile scandals, and fearing government censorship, in 1922 established what came to be known as the Hays Office, run by attorney Will Hays, designed to bring respectability back to the industry. The office blacklisted stars, sought to regain favorable publicity for Hollywood, and in 1930 instituted a Production Code that detailed what was morally acceptable on the screen. In addition, fearing actors would undo their hard work and careful grooming, studios began including "moral turpitude" clauses in actors' contracts. The signees had to agree to conduct themselves with "due regard to public convention and morals" and not to do anything that would arouse "public hatred, contempt, scorn or ridicule" or that would "shock, insult or offend the community."[47] (Outside of Hollywood, Babe Ruth would become the first athlete thought to have signed such an agreement, promising to abstain from alcohol and be in bed by 1:00 a.m. during the baseball season[48]). If they behaved immorally, they could be fired.

Standards were enforced with threats that Parsons or Hopper would expose them if they didn't shape up. Conversely, Parsons and Hopper could also be bought off to remain silent about the behavior of stars who were big at the box office; because both owed their positions and success to power brokers in Hollywood, there were certain stories, especially about the extramarital affairs of major stars, that they did not print. Nonetheless, they did take on major actors, like Charlie Chaplin, whose success in early silent films became eclipsed by his reputation as a womanizer (he pursued and married much younger women), and, later, in the 1950s, Ingrid Bergman, whose extramarital affair with director Roberto Rossellini created such negative press that the Academy Award–winning actress chose to live in Europe, away from the spotlight. Hopper and Parsons contributed to the coverage, writing often vindictive and destructive stories that fueled major scandals. As the gossip columnist Liz Smith noted, "The studios created both of them. And they thought they could control both of them. But they became Frankenstein monsters escaped from the labs."[49]

Sound and Color

In the late 1920s, sound arrived. Early films were silent, and while some were accompanied by live music, like organists accentuating the drama of a film, or sound effects, the actors' voices were unheard. In 1927, the first feature-length "talkie," *The Jazz Singer*, debuted and after that audiences could hear the tenor and tone of voice of their favorite stars. The sound of the human voice added an additional layer of intimacy and connectedness, making films and their players seem all the more real.[50] Whereas stars of the silent era may have been presented as aloof gods and goddesses, known for their talents, beauty, or skills, the advent of sound shattered "the psychological distance between stars and their audience" and made the actor appear ever more immediate.[51]

Because one's voice—its timbre, accent, range of expression from despair to elation—is also such a distinctive marker of who we are, the talkies further required, and celebrated, individuality. Sound required that actors be not only attractive and directable but also natural and charismatic in speech and affect. Some silent actors managed to make the transition; Greta Garbo, who began her Hollywood career in silent roles, went on to find success in talking features like *Anna Christie* and *Grand Hotel*. Others were not so lucky; silent movies meant that a man with a Swedish or German accent could play a cowboy, but not when sound revealed he was no born-and-bred western cowpoke. The successful comedian Raymond Griffith, who had suffered an injury to his throat as a child, found his hoarse voice could not project through the microphones.[52] Mary Pickford and Lillian Gish, two of the brightest silent stars, pursued work offscreen when they found their wholesome image and exaggerated expressions no longer appealed to audience tastes.[53] Silent film required physically and facially broad dramatic gestures; these seemed absurd with the arrival of talkies. The 1930s and '40s required a new kind of star who relied not primarily on a kind of ethereal distance, but on a sense of likability and everydayness that could be conveyed through speech and demeanor.

The 1930s then saw the rise of a yet new kind of movie star, one who could sing, dance, or both. Fred Astaire and Ginger Rogers, beginning in 1933, became top box office stars through the ten movies they made together. Jeanette MacDonald, a soprano who introduced millions of moviegoers to opera, paired with the baritone Nelson Eddy in the mid-1930s, appearing with him in *Naughty Marietta* (1935), which won an Oscar for sound recording and was voted one of the best pictures of the year, and in *Rose-Marie* (1936), one of the top grossing films of the year, with their famous duet "Indian Love Call." Now being able to sing or dance (but not necessarily to act) became convertible to being a movie star.

The next influential shift in the presentation of actors on-screen came with the arrival of color film. The 1930s and '40s saw the arrival of Technicolor, a motion picture process that allowed for the creation of richly saturated color films. Early improvements in the process, which originally resulted in grainy, difficult-to-see footage, eventually allowed for a clear, colorful picture. Walt Disney was one of the earliest adopters of the technology, producing the first commercially released, full-color animated cartoon, *Flowers and Trees*, in 1932. Toward the end of the decade, Technicolor was wowing audiences in films like *The Wizard of Oz* (1939), *Gone with the Wind* (1939), and the first feature-length animated film, Disney's *Snow White and the Seven Dwarves* (1937). Like sound, color also worked to transform the fantasy world of cinema into a more realistic, lifelike landscape. The big screen, once silver, was now bursting with colors even more intense than those experienced in everyday life.

Color made some stars seem even more vibrant. Betty Grable, for instance, was fabulous in color. Film historian Jeanine Basinger describes her as "a strawberry cream puff. Her blonde hair, her creamy complexion, her full and sexy mouth made up in vibrant reds, and the red-white-and-blue outfits she wore—not to mention the lime green, the hot pink, the shocking aqua, the cherry red, and the royal purple—knocked audiences out."[54] Grable famously became one of the most popular pinups for soldiers during World War II. Not only did the color presentation help to enhance the allure and charisma of the stars, it also helped the audience to further appreciate the actors' features—the color of their eyes, the tone of their complexion, the highlights in their hair. It is, perhaps, not surprising, then, that the 1930s and '40s marked the height of the Hollywood era, for it is during this time that the audiences were urged to feel like they could come to know the stars like never before.

A Golden Age, a Great Depression

This era came to be called the Golden Age of Hollywood, during the 1930s and 1940s, where film stars enjoyed a vaunted place in popular culture. Icons like Bette Davis, Katherine Hepburn, Clark Gable, Humphrey Bogart, Judy Garland, Spencer Tracy, and Lauren Bacall, to name just a few, embodied the ethos of the American dream and the promise of American exceptionalism. Hollywood stars personified the promise of individuality, self-expression, and success in the midst of the Great Depression. As Karen Sternheimer notes in *Celebrity Culture and the American Dream*, star narratives served both as "a distraction from the faltering economic system" and a reassurance "that it was still possible to become rich in America."[55] Celebrities embodied "self-expression over conformity" and "hedonism above responsibility,"[56] serving as heightened examples of individual achievement, challenging the rigidity of class-based society while representing the potential for all to transcend their station in life.[57]

Film attendance soared even as the economic system collapsed. On October 29, 1929, the stock market crashed, producing a shockwave so deep and immediate that the day would go down in history as "Black Tuesday." The global economy was rapidly contracting. Demand for products, goods, and services fell and unemployment skyrocketed: from 1929 to 1933, the U.S. Gross National Product dropped by 29 percent, construction by 78 percent, and investment by 98 percent. Unemployment rose from 3.2 percent to a staggering 24.9 percent. Throughout the 1930s, Americans struggled to keep their families and their spirits afloat in this difficult landscape. Confronted with a time of economic despair, audiences looked to films for a sense of hope and escape and an affirmation of American ideals.

Hollywood stars were special individuals who transcended the economic catastrophe. They weren't working tedious jobs under harsh conditions, didn't have to watch what they spent, and could marry how they liked and still be celebrated. Their relative freedom offered the audience an opportunity to vicariously and fleetingly enjoy the pleasures denied them by Depression life. Indeed, many films, like the enormously popular Ginger Rogers–Fred Astaire movies, showcased luxurious clothing, living conditions, and lifestyles, transporting viewers to a glamorous and carefree world. The paradox at the core of this is that while celebrities are often seen as having "charisma"—exceptional, unique, and magnetic qualities that set them apart from others—they also lure ordinary spectators into the reverie that we, too, can break out from the pack.

But actors were not immune to the constraints of modern bureaucracy. Between the mid-1920s and early 1930s the Hollywood studio system was established, dominated by the Big Five: Warner Brothers, Paramount, RKO, MGM, and Fox. They typically used a regimented model to produce their stars, against which some of them chafed, especially by being typecast. By this time, Hollywood had developed a "star machine" through which celebrities could be "discovered," shaped and sold to the public.[58] The production of successful "types" continued—the ingénue, the girl next door, the spunky working girl, the rebel, the villain. Thus, while movie stars might seem distinctive—Rita Hayworth and Katherine Hepburn looked and acted very differently—they, too, were subject to Hollywood's mass production process, a system that favored easily recognizable characters. This is what German theorists Theodor Adorno and Max Horkheimer meant when they coined the term "pseudo-individuation." They argued that such cookie-cutter production and recycling of star types limits the kinds of people and stories one saw on-screen, stunting "consumer's powers of imagination and spontaneity."[59]

Moreover, the need to fill certain identifiable types justified and perpetuated denigrating stereotypes. This was especially true when it came to race. Actors like Stepin Fetchit (Lincoln Perry) became famous for their movie performances, in which they portrayed black people as slow, lazy, dimwitted, and unsophisticated "Uncle Toms." Roles for black actors were limited, and those that did exist often called for them to play subservient employees, or buffoons, or even to learn to speak in racist dialects marked by malapropisms that the actors were not familiar with and never used in real life. Black women were most frequently cast as mammies or domestic servants. So while some black performers earned fame and praise, to do so often required that they perform a caricatured version of self.

In 1939, Hattie McDaniel became the first African American to win an Academy Award for Best Supporting Actress in *Gone with the Wind* for

Figure 3.4. Hattie McDaniel with the Academy Award she received in 1940 for her role in *Gone with the Wind*. Getty Images. Reprinted with permission.

her role as Mammy, a slave on a Southern plantation. Despite her success and the critical praise she received, and the fact that Mammy displays subtle moments of resistance in the film, some criticized *Gone with the Wind* for what they saw as its favorable and empathetic depiction of the slave system.[60] And in the South, Mammy did not appear on any of the promotional materials for the film, for fear of alienating white audiences. Offscreen, McDaniel was barred from the film's premiere in Atlanta because of Jim Crow laws. She was forced to sit away from her cast mates, in the back of the theater, while attending the Academy Award ceremony at which she won, and was not invited to any of the award parties.

Movie stardom was denied to other people of color who, whether the characters were Asian, American Indian, or mixed race, were portrayed by white stars. And stars of color were ignored by the fan magazines. The 1937 film *The Good Earth*, about struggling Chinese farmers, featured an all-white cast. Asian men were either fiendish, conniving villains like Fu Manchu (initially played by Swedish American actor Warner Oland), or subservient, asexual, and unable to speak proper English, like the detective Charlie Chan (also played by Oland). Forty-seven Chan movies between 1926 and 1949 cemented such stereotypes. Asian women, when they appeared at all, were also either extremely subservient or, on the other end of the spectrum, hypersexualized, deceitful "Dragon Ladies." Possibly the most repeatedly stereotyped group has been American Indians, for decades played primarily by white actors like Rock Hudson or Burt Lancaster and characterized as uncivilized savages and one-dimensional men whose main word was "How."

Thus, the film industry's desire to attract audiences via a kind of consistent, repetitive product worked to both reflect and reinscribe some of the era's most damaging stereotypes, the results of which could be seen offscreen as well as on. This model also bolstered normative ideologies around gender, as stars like Douglas Fairbanks and Rudolph Valentino played swashbucklers and exotic heartthrobs while Lillian Gish and Louise Brooks combined female youthful fragility and steely resolve. To promote these actors, the studios used the techniques of modern advertising, developing and honing a heretofore unrivaled publicity machine, highly skilled at utilizing and manipulating the press to its advantage to create known name performers to attract an audience.

Decline of the Studio System

Moviegoing reached its peak during the Second World War, with more than 60 percent of Americans in weekly attendance during the early 1940s.[61] But several factors reshaped moviegoing and the power of the studios. In 1948, the Supreme Court ruled on the U.S. government's long-running antitrust lawsuit against Paramount Pictures and seven other Hollywood studios. The studios enjoyed an oligopoly characterized by vertical integration—they controlled both the production and distribution of films, either by owning movie theaters outright or by compelling independent theater owners to accept "block booking," meaning they had to show a certain number of a studio's films, and if they wanted those with name stars they also had to accept less desirable "B" movies. In *U.S. v. Paramount et al.*, the court ruled that the studios had to divest themselves of their theater chains and sell films on an individual basis.[62] This seriously eroded their power, and opened the way for more independent producers to get their films shown. The studios also began releasing stars from their ironclad contracts. In fact, some stars, like Bette Davis and Marilyn Monroe, had started battling with studio heads over which parts they would and would not accept, and even suing to get out of their contracts. Up and coming actors thus knew about the restrictions imposed by the studios and chose to become free agents instead. On top of this, a new medium was quickly becoming a central part of American life and, this time, you didn't even have to leave your living room to be entertained. This coincided with the baby boom, when couples who had postponed having children because of, first, the Great Depression, and then World War II, began having children, took advantage of the new medium rather than finding babysitters or trying to take their kids to the movies.

Thus, box office receipts declined; in 1948, about ninety million people were regular moviegoers; by 1953 it was just over half that at forty-six million.[63] Movie stars, no longer reliably protected or promoted by the studios, had to adjust to this new regime. And press coverage of celebrities was changing. It no longer focused solely on the glamorous lives of the stars and their lucky breaks. The immediacy of television, combined with the lack of studio control over celebrities' press coverage, changed the discourse around famous figures. Reverence and glamour no longer provided the protective aura they had in the past.

It was during this era that the industrial production and management of movie stardom changed, leading to the proliferation of professionals to help produce and manage celebrities. The growth of early agencies like MCA (the Music Corporation of America), superagents like Lew Wasserman, and publicists worked to sell the services of their stars and to maximize their profits, by having, for example, stars forego a salary in exchange for an interest in the box office take of the film, which could be much more lucrative. The difference here was that while in the past the studios had employed the actors, here the actors had to employ the agent and publicist. But increasingly a celebrity's image was now his or her own to create.[64]

Off Their Pedestals

By the early 1950s, a new breed of star coverage had emerged in magazines like *Confidential* and *Inside Story*, which harkened back to "jazz journalism" with their penchant for revelation, innuendo, and scandal. The success of these publications, as historian Mary Desjardins argues, was made possible by a number of factors. With the decline of the Hollywood studios, official narratives about the stars were harder to promote, and the studios no longer had the power to hush up the indiscretions of their stars. As studios began cooperating less and less with the magazines and the magazines had to dig for their own stories, the content got sleazier. Magazines like *Confidential* were able to produce their own narratives about celebrities, even if their stories were far-fetched or scathing, in part because the official voices of Hollywood were no longer in control. In addition, during this period, legal principles of obscenity, libel, and defamation were unclear and inconsistently applied in California courts.[65] Such magazines would employ multiple sources to spread the responsibility for the story among informants, thus protecting the publication. If a star did decide to sue over a story, he or she would likely have to testify at trial, a process that would almost certainly generate even more coverage of the scandal. In all of these ways, celebrities were vulnerable to increasingly invasive and unsympathetic reporting.[66] Stories about alleged homosexuality, affairs, and sexual liaisons were favored topics, the juicier the better. Sample *Confidential* headlines included "Why Sinatra Is the Tarzan of the Boudoir" (May 1956), "Joan Crawford's Back Street Romance with a Bartender" (January 1957), and "Louella Parsons: Hatchet Woman" (April 1959).[67]

Scandalous or otherwise illicit celebrity coverage was reinforced by the emergence of paparazzi photography. The term *paparazzo* was coined in the 1960s by Italian director Federico Fellini when he gave the name, which roughly translates to "the noise of a buzzing mosquito," to a frenetic, fictional photographer in his film *La Dolce Vita*. But his filmic inspiration came from the actual photographers who had begun snapping images of film stars as they darted around Europe shooting the latest picture, enjoying a holiday, or canoodling with a certain someone. Italian photographers combed the luxurious Via Veneto—a hangout for the wealthy and fabulously famous—in hopes of snapping a shot of the stars who frequented the area's bars and restaurants.

The profession caught on in Los Angeles and by the 1970s American photographers like Ron Galella—regarded as having invented America's paparazzi market—became famous in their own right for capturing elusive images of megastars from the entertainment, political, and cultural scenes.[68] Galella began photographing celebrities as they came to movie premieres and became known for catching them in unguarded moments, out of the spotlight, often surprising them on the street or using telephoto lenses to capture their image. Indeed, Galella was hoping to snap stars during those back-stage, ungoverned moments. He became extremely controversial as a celebrity stalker, most famously of Jacqueline Kennedy Onassis, with whom he was obsessed and whom he photographed relentlessly against her will until she was granted a restraining order in 1972 requiring him to stay fifty feet away from her and her children. Marlon Brando did not go to court; he simply punched Galella in the face for following him, knocking out five of his teeth and breaking his jaw.[69] Galella pioneered, for better and, from the stars' point of view, for worse, in pushing against celebrities' notions of and desire for privacy. Galella personified the notion that if you were well known, losing your privacy and your ability to control images of yourself was simply a price you had to pay for fame.

Increasingly, the privacy of stars was more aggressively violated. The candid, unscripted, often unwanted nature of paparazzi photos lent itself to unsanctioned celebrity narratives, in which the stars were on display and available for our scrutiny. In the 1960s, the beautiful, mercurial Elizabeth Taylor was a favorite subject, including of Galella's. Her many affairs, engagements, and marriages drew attention from the press and public alike. In 1962, while filming *Cleopatra*, Taylor was surreptitiously photographed sunning and smooching on a yacht with her costar Richard Burton. Both were married to other people at the time, and the images generated an international scandal, especially as Taylor was already known for having "stolen" Eddie Fischer, her then husband, from "America's sweetheart," Debbie Reynolds.[70] The paparazzi coverage, and sensationalized reporting that followed helped to bolster Taylor's infamy while feeding the public's appetite for news, and photographic evidence, of the star's most intimate moments. But where scandal and bad behavior only fueled Taylor's fame, and success, it could also ruin reputations in an instant.[71]

Within this milieu the traditional fan magazine began to decline. Although fan magazines continued to drive ticket sales into the late 1960s (*Modern Screen* and *Photoplay* reportedly accounted for more than one out of every two theater tickets sold), movie studios weren't interested in cooperating with them because of their increasingly immoral tone.

Figure 3.5. Elizabeth Taylor and Eddie Fisher surrounded by photographers, 1959. Getty Images. Reprinted with permission.

Nor were many of the new, more independent, and rebellious young actors, like Dustin Hoffman, Jack Nicholson, or Jane Fonda, remotely interested in supplying fan magazines with their traditional pabulum, particularly about their personal lives. Some of these stars wanted instead to talk about politics—Jane Fonda, who was adamantly opposed to the war in Vietnam, being noteworthy on this score—yet the fan magazines and their readers were not interested in such content at all. By the 1970s, according to author Anthony Slide, "fan magazines had long since passed the zenith of influence both within the film industry and among their readership. With an overemphasis on Jacqueline Kennedy, the fan magazines acknowledged that nobody who was part of the entertainment community had the celebrity of the former First Lady." And what the fan magazines seemed to be serving up was "from the same, tired, old menu."[72] Their circulation began faltering in the late 1960s; *Photoplay* ceased publication in 1980 and *Modern Screen* hung on until 1985.

Star Production in the Poststudio Era

Despite all this, there were—and are—still movie stars, and for the most part they remain at the top of the celebrity hierarchy, although now rivaled by pop, rock, and hip-hop stars. Top stars develop (and have cultivated, through how they are filmed and how they are promoted) branded identities that remain essential to film celebrities. As brands they are an amalgam of the roles they play, their qualities or traits as individuals—facial features, how they walk and hold themselves, their voice, their personality—the quality and nature of their performances, and their appearances in other media.[73] And their brand can be enhanced or undermined by the filmic apparatus—how they are lit, shot, framed, and accompanied by music and sound effects in each movie.

One such star was Tom Cruise, who, especially after *Risky Business* (1983), enjoyed over two decades as an A-list star until various public comments and his ties to Scientology began to damage his brand. In fact, from 1990 to 2009, Cruise was that era's most enduring moneymaker, his box office hits rivaled only by Tom Hanks.[74] And Cruise is an exemplar of the star as a "performed brand"; his star quality—the chiseled good looks, the trademark, dazzling smile, his physicality, the black Ray-Bans—was enhanced by how he has been filmed over the years. As Paul McDonald emphasizes in his study of Hollywood stardom, how Cruise entered scenes—how he was shot—helped make him a spectacular figure; such star entrances, McDonald argues, are used to carefully stage and display the star's attraction, his charisma. Cruise's famous sliding into the scene in his socks and underwear while lip synching the words to Bob Seger's "Old Time Rock and Roll" in *Risky Business*, hanging from a rocky ridge at a dizzying height in *Mission: Impossible 2*, springing out from behind a bank of television sets in *Jerry Maguire*, all conveyed his youthful energy, his cool self-confidence, his bravado and derring-do.[75]

At the same time, for bankable stars to become prestige stars, and to extend and maintain their celebrity status, they need to transgress their established, often safe, film or television persona. For Cruise, this involved appearing in serious, nonaction roles in *Rain Man* (1988) opposite Academy Award winner Dustin Hoffman, and in *Born on the Fourth of July* (1989) as a paraplegic Vietnam veteran. Farrah Fawcett, formerly of the TV series *Charlie's Angels*, transgressed her image as a gorgeous "pinup girl" portraying an abused wife in *The Burning Bed* in order to be taken seriously as an actress. Robin Williams, the stand-up comedian who got his start as an alien in the TV show *Mork & Mindy*, also took on serious, dramatic roles in movies like *Good Will Hunting* (for which he won an Oscar as Best Supporting Actor). It is through such transgressions, P. David Marshall argues, that film stars avoid being stuck in one type of character or role and can extend their symbolic value and, thus, their longevity and economic value.[76]

Cruise, however, has not been as successful, more recently, in managing his back stage, and thus the erosion of his symbolic power has hurt his economic clout. His 2017 movie *The Mummy* performed poorly in the United States, and now stars like Cruise must confront a key feature of stardom in the twenty-first century: increased audience involvement in celebrity success, here in the form of the reviews on the website *Rotten Tomatoes*, with comments like "an utter bore," "full of embalming fluid," and, simply, "a mess."

The production of movie stardom is quite different from that of the vertically integrated studio system of the 1930s and 1940s, when the studios enjoyed pretty much exclusive control over the stars and their image. With actors in the 1950s and beyond primarily on their own, as freelancers, a new, elaborated machinery of celebrity production and maintenance emerged, with agents, managers, attorneys, and publicists constituting a "network of external service providers." In this new environment, some stars formed their own production companies in collaboration with producers or agents to allow them more artistic freedom. The ongoing conglomeration of media companies into fewer and larger entities has meant that there is still oligopoly control over film distribution and thus over what the star needs most: visibility. Yet despite massive changes in the industry, many of the constitutive elements of film stardom remain the same. The movie star must be, through his or her team, a talented, creative actor, a recognizable brand, a commercial asset, a "textually constructed identity" through profiles and interviews, and, still, someone who fans admire, even adulate, and identify with, seeing them as, simultaneously, far above us yet "just like us."[77]

Today, A-list stars—those who can "open" a movie, their mere presence in a leading role ensuring the profitability of high-budget films—remain at the top of the celebrity hierarchy. Indeed, in an increasingly crowded celebrity marketplace, movie stars, especially those who are respected and celebrated for their acting ability, artistic prestige, and commercial value, retain an unmatched cachet.[78] But it is now rare for an actor, especially a female celebrity, to maintain a stardom based primarily on aloofness and inaccessibility. Stardom today requires an active maintenance of one's public face, an ability to purposefully and strategically engage the press, and an ability to connect with fans and followers across media platforms. Twenty-first-century actors must appear authentic and engaged, accessible and down-to-earth, even as they cultivate their stardom.

4

Radio

The Stars in Our Homes

With our iPods, smartphones, streaming music, podcasts, in-car stereos, in-home sound systems, and the like forming an ever-available audio environment, it's easy to forget what a complete auditory revolution Americans experienced in the 1920s when radio burst on the scene. Music is such a deeply structuring part of our emotional and psychic lives, it powerfully connects us to friends, family, and lovers. Today we can access it whenever we want, so that we simply take its availability for granted. Certain songs define the memorable moments in our lives; couples have "our song"; and many of us use music to manage our moods, to cheer us up or, also, to enhance feelings of sadness and loss. As P. David Marshall reminds us, when we listen we invest our own personal experiences in the meaning of the song, giving us a sense of possession of both the song and the performer.[1]

And, of course, we have become powerfully tied to musicians we've never met—folk singers, rock stars, hip-hop artists, jazz virtuosos, opera divas, pop stars, country singers, and more—whose artistry we admire, whose performance style speaks to us, and whose music gives voice to our desires, hopes, and fears. This is one of the reasons our fandom of musicians is so deeply personal and keenly felt. When we purchase, listen and relate to, and consider ourselves fans of a particular musician, we often develop a profound sense of investment in the music and a feeling of personal connection with the musicians who produce it. Key to our fandom is our belief in the singers' authenticity—that they are expressing their true emotions and are not "manufactured." It was through the development of electronic means of musical reproduction that we could connect to such musicians who, in turn, became national and international celebrities.

This was new—that someone could become a national star primarily, even exclusively, because of his or her voice. The phonograph enabled this, and with the advent of radio this was true not only for singers but also for comics and other performers. Once you bought a radio, the entertainment on it was supported by advertising and thus "free," a crucial feature during the Great Depression. Radio revolutionized fandom and celebrity because now, for the first time, a mass medium penetrated directly into your home, bringing stars into your domestic space, further eroding the distance between audience and star and generating a new, unprecedented form of intimacy between star and fan. The radio star had to seem to be speaking directly to you, the individual, and also to the larger you, the audience, to whom you and the star were also connected. As Michael Pitts and Frank Hoffman explain, "The trial and error of the early 1920s revealed that a natural type of voice—effortlessly modulated rather than classically trained—was best suited to the radio mike. An everyday, casual, off-the-street and into your living room voice . . . [radio] preferred friendliness."[2] Thus, this technology, radio, also demanded new modes—mostly vocal—of establishing a distinctive celebrity persona. And it required the vocal performance of sincerity, of seeming genuine and real.

This chapter explores how the technological affordances of this mass medium, radio, which denied sight to its audience, gave rise to familiar, but also quite new types of celebrities. Radio especially favored those who knew how to use voice and language to create a familiarity, a powerful form of identification, and the first real-time parasocial interactions between star and listener based on sound alone. Because of the power of listening to these often very personal addresses on the radio, especially by singers, radio helped produce new, often intense structures of feeling between celebrities and fans. Unlike some silent film stars whose careers were over with the advent of the talkies, those who knew how to modulate the tone and registers of their voices, and to use language to create mental images, became major celebrities in the 1930s and 1940s. Unlike in the movies, your appearance—especially for women—was less important to stardom. What was important was the sense of authenticity, that the performer was genuine, sincere, and genuinely talented.

Radio also pioneered, however fitfully, in forging new forms of affinity, and even identification, between African American stars and white audiences. It was precisely because radio both showcased musical virtuosity and denied sight to its audience that it could lay the ground-work for the production of African American stars. This too was new in the evolution of celebrity culture. And it was highly resisted and contro-versial. Like the other new media form and its stars, the movies, radio pushed boundaries around race and gender that challenged tradition and simultaneously reinforced yet upended traditional mores.

Recorded Sound and Mass Intimacy

In the late nineteenth century, music could only be heard by attend-ing public performances or through one's own ability to sing or play an instrument. Singing along with accompaniment was a popular at-home pastime, typically performed by women, and the sales of pianos skyrocketed between 1870 and 1910. Piano literacy, as the historian Ann Douglas puts it, was almost as high as print literacy among well-bred American women, and the sheet music industry made sure there was plenty to play.[3] To popularize a new tune, vaudeville and music hall per-formers were commissioned to sing and promote the songs, their faces and names often appearing on the cover page of the song sheets. The most popular songs sold millions of copies and further propelled their singers into the public eye.[4] But soon a series of technological develop-ments would fundamentally shift the relationship between audiences, music, and the famous voice.

Thomas Edison's invention of the phonograph in 1877 and the sub-sequent development of the gramophone—which played easily mass-produced discs instead of wax cylinders—further transformed the act of listening. The gramophone record allowed listeners to select and enjoy previously recorded music any time they wished. Sales of phonographs took off in the early twentieth century, and rose from $27.1 million in 1914 to $158.7 million in 1919. In 1921 Americans bought more than 100 million records, spending "more money for [records] than for any other form of recreation."[5] This technology made talented voices of the day accessible, bringing the voice into the intimate space of the home and allowing musi-cal performances of the famous to become a part of everyday life. Further, the act of purchasing the record marked the listener as an active con-sumer, solidifying the relationship between audience and artist. The same performers used to promote sheet music sales now provided a system of stars to help propel the new recording industry.[6] With the invention and adoption of the phonograph, singers became household names.

One of the most famous performers was Enrico Caruso, the Italian operatic tenor, who began recording in 1901. Enormously talented and charismatic, he was the first recording artist to sell over a million records. Thus, he could be heard not just in opera houses but also in people's own homes, vastly expanding his fame. During his career he made approximately 260 recordings and can be rightly regarded as the "first global superstar" singer.[7]

Although phonographs, which by the teens had become a fixture in most middle-class homes, had brought people Caruso as well as ragtime, classical music, and the popular songs of Tin Pan Alley, we must remember that "talking machines" were still hand cranked, and the maximum playing time on each side of a record was about four minutes. Nor was there any such thing as a record changer. To listen to Beethoven's Fifth Symphony, for example, the listener would have to put on and remove five records while keeping the phonograph cranked up.[8] Audio quality left much to be desired. Listeners responding to a survey done by the Edison Company in 1921 complained about the scratchy surface noise of Edison records and their tendency to warp.[9]

But by the mid-1920s, radio supplanted the phonograph as the device people used to bring music into their homes. With radio, listeners could have music on demand, and not just piano music or the same scratchy recordings, but that produced by the country's finest bands, orchestras, and singers. While the music they heard might have been "canned" rather than live, they no longer needed to leave home to hear it.

The discovery of the radio wave, and of mechanisms by which to amplify and control it, pioneered between 1896 and the 1910s by inventors including Guglielmo Marconi, Reginald Fessenden, and Lee De Forest, produced a new mode of communication by which voices could be transmitted over long distances without wires. While previous advances in telegraphy, such as Morse code, emphasized the transmission of information from a single sender to a single receiver, radio, with its ability to convey sound across space to reach an audience of many, became the first electronic broadcast technology.[10]

In 1920, the first commercially licensed radio station, Pittsburgh's KDKA, began broadcasting; by 1924 there would be 500 licensed stations. The speed with which the radio craze swept the country between 1920 and 1924 prompted analogies to tidal waves and highly contagious fevers. By 1922, sales of radio sets and parts totaled $60 million (Westinghouse was manufacturing 25,000 sets a month and couldn't keep up with orders); in 1923, $136 million; by 1924, $358 million.[11] "The rapidity with which the thing has spread has possibly not been equaled in all the centuries of human progress," gushed the *Review of Reviews* hyperbolically. "Never in the history of electricity has an invention so gripped the popular fancy."[12] In the record-breaking time of twelve months, reported the *New York Times* in 1922, listening to the radio "has become the most popular amusement in America."[13] The act of "listening-in," as it was called, was hailed as the new national pastime. Where more than 40 percent of American homes owned a radio set in 1930, ten years later an overwhelming 83 percent would be tuning in.[14]

Through radio, music became more fundamental to the American experience than it ever had been before. In fact, it began to structure social relations much more thoroughly and ubiquitously. The commonality of the experience was on an entirely new level: now more people listened simultaneously to the same bands and the same songs as they passed through their time in history. Within a few weeks, radio could make a song a hit—and a performer a celebrity—across the country.[15]

With radio, music played an enormous role in structuring peoples' emotions, sense of time and place, their sense of history, and certainly their own autobiographies.[16] After radio, particular styles of music, and particular songs, were inextricable from peoples' memories of their youth, their courtships, their sense of separateness as a generation. Reinforcing the intimacy of recorded sound was the development of the microphone, which allowed the voice to be transmitted and experienced in new ways.

The radio craze seriously undercut the sale of phonographs, and, in 1923, ASCAP (the American Society of Composers, Authors and Publishers), which represented those who made their living selling records and sheet music, forbade radio stations from playing phonograph music without paying royalties. This prohibition pushed the use of live singers, who sounded better than records, and most stations preferred local talent to records.[17] But with the formation of the networks in 1926 and 1927, which brought the same programs to people around the country, local talent gave way to national stars.

Rise of African American Musical Stars

Radio created a range of celebrities—singers, bandleaders and other kinds of musical stars, comedians, reporters and news commentators, gossip columnists, and radio actors, most of them white. But radio, because it denied sight to its audience, and emerged during what came to be called the "jazz age," also made an unprecedented number of African American musicians national stars, during a time of heightened racism and enforced segregation. This was a major change in the construction and culture of celebrity.

By the mid-1920s, African American music, particularly "hot" jazz, as performed by African American musicians, got on the air in certain places like Chicago or New York. Alliances quickly grew between radio stations, hotels, and nightclubs, which competed with each other over which dance bands or orchestras they could book. The stations got live music—some of it the finest of the period—and the ambiance of a glamorous nightclub, and the hotels got free publicity. Radio hastened the acceptance of this music among many who would not have heard it otherwise.[18] In the 1920s, radio (along with phonograph records) opened a small crack between white and black culture, and Louis Armstrong, Bessie Smith, Duke Ellington, and a few others slipped through. By the end of the decade, most would agree that the radio industry and the white bands it rewarded had co-opted, domesticated, and often bastardized black jazz. But African American music crept into white culture and white subjectivity, and this was critically important for the enlivening of American music, and for the long, slow struggle out of Jim Crow America.

The rise of jazz on the radio was especially dramatic in a city like Chicago, which was, arguably, the radio capital of America in the 1920s. Because of the wartime migration of nearly 60,000 African Americans to Chicago, a migration that included some of New Orleans' finest musicians thrown out of work when the U.S. Navy—as a "wartime precaution"—closed down the city's red-light district, Chicago became a major jazz center. Although its recent arrivals may have been a benighted minority, they also became something else: a market. And what they wanted was blues and jazz.

While the "Big Three" in the phonograph industry—Edison, Victor, and Columbia—struggled to stay afloat in the face of radio by continuing to record classical music and Tin Pan Alley songs, small independent companies, looking for new music and new markets, recorded jazz and the blues. They also marketed phonographs to urban blacks. It was these listeners who, in February 1920, made Mamie Smith's "Crazy Blues" a smash hit that sold 8,000 records a week; within seven months, it had sold a million copies.[19]

Suddenly "race music" became big business, and it is widely agreed that Bessie Smith, who signed with the nearly bankrupt Columbia in 1923, single-handedly saved the company's fortunes by selling approximately six million records in the next six years.[20] At first, these kinds of sales came primarily from the black community, which bought at least six million records a year.[21] By the end of the decade, white fans flocked to race music too, to jazz and the blues, finding in both a skepticism, a sexual vitality, and a revolt against repression and propriety. In other words, what they found was authenticity.

Because it was African American music, the blues and especially jazz became enormously controversial throughout the early part of the decade. Louis Armstrong and Bessie Smith—a huge star, probably the most popular singer of her time—were banned from many radio stations in the early 1920s. The word "jazz" itself had, in some quarters, referred to sexual intercourse, and that's exactly what critics claimed it encouraged. To support this contention, they cited the scandalous new dances—the Charleston, the fox-trot, the shimmy, and other "lewd gyrations"—that people performed while listening to jazz bands. Given its associations with brothels, dives, and African Americans, its reliance on the sinfully suggestive saxophone, its often earthy lyrics, and its insistence that listeners let loose their backsides to shimmy and shake, critics saw jazz as the major indication that American society was going down in flames.

The discourse surrounding jazz was, of course, a discourse about race, about fears of miscegenation, pollution, and contamination. Even articles praising jazz referred constantly to "the jungle," "savages," and "primitivism," noting how staid, white, European culture was being forced to respond to more exotic, feral influences.

It is not surprising that such attitudes, coupled with the race hatred and segregation of the times, would at first keep black singers and musicians off most radio stations. But soon several white bandleaders, whose mission was to make jazz less threatening and more respectable to white audiences, began to adapt various elements of jazz and incorporate them into white music, producing what some called "sweet jazz." Paul White-man was the most successful of these, who earned the title "King of Jazz"—and a gross income of over one million dollars in 1922—by ap-propriating and diluting black jazz (without, one might note, hiring any black musicians) and selling it as "the real thing" to whites.[22] Whiteman remained on the radio for twenty-five years.[23]

Despite the denunciations of jazz—and certainly, in part, because of them—this music's enormous popularity escalated throughout the 1920s and beyond. As early as 1924, the *Outlook* reported, "you can scarcely listen in on the radio, especially in the evening, without hearing jazz."[24] What this meant was that more black performers began getting airtime. It is not surprising, given the desperate racial politics of the 1920s, with the epidemic of lynchings, the spread of the Ku Klux Klan, and new restrictions on immigration, that segregation and discrimination would block African Americans from being allowed on the radio. What *is* sur-prising is that they got on at all—but get on the air some of them did. And they became stars, and not just to African Americans.

In 1922, a concert at New Orleans' Lyric Theater featuring Ethel Waters, backed up by Fletcher Henderson's jazz band, was broadcast by WVG and was reportedly heard in at least five states and Mexico. Waters, a pioneer who "helped invent pop-jazz singing,"[25] was, accord-ing to one paper, "the first colored girl to sing over the radio."[26] Bessie Smith, whose classic "Empty Bed Blues" was banned in Boston, had her music broadcast over WMC in Memphis and WSB in Atlanta as early as 1923. The audiences of both stations were almost entirely white (that's who could afford radio in the South in the early years) and on occa-sion they flooded the stations with requests for her to repeat songs like "Outside of That He's All Right with Me." In 1924, WCAE in Pittsburgh broadcast one of her concerts to accommodate the thousands who had been unable to get tickets to see her, despite a one-week extension of her booking.[27]

By 1925, the African American music critic Dave Peyton could re-port in the *Chicago Defender* that there was actually a "great demand for race musicians."[28] As this demand increased, stations did more remotes, broadcasting live from nightclubs where popular bands were perform-ing. Several stations in New York City were especially noted for seeking out black bands and putting them on the air.[29] Duke Ellington and his band appeared as early as 1924 over WHN in New York City, as did Fletcher Henderson and his band, which led to live broadcasts of Henderson's band from the Roseland Ballroom in New York. The band was hugely popular between 1926 and 1928, when they were on WHN three times a week and WOR once a week.[30] And here Henderson was joined by the incomparable Louis Armstrong.

Writing about the effect Louis Armstrong's bluesy yet swinging cornet playing had on Henderson's band at Roseland, historian Philip Eberly writes, "One can only guess at the reaction of listeners, heretofore accustomed to tuning in Roseland broadcasts featuring conventional dance music, now hearing on WHN a joyous, new, stomping kind of music, thanks to Armstrong's New Orleans injections."[31] Armstrong was a genius at combining African American rhythms, vocalization, and blues cords with Western harmonies, embodying the quixotic notion that black and white music—and thus culture—could happily coexist. By 1927, Duke Ellington became famous nationally as a result of his nightly broadcasts from the Cotton Club over the newly formed network CBS, and so did Cab Calloway.[32] So it was radio that gave Armstrong, Duke Ellington, and others exposure to a huge audience they would never have had otherwise. Radio made them international stars.

At the same time, it is also true that the networks refused to hire black studio musicians until the late 1930s.[33] In addition, the music of black jazz bands was more likely to be censored by the radio networks. Black musicians realized that they had to be more polished, more deferential, more circumspect to get bookings—both in white clubs and on the air—to overcome the barbed stereotypes that sought to keep them out of white preserves. Tuxedos with tails, mirror-shiny shoes, crisp white shirts, and an air of reserve became the "dress uniform" for those seeking to combat the old bromides that blacks were, as Dave Peyton complained, "unreliable, barbaric and huge liquor indulgents."[34] Smiling a lot and appearing grateful to white audiences and employers was essential.

Here began the ongoing dilemma of becoming a crossover star as an element of African American celebrity. Crossing over was good for the music, the performer, the race; but it could also corrupt the black artist's musical and personal integrity, bring charges of diminished authenticity, and force the musician to assume a highly constricting, dishonest masquerade.[35] While radio did indeed remove and "contain" a "black presence on the airwaves,"[36] some of these performers nevertheless became household names by the end of the decade. Because of radio, black culture—or, at least, those narrow, fetishized slices of black culture forced to represent the whole—"became part of mainstream American expression."[37] Radio took the music of black America into the heart of white America and made it our first genuine national music and one of the most important cultural exports of the century.[38] It is in radio's relationship to jazz that we see the beginnings of this invention's nearly century-long role in marrying youthful white rebellion to African American culture. Now African American music would play an increasingly important role not just in constituting the identities of blacks but of whites as well. As a result of this marriage, middle-class cultural repression was challenged.

Crooners

By the 1930s, a new cohort of mostly white male singers had emerged, bringing with them a fresh sound and style, made possible by the microphone. Prior to the 1920s, classical singers and vaudeville performers had to project their voices loudly and clearly in order to reach large audiences in theaters and playhouses. This took skill and practice, but also limited the range of cues that a performer could convey in an almost declamatory style of singing. Subtle changes in volume or emotion might not transmit to those in the deepest rows of the balcony. The development of microphone technologies, which allowed performers to amplify—and to control the directionality of—their voices changed the listening relationship between audience and performer. Once distant, removed from the crowd by virtue of their placement on the stage, their training and skill, now singers could provide a sense of being close by, conversational, even intimate. The microphone highlighted the range of qualities of the human voice: the subtleties of whispers and coos, vocal smirks and winks, even the catch of the voice in a moment of emotion. The microphone, which was sensitive, also required artists to use "soft, often caressing tones lest a loud or high

Figure 4.1. Rudy Vallee, c. 1930s. Getty Images.
Reprinted with permission.

note shatter a transmitter tube."[39] All of these could now be projected clearly and directly to the listener. As Andre Millard writes, "Recorded sound was a technology for the masses, and these recordings were at the heart of a new mass culture of entertainment."[40]

Thus, a new style of singing—what came to be called crooning—was a direct consequence of the affordances of radio and the radio microphone, technologies that created a new type of celebrity with passionate female fans. Unlike Caruso, who focused on the technical perfection of the voice, crooners showcased the emotionality and personality of the voice.[41] Rudy Vallee, Bing Crosby, and Frank Sinatra became sensations with female listeners, speaking and singing close to the mike, directly addressing the audience with a casual, soft, and even yearning tone.[42] The style of crooning often involved hitting a note just slightly above or below the intended note and then sliding your voice up or down to hit the note you wanted. In addition, crooners sang in the common vernacular, taking a "plain truth approach," incorporating the common language of the street with all its colloquialisms.[43] These vocal techniques pulled the listener in, helping to close the distance of the airwaves; tuning in at home, one could image that the singer was right beside you, cooing softly into your ear.

Rudy Vallee was "the first national network star created by radio"; as radio's answer to Rudolph Valentino, he was the first crooning idol, and, really, the first male pop star, with millions of devoted female fans. He gave the radio singing voice sex appeal.[44] When Vallee's performances at the Heigh-Ho Club in New York were broadcast over WABC, he became an instant hit and got a national show on NBC in 1929 that generated thousands of fan letters every day. Vallee's style was perfectly suited to radio; he stressed the song's lyrics, choosing simple songs and emphasizing the chorus, in a way that allowed the listener to learn the words and sing along, which promoted the listener's own emotional involvement and identification with him. He showcased love songs that typically contained an I-you direct address, seeming to sing to just one person, you. Vallee understood, as historian Allison McCracken notes, "the value of repetition in fostering audience familiarity and anticipation." What this marriage between radio and Vallee meant for fandom was that the voice of a nationally famous singer was coming right into your home, seeming to sing love songs straight to you. With songs about newfound love, or lost love, the audience is the stand in, that object of desire. This is an experience we know all too well today.

But as with jazz, crooning too was controversial, prompting moral watchdogs to worry about the singers' impact on young women, and to criticize the music itself as mushy. As McCracken has found, Vallee's fan mail verged on the orgasmic, with women writing "I enjoy your programs so frightfully much that I just have to speak of it or I will burst with admiration of your talents," and "A long time ago, I listened to you sing 'Rain' and all sorts of shivery thrills ran up and down my spinal column. Is it possible I've fallen in love with a voice?" One woman reported "jumping three feet in the air" when she heard his voice; another wrote "I'm burning up."[45] Also, because some of Vallee's songs were sung from a woman's perspective, like "The Man I Love," or expressed sadness and emotional vulnerability at losing a woman he loved, some questioned Vallee's masculinity with charges he was too effeminate.[46] The cardinal of the Boston Roman Catholic Archdiocese denounced crooning as "[i]mmoral and imbecile slush. A degenerate, low-down sort of interpretation of love . . . [with] a man whining a degenerate song. . . . It is a sensuous, effeminate luxurious form of paganism."[47]

Golden Age of Radio

Illustrating the country's deeply ambivalent and problematic attitudes about race, radio's first really big national hit was *Amos 'n' Andy*, a show in which its main black characters were played by white men, Freeman Gosden and Charles Correll, partners in the "Fresh Air Taxi Company, Incorpulated." *Amos 'n' Andy* became a daily network show in August 1929, just a few months before the stock market crash, and it quickly became the most popular program on the air, reaching an estimated forty million listeners, or approximately one-third of the population.[48] It was a national addiction: hotel lobbies, movie theaters, and shops piped the show in from 7:00 to 7:15 so as not to lose customers. Telephones remained still, toilets weren't used, taxis sat unhailed while the show was on.[49] Within short order its stars were making a staggering $100,000 a year and up to $7,500 a week when they did personal appearance tours to packed houses. Soon there were *Amos 'n' Andy* toys, candy bars, and other related merchandise.[50] And it stayed on the air as a daily show for a decade-and-a-half.[51] Gosden and Correll were the first major radio celebrities—and they were huge—who were not musicians or singers.

What made them and their show such a hit? As Gilbert Seldes noted at the time, the show fused two already successful pop culture genres, black-face minstrelsy and the "story comic strip," because there were ongoing story lines.[52] Most of the humor came from the pair's mangling of conventional English, from the incessant malapropisms, inadvertent puns, and total misunderstanding of regular terms and phrases. The linguistic mutilations of the show allowed listeners to feel superior to these illiterate, verbally stumbling men, whose language deficiencies were meant to reflect cognitive deficiencies. But the malapropisms also ridiculed mainstream, white America, especially the arbitrariness and high-handedness of government bureaucracy and big business during the depths of the Depression. Letters Andy "de-tated" to Amos were address to the "secketary of de interior o' labor," and nationally known figures were renamed "J. Ping-Pong Morgan" and "Charles Limburger."

Executives discussed "propolitions," the economic crisis was "de biz-
ness repression," and garbled explanations of the causes of the Depression were not all that far off from the incomprehensible and reckless
machinations of Wall Street manipulators.[53] This use of blacks—or faux
blacks—to attack the pretensions, snobbery, and frequent inhumanity of
the upper classes had begun in minstrel shows, in which the Dandy Jim
caricature lampooned not just the urban black dandy but also the prissy
and pompous upper-class *white* dandy.[54]

So it is important to move beyond the "was it racist or not" questions
surrounding the show. Of course it was racist. It took the most demean-
ing aspects of minstrelsy and enshrined them on the air. But as Melvin
Patrick Ely argues in his definitive study of the show, millions of white
listeners were not glued to it every night at 7:00 simply so they could
laugh at the stupidity and naiveté of black folks. Remember, the country
was now in the throes of its greatest economic crisis ever, which had rav-
aged millions, blacks and whites alike. The show's power came from the
way it dramatized the collapse of paternal authority in the home, in the
government, in the marketplace. White culture has often projected onto
"Stage Negroes" its worst fears about itself.[55] This was certainly true of
Amos 'n' Andy, in which black men (portrayed by white men) struggled
to earn a living, conquer bureaucracy, and retain some shred of mascu-
line dignity in the face of breadlines, an indifferent government, and up-
pity women. Using what writer and editor Mel Watkins has called "racial
ventriloquism," white men put into the mouths of blacks their sense of
helplessness in a world when all too many men suddenly felt superflu-
ous, stymied, throttled.[56]

The huge success of *Amos 'n' Andy* showed that there was a national
audience for radio comedy and that it could make on-air performers into
major stars. With the popularity of radio and movies, and the devastation
of the Great Depression, the 2,000 vaudeville theaters that had thrived at
the turn of the century had shrunk to fewer than 100 by 1930.[57] By the
early and mid-1930s, with advertisers and networks searching for similar
shows with national appeal, a host of vaudevillians signed up to do their
own radio shows—Joe Penner, Will Rogers, Ed Wynn, George Burns and
Gracie Allen, and Jack Benny—and their voices came right into your
home. As new performers and programs emerged to fill airtime, they
quickly gained a mass following. Movie stars like Mae West and Tallulah

Bankhead would also appear on radio shows as a way to cross-promote their films and their stardom (although Mae West got banned from NBC for fifteen years for doing a provocative reading of a skit about Adam and Eve on the *Charlie McCarthy Show* with Edgar Bergen).

One of the biggest early radio stars was Will Rogers, who assumed the persona of a cowboy from Oklahoma and was known for his folksy humor and political commentary. Rogers embodied an emerging aspect of celebrity in the 1930s, appearing on multiple platforms, as he wrote newspaper columns and books, appeared on the lecture circuit and in movies, and had his own radio shows. In 1934 he was voted the most popular male actor in the country.[58] His specialty was the monologue, perfect for radio, in which he commented in simple, accessible, and ironic language on current affairs and also impersonated famous people. He labeled Congress "the national joke factory."[59] In one bit he imitated the high-pitched voice of President Calvin Coolidge and was so convincing that listeners believed they were actually hearing the president. By the early 1930s, he was reaching forty million people through his columns and broadcasts and his income was reportedly $600,000, a staggering amount back then.[60] When he was killed in a plane crash in 1935, NBC and CBS went off the air for thirty minutes as a tribute to him.[61]

Radio comics in particular had to develop an identifiable, distinct persona and entertaining "personality." The show, of course, could refer to the clothes the comic wore, his face, and body movements. In fact, radio had to overdescribe everything in a way you never would in real life—"Oh, look, here's Jack coming into the room now"—which made the discourse of radio comedy uniquely quaint. But for the most part, comics really had to rely on their voice and words to set themselves apart from the others. So radio celebrity required, in part, the development of "vocal trade-marks" by which the comics were known, phrases, modes of delivery, vocal gymnastics.[62] What prompted the audience at home was the institutionalization of the studio audience, who helped comics time the delivery of their jokes and helped those at home visualize themselves as part of a larger, public audience in which it was perfectly fine—even expected—to laugh out loud in front of a box in your living room.[63] Radio stars also fabricated fake "feuds" to cultivate regular followers and interest in what would happen next. Jack Benny and Fred Allen (friends in real life) started such a bit, trading insults on the air, as did Bob Hope and Bing Crosby (who also appeared in numerous films together).

Over the years, radio produced hundreds of celebrities, some of them fleeting and others that endured for decades, especially those who made the transition to television. This kind of relationship with the star had its special pull. With radio, whether listening to a singer, or a comic, or a dramatic actor, you had to imagine them, create your own image of them, and one you suspected might be like that of others', but was also distinctly yours.

Political Celebrity

Radio also helped transform the relationship between one of the most famous people in the country, the president, and its citizens. Presidents, of course, had always been famous, but there had been a distance between them and everyday people except when they traveled to give campaign speeches. Radio changed that. During his tenure in the White House, and in stark contrast to his predecessor Herbert Hoover, President Franklin Roosevelt recognized radio's influence and its potential to create a personal connection between speaker and audience. Between 1933 and 1944, Roosevelt famously used the medium to broadcast his live fireside chats, personal addresses that spoke directly to the American people during a time of economic and political turmoil. Indeed, you can't say Roosevelt's name without immediately thinking "fireside chats," so effective was FDR's command of the relatively new technology of radio. Not unlike contemporary presidents—Barack Obama through e-mail and the Internet, Donald Trump through Twitter—Roosevelt sought to use radio to circumvent the gatekeepers of the dominant newspapers, many of whose publishers were Republican and opposed the New Deal; indeed, in both the 1936 and 1940 elections, two-thirds of the nation's newspapers editorially opposed Roosevelt's reelection. Thus, his use of the new medium was crucial to his political survival.

In addition, as a communications medium that denied sight to its audience—especially important for Roosevelt who was a paralytic and worked assiduously to keep his disability from public view—radio allowed him to convey both enormous authority and empathy and to

Figure 4.2. FDR fireside chat, September 6, 1936. Photograph by Harris and Ewing, Library of Congress.

utterly avoid any suggestion of his disability. Roosevelt and his aides understood that radio was a very intimate medium that could make the listener feel like you were speaking to him or her personally. He thus deliberately imagined his audience as a few people sitting around his fireplace with him; he did not use the stentorian political oratory of the stump, but the intimate "I-you" mode of address that had proven to work so well in the medium. He opened the chats with "My friends," and was careful to use simple, direct, informal language. While each chat indeed sounded relaxed, informal, unrehearsed, each talk "was the result of extensive preparation, having gone through perhaps a dozen drafts."[64] Having discovered that a separation between his two front lower teeth produced a slight whistle on the air, he had a removable bridge made that eliminated the sound. That's called paying attention to the affordances of a particular medium!

In a 1943 chat, delivered on Christmas Eve, FDR spoke from his home in Hyde Park, New York, where, as an announcer informed listeners, "he ha[d] gathered with his family to simply celebrate Christmas," the president directly addressed members of the armed forces, naming specific locations in which they were stationed. "Tonight," Roosevelt said, "on Christmas Eve, all men and women everywhere who love Christmas are thinking of that ancient town and of the star of faith that shone there more than nineteen centuries ago." The fireside chats employed the intimacy of radio to bolster public morale, enhance support for his policies, and humanize the presidency.

Getting behind the Scenes

In 1936, *Life* debuted as a weekly national magazine that would become a kind of who's who of the American public scene. *Life* pioneered the use of photojournalism as a narrative tool, one that emphasized the centrality of the image in American life, so it became an important counterpart to radio and its emphasis on aurality. The magazine also blended news and information with popular entertainment. In December 1937, *Life* ran a story about Detroit's WXYZ, commending the station for its innovative programming and highlighting a montage of behind the scenes photos of the productions. Readers were treated to photographs of the performers in action; four young men used "toilet plungers swathed in cheesecloth" to create the sounds of the trusty steed Silver riding beside the Lone Ranger, while another image featured Earle Grasser, the Ranger himself, sporting a black mask and western hat as he bellowed his lines into the microphone, hand raised high in a moment of exclamation. Other photos showed *The Green Hornet's* Al Hodge perusing a script while the musical group the Mountaineers perform live.[65] These images gave readers a glimpse into the world of radio production and furthered the renown of popular performers, heretofore known only by their on-air voices, who could now be seen in action across the magazine's pages.

Thus, with the rise of the film and then radio industries, celebrity production—by the studios, advertising agencies, and newspapers and magazines—had become a well-oiled and predictable machine. Gossip columnists were key conduits of news, alleged back-stage inside info, and scandals. And accompanying and promoting radio's meteoric rise as the most popular form of entertainment in the country was the radio fan magazine. As with the movie fan magazines, there were stock features we still recognize and see today. New magazines like *Radio Mirror* (geared primarily to women) that sold for ten cents put pictures of radio stars on the cover (so fans could see what they looked like) and featured the new, chatty, "inside story" style of celebrity features. For example, it featured "late news and hot gossip of the radio artists," profiles of stars like Will Rogers, "at-home-with-the-stars" pieces, accounts of celebrity romances ("They Sing Their Love Every Day, the Romance of Ozzie Nelson and Harriet Hilliard"), and articles allegedly by celebrities like Bing Crosby ("There's Only One Marriage for Me").[66] Such ridiculously idealized (and phony) profiles enhanced the fame and enviability of radio stars by putting faces to voices and, of course, letting listeners in on "behind-the-scenes" stories.

But it was Walter Winchell who brought gossip to the airwaves.[67] Nearly forgotten today, Winchell was a major, self-made celebrity, with a lasting impact on the role that celebrities play in our culture. The gossip column moved from the newspaper columns to radio, almost exclusively through Winchell's broadcasts. From the early 1930s until the mid-1950s, he was a superstar, one of the most influential men in the United States. He made and broke the careers of entertainers and politicians, endorsed or damned American foreign and domestic policy, and powerfully shaped the values and attitudes of millions of Americans. Thus he was widely courted and deeply feared. So much of what characterizes our media landscape today—the incursion of celebrity gossip into mainstream journalism, the powerful role that some radio and TV commentators can play in American politics, the move from reporters reporting on a story to being a central part of the story—began and advanced with Winchell.

Winchell started as a newspaper gossip columnist in the 1920s and in the 1930 brought his mix of gossip and crime reporting to radio; in short order, twenty million people listened to his show, which was, by the late 1940s, the top rated program on the radio. Listeners recalled being able to walk down the street at night and hear Winchell's trademark rapid-fire "flashes" coming out of nearly every house on the block. In his column, Winchell had seized on the post–World War I delight in slang, lacing his column with gaudy, inventive wordplay: "made whoopee" meant "had fun"; "Reno-vated" or "phffft" meant "divorced"; "Adam-and-Eveing it" meant "getting married." Such wordplay worked perfectly on the radio and helped brand Winchell and his distinctive style. Now, on the air—at 200 words a minute—such language intermixed with sound effects and Winchell's personal, direct address to the audience. Winchell's biographer Neal Gabler perfectly captures Winchell's voice—"clipped like verbal tap shoes"—and reports that his voice went up an octave went he went on the air. Winchell opened the show with the urgent tapping of a telegraph key, which wasn't really tapping out anything resembling the Morse code, but which did signify news "hot off the wire." "The Big Idea is for sound effect," Winchell noted, "and to set the tempo." The tapping bracketed the beginning and end of each story, and was coded to let the viewer know what was coming: low-pitched clicks for domestic news, high-pitched beeps for international news.[68] He then greeted "Mr. and Mrs. America and all the ships at sea," suggesting, in his classic telegraphic form, that his broadcasts spanned oceans, and that Mr. and Mrs. America was a common, national category all his listeners fit into. "I want to create as much excitement as a newsboy on the streets when he yells 'Extry, extry, read all about it.'"[69]

At first, the program focused almost exclusively on celebrity marriages, divorces, and love affairs, but gradually it combined a mix of celebrity and gangster gossip and national and international news. He would open with an urgent "flash," often a train wreck, murder, or other disaster story. An assistant combed foreign newspapers for his "By Way of the High Seas" segment, which he introduced with the beeping sound of wireless dots and dashes.[70] As Gabler emphasizes, Winchell turned gossip into a commodity that coexisted on the same pages—or in the same broadcast—with news. In the process, then, he helped to redefine what *was* news, and stirred up heated debate about who had the right to shape listeners' tastes in and expectations of broadcast news.

The kidnapping of Charles and Anne Morrow Lindbergh's twenty-month-old baby in March 1932 was such a huge story it too was described as the "Crime of the Century" (superseding the 1906 Nesbit-Thaw-White scandal) and the 1935 trial of the accused, Richard Bruno Hauptmann, became the first nationally broadcast murder trial. After a seventy-three day drama involving multiple ransom notes demanding an ever-increasing amount of money, the baby's body was found on May

12. A massive investigation by the FBI and state police ensued, all fever-ishly covered by the press.

After being the first person to fly solo across the Atlantic, landing just outside of Paris on May 21, 1927, Charles Lindbergh became an instant hero, "the hottest name in the newspaper business." The feat had seemed miraculous, near impossible, and he had endured sleet, fog, and minimal visibility to achieve it. Of course he was a hero, not because of his personality but because of this singular, courageous achievement. Within a week he had become "the most highly publicized person in the world," dubbed "Lucky Lindy."[71]

Lindbergh was unprepared for the avalanche of attention and especially for the focus not on the aviation feat but on his personality, on tidbits about "Lindbergh the man," much of which was false or made up by a ravenous press desperate for copy. On the one hand, upon his return, New York City gave him the largest ticker tape parade ever, attended by an estimated four million people, and the president awarded him the Distinguished Flying Cross and then the Congressional Medal of Honor.[72] On the other hand, he and his wife were besieged by a celebrity-hungry press that bribed servants to get the inside scoop on the Lindberghs' private lives, and who stalked them to get candid, unauthorized photos. Lindbergh hated the incessant quest for and publication of these "human interest" stories, and the often unscrupulous ends reporters would resort to, and his resistance to the unrelenting attention led to one of the first "journalistic introspection(s) about America's culture of celebrity," some wondering if they had indeed gone too far.[73]

But not Winchell. Already famous and controversial, he inserted himself into the trial in ways many found utterly inappropriate. Indeed, Winchell was one of the founding fathers of the broadcast "media circus," which both enlivened and perverted on-air journalism. He was Jewish and came from the lower middle class, and so raised questions about what kinds of people, of what class and ethnicity, should be national opinion makers. There were also tensions here about masculinity, about what kind of *men* deserved such celebrity and such power, and about what kinds of things such men should discuss and how they should discuss them. Winchell fused male power, authority, and interest in the political with hysteria, irrationality, and an interest in the interpersonal and romantic. Winchell's appeal came, in part, from his emotionalism and urgency, from the permission he gave men to be passionate and even irrational about issues and events. Winchell remained hugely popular and influential until the 1950s, when his support for the rabid anticommunist Senator Joseph McCarthy led to his downfall.

Talent Shows and Stardom

Radio also set the precedent for making everyday people stars, and its shows established the template for how television talent shows over seventy years later, like *American Idol* and *The Voice*, would be structured. Radio talent shows became a craze during the Great Depression, not surprising given the unemployment rate and the huge salaries paid to radio and move stars. The most successful of these was *Major Bowes Original Amateur Hour*, which premiered in 1935 and was an instant hit. Contestants came on to sing, play an instrument, dance, and the like; if their performance was deemed a dud, Bowes banged a gong to end it. Listeners were also asked to telephone or send in a postcard naming their favorite. At the height of the show's popularity, over 10,000 people applied each week for the twenty available slots on the program and the chance to become famous.

While very few contestants actually landed show business careers, a few, like Frank Sinatra and Beverly Sills, did become superstars, stoking the myth that anyone with talent could make it.[74] Sinatra performed as a solo artist and as part of a group, which garnered a record 40,000 calls to the show. Sinatra left the group and in 1940 joined Tommy Dorsey's band, where he enjoyed huge success, due, in part, to Dorsey's impressive publicity machine. In short order Sinatra became a sensation with young female fans called "bobbysoxers." By December 1942, after Sinatra had left Dorsey's band and performed solo at New York's Paramount Theater, he was greeted by deafening roar from his fans, marking what came to be known as "Sinatramania."

As with many singing stars, Sinatra was of course very talented, with an impressive vocal range and smooth phraseology. He also had a shrewd press agent, George Evans, who dubbed him "the Voice" and "Swoonatra," and his fans "Sinatrics," who were gripped by "Sinatrasms." But Sinatra also filled his voice with emotion and when performing live seemed to be looking straight into the eyes of his fans. Critics likened his

Figure 4.3. Frank Sinatra surrounded by audience. c. 1950. NY Public Library, Billy Rose Theatre Division.

voice to "worn velveteen" and one suggested "it was like being stroked by a hand covered in cold cream."

Historical context matters as well here. The success of some celebrities can be attributed, in part, to how they compensate for a sense of loss, how they address a sense of longing during difficult and even scary cultural moments. Remember that by the time of Sinatra's Paramount performance, the United States had been at war for a year, with millions of young men drafted and deployed, and some of them already killed. Sinatra filled that void, however symbolically, and at a distance, for millions of young women during World War II. And while young people in the 1920s and '30s had of course been fans of jazz and crooners, it was Sinatra who really tapped into and helped define young people, and especially young women, as distinct, significant, and passionate fans of popular music.

Sports Heroes

Radio not only brought musical performance and storytelling into the home, it also played a central role in turning athletes—including African American athletes—into mass idols on a par with movie stars. Nearly all of these athletic celebrities were men, and unlike for women (or many male movie stars), appearance mattered much less than their achievements. Also, unlike women, their greatness was typically established and measured in numbers, statistically—how many runs, how many knockouts, and the like. Because of their prodigious athletic skills (which sometimes seemed superhuman) and because they represented the identities and aspirations of particular cities, or even the nation, some were seen not just as stars but as heroes, admired for their extraordinary efforts, even courage under competitive pressure and constant national attention.

Sports celebrities emerged in the late nineteenth century when, with the expansion of newspapers and their push for ever larger circulation, they began devoting even more coverage to commercial amusements. By the 1880s and 1890s, many large city papers inaugurated something we take for granted today, the sports page, recognizing it was yet another circulation booster. In doing so, as Charles Ponce de Leon has argued, sportswriters sought to bring together both working-class readers on the one end of the class spectrum and more middle and even upper-middle-class readers on the other, many of whom disdained what they saw as the vulgarity of a sport like boxing. The sportswriter's job depended on athletics being seen as a character-building, wholesome pursuit that millions could follow. Thus sportswriters played a central role in delineating the difference between a true hero and the overrated "pretender."[75]

Athletic heroes, those who aroused devotion from their fans, embodied traits Americans admired and wished (or even imagined) they possessed themselves, both on the field (or ring) and off. A journalistic frame that reporters helped construct suggested that athletic models of success could be transferable to the "game of life." A review of these idealized traits shows that, with few exceptions, these expectations of what constitutes a true athlete-hero still holds powerful sway today.[76] Most of these stars did not come from wealth or privilege (indeed many were working class) and so gained their fame from constant practice and a drive to succeed, embodying the American work ethic. Thus, whatever the athletes' inherent gifts were, sportswriters emphasized their constant desire to improve further, to be disciplined to get even better. Mental attributes were essential as well. The athlete-hero had to be confident, to "withstand the doubts and fears that arose in the heat of competition" and to conquer the nervousness to which we are all susceptible "in clutch situations."[77] Yet he could not be cocky. He had to remain calm and know how to handle pressure, so as a man he knew how to restrain his emotions.[78] They played fair, and were supposed to embody good sportsmanship and not be sore losers, letting their desire to win get the better of them.[79] Thus, a kind of nobility was ascribed to them, but one they also had to personify and nurture as humble, "regular" guys, just doing their best for their fans, their town, their country. They had to be team players who were not prima donnas, only out for themselves. And they were supposed to engage in the sport for the "love of the game," not primarily for personal gain. The ideal of sport "was highly critical of excessive competition, rule breaking, acquisitiveness, and self-aggrandizing individualism."[80] Athletes whose off-field behavior violated this notion of nobility typically did not garner the same kind of fan loyalty. Athletes that "transcended the game," who moved into the realm of popular culture especially through other venues than the playing field, became bigger celebrities than others.

Sporting events—college football games, the World Series—were some of the first live events broadcast on radio, as early as the 1921 World Series and the 1922 football game between Princeton University and the University of Chicago.[81] At first many team owners feared radio broadcasts of baseball games, believing they would hurt ticket sales.[82] Nonetheless, the often highly colorful play-by-play of radio sportscasters helped make certain players national heroes. And, of course, radio meant that millions unable to attend sporting events in person could follow famous teams or athletes and hear about their victories or defeats as they happened.

It was especially boxing and baseball that gripped the public imagination and, with the help of radio, made its stars household names. The intersection between seeing photos of athletes in America's newspapers and magazines and hearing, live, the contests they were in created sports heroes that men, in particular, could admire and seek to emulate. By

one estimate fifty million listeners tuned in to the 1927 Jack Dempsey–
Gene Tunney boxing match. Yet it was Joe Louis, nicknamed the "Brown
Bomber," whose boxing matches on radio revitalized prizefighting and
turned him into one of the first African American national sports heroes. For African Americans, some of the most important broadcasts
of the 1930s were Joe Louis's matches, whose victories over white opponents galvanized black pride and spirit and suggested that, even in a
deeply racist society, black men could occasionally embody the national
will. In 1935 he beat Benito Mussolini's favorite boxer, Primo Carnera,
and then, a few months later, he beat Max Baer in a fight broadcast
around the country and to Europe over shortwave radio. It was a hugely
important mixed-race fight. "In New York's Harlem, Negroes who had
listened to radios in taxicabs, saloons, restaurants, pool-rooms and private homes surged through the streets, blew horns, turned hand springs,
paraded, swarmed onto buses," reported *Literary Digest*. The same thing
happened in Detroit, Louis's hometown.[83]

Then, in 1938, Louis knocked out Hitler's favorite, Max Schmeling,
in two minutes, a match 64 percent of American radio owners tuned in
to. This wasn't just a victory for blacks, it was a victory for America.[84]
As Lew Erenberg noted, because of this instant victory over Schmeling,
a stand-in for Hitler, this was "the first time in history that an African
American male enjoyed such widespread devotion and popularity."[85]
Indeed, *Time* magazine reported in 1941 that Joe Louis boxing matches
attracted the largest audiences in U.S. radio history with the exception
of two prewar addresses by President Roosevelt. That year he appeared
on the cover of *Time*, was dubbed "the black Moses," and a year later
promoted the U.S. war effort before 20,000 fans at Madison Square
Garden.[86]

Baseball stars, like boxers, represented "achieved celebrity"; they
earned it through their athletic virtuosity. And in the 1930s, '40s, and
'50s, baseball was the dominant sport in the country.[87] The first mas-
sively successful star was George Herman "Babe" Ruth, widely considered the greatest baseball player of the twentieth century and certainly
one of the sport's biggest draws for fans. Ruth started out as an excellent
pitcher who could also hit, a very unusual combination in a player;
during his time with the Red Sox he won eighty-nine games in six years
and set a World Series record for consecutive scoreless innings.[88] In

Figure 4.4. Joe Louis, c. 1936. Library of Congress.

1919 he was traded to the Yankees and became a full-time outfielder, but it was as a batter that he revolutionized the game, bringing enormous power to his swing, which also produced higher scoring games. In 1920, he hit a staggering fifty-four homeruns (no other player hit more than nineteen), and in 1927 he hit sixty, a record that stood for thirty-four years.[89] He was soon dubbed the "Sultan of Swat" and the "Colossus of Clout." He led the Yankees to seven American League pennants and four World Series titles.[90] With the emerging multiplatform appetite for and promotion of famous people, Ruth did vaudeville, appeared in movies, was of course on baseball cards, and had a candy bar named after him in 1921.

Ruth also personified how celebrities can rise, fall, and then rise again as a "new" version of their previous selves through shrewd presentation of self. Because he was such a star, Ruth was exempted from curfews and other regulations affecting his fellow players. He became known for his large appetite for food, alcohol, and women, as well as lavish spending and high living, which partially meshed well with the pre-Depression "jazz age" zeitgeist. But in 1925, after highly public fights with the Yankee manager and owners, and accusations of having a "swelled head," he experienced a physical "collapse" and seemed doomed to become a "has-been." But as his health improved he rededicated himself to the game, vowed to reform, got married, and gave interviews acknowledging it was time for him to follow the rules. As a result, "journalists proclaimed the 'new' Ruth vastly superior to the 'old.'"[91]

Ruth's status as a sports hero was amplified by radio, once stations began broadcasting the World Series in 1921. The Yankees were in the series six times in the 1920s, winning three of them, including in 1927 when Ruth set his home run record. In 1934 he began hosting his own radio show consisting of jokes, interviews, and predictions about upcoming games, and was a frequent guest on the shows of other sportscasters.

By the 1940s, baseball was a fixture on radio and its pacing made it especially conducive to oral presentation by skilled announcers who themselves also became stars. Major baseball heroes of this era included Joe DiMaggio, who had a fifty-six-game hitting streak in 1941; Lou Gehrig, a seven-time All Star player; and the legendary hitter and seventeen-time All Star Ted Williams. Yet the Red Sox's Williams had an uneasy relationship with the Boston press because he disliked coverage that focused as much (or more) on his personal life as on his baseball performance, which he regarded as an invasion of privacy. He also reacted very negatively to any press criticism of his play, complaining that "the newspaper men have been on my back" and adding further that he didn't like Boston or its people.[92] Thus, Williams came off as arrogant and ungrateful, two traits sports heroes are not supposed to exhibit.

Celebrities and "Giving Back"

During World War II, musical stars, including African Americans, cemented their popularity. The orchestras of Glenn Miller, Tommy Dorsey, Duke Ellington, and Harry James had serial hits on the radio, as did Nat King Cole, Billie Holiday, and Lena Horne. The advent of the war made radio even more central to American life; millions had been following the daily broadcasts about the war in Europe and first heard about the bombing of Pearl Harbor on the radio. With the seemingly endless documentaries made, and still being made, about World War II, we tend to think of this as a highly visual war, experienced by Americans back home primarily through pictures. And certainly, with eighty-five million people going to the movies each week, Americans saw the progress of the war through newsreels, as well as through photographs in newspapers and magazines. But the way we have come to remember the war—through this visual record—misrepresents how people followed and imagined this war on a daily basis. This was an audio war, one that people *listened* to. This was, quite simply, a total revolution in American life: the bringing of eyewitness accounts, the sounds of air raid sirens, or gunfire, right into peoples' living rooms, bedrooms, and kitchens. World War II was a radio war.

Once again, because of the war, radio reconfigured the role of celebrities, many of whom now wanted and needed to support the war effort and be seen as selfless, charitable, and patriotic. Some, like Joe Louis, joined the army, and he became even more beloved when he fought and won a benefit bout in 1942 and donated the entire purse to the Navy Relief Society.[93]

For other stars—men who used their family exemptions or were too old to be drafted, most women—it was participating in USO (United Service Organizations) tours and performances that established their bona fides as committed to the war effort, charitable activities, and the broader social good. It was now imperative that celebrities were seen as "giving back." Entertainers went to "Camp Shows" to entertain and boost the morale of the troops, sometimes in the face of great personal danger. Thirty-seven entertainers died during the war, the most famous being bandleader Glenn Miller, whose plane disappeared over the English Channel. The most legendary USO performer was Bob Hope, already a major radio star. Hope's rapid fire delivery of jokes, sometimes as many as seven a minute, worked very well on radio, and he developed an irreverent style with many allusions to current affairs. Hope traveled to Sicily, North Africa, and the South Pacific, and broadcast 144 shows during the war, some of them heard primarily on the Armed Forces Radio Service.[94]

One of the most famous wartime broadcasts by a celebrity aired on September 21, 1943, when radio star Kate Smith hosted a war bond pledge drive that lasted eighteen hours. Throughout the broadcast,

Figure 4.5. Kate Smith, CBS, 1943. Getty Images. Reprinted with permission.

Smith spoke directly to her listeners, imploring them to participate and purchase bonds. Incredibly popular at the time, with twenty-three million Americans tuning in to her daytime program each week, and twenty-one million listening to her evening show, Smith was tremendously successful in prompting donations, at least in part because she presented the drive, as Robert Merton would famously report, as "a personal message, iterated and reiterated in a voice often broken, it seemed, by deep emotion."[95] Thirty-nine million dollars in bond pledges were made in the course of a single day.

Smith's listeners perceived her to be sincere, according to Merton's analysis of the broadcast, and reported a personal connection with her, a sense of being part of this marathon experience. As Merton wrote, "The presumed stress and strain to the eighteen-hour series of broadcasts served to validate Smith's sincerity. . . . Not merely the content of her messages, but the *fact* of the all-day drive, believed to be unique in radio history, was taken to testify to her distinctive willingness to serve."[96] Because Smith tailored her broadcast to respond to listeners who telephoned in throughout the day, "the usual radio monologue became something of a conversation."[97] The reciprocal interplay between Smith and her audience, the sense of personal connection, worked to enhance not only the success of the war bond drive but also the esteem that listeners felt for Smith herself.

Radio and Imagined Communities

During the Great Depression and World War II, radio and its stars helped cultivate what the scholar Benedict Anderson termed "imagined communities."[98] Stars publicly performed "being American," and their patriotic dress, volunteer work, and emphasis on the collective spirit modeled patriotic engagement for a mass audience. Anderson asked how nationalism—the notion of a country with a distinct identity, interests, and borders to which one belonged—came to emerge so concretely by the end of the eighteenth century. And he insisted that while political states indeed have borders, leaders, and populations, the notion of nationality, of nationhood, is *imagined*, because most of its members will never actually meet each other, "yet in the mind of each lives the image of their communion." Despite divisions based on class, race, gender, age, and geography, people still need to conceive of the nation "as a deep, horizontal comradeship."[99] In addition, the nation became imbued with a sense of destiny, and historical upheavals and discontinuities become part of a national story of historical trajectory guided by and directed toward some larger, grander purpose.

The most pivotal development, Anderson argued, which transformed hunks of populated territories into imagined communities of nations, was the newspaper. Every morning, at roughly the same time, people read the same stories about the nation, its leaders, and about some of their fellow citizens in the newspaper. It was this daily ritual, powerfully infused with a sense of simultaneity, of taking in the same stories, the same knowledge, at the same time as you knew your countrymen were that forged this sense of comradeship with unseen others. The paper, through its stories and, later, its images, was a concrete representation, one you held in your hands every day, that such a nation *did* exist, and *did* have very particular, distinctive characteristics.

Reading the newspaper may have been a crucial first step in cultivating this sense of national communion. But radio broadcasting did
this on entirely new geographic, temporal, and cognitive levels, inflating
peoples' desire to seek out, build on, and make more concrete that notion of the nation. For it wasn't just that this technology made imagined
communities more tangible because people now listened to a common
voice and a common, shared event at truly the exact same moment as
others around the region, or the country. Listeners themselves insisted
that this technology enhance their ability to imagine the people of their
country, as well as their ability to be transported to "national" events
and to other parts of the country. The sheer geographic scope that these
new simultaneous experiences now encompassed—when forty million people, for example, tuned in to exactly the same show or event—
outstripped anything the newspaper had been able to do in terms of
nation-building on a psychic, imaginative level. This mattered especially
during World War II.

At the same time, we must remember that people also used radio to
tune in on difference, which radio's many multiple and various stars
embodied. So while it has become a commonplace to assert that radio
built national unity in the 1930s and beyond, what radio really did (and
still does today) was allow listeners to experience multiple identities
at the same time—national, regional, local—some of them completely
allied with the country's prevailing cultural and political ideologies,
others of them suspicious of or at odds with official culture. And the
agents for this were radio stars—the comedians, actors, singers, athletes, reporters, and gossip columnists who individually and collectively
embodied the country's national character and its individual, distinct
features as well.

Radio in the 1950s and Beyond

By 1954, television was in over twenty-six million American households,
or 56 percent. The number of television stations had soared, from six in
1946 to 354 in 1954. Who was going to listen to sound alone when this
new box brought you voice, music, *and* pictures, right in your own living
room? By the early 1950s, radio was thought to be dead, a victim, like the
movies, of television. The famous "talent raids" of 1948–49 lured stars

like Jack Benny, Bing Crosby, and Ozzie and Harriet away from radio to television, inaugurating the death knell. Thus, by 1954, network radio, with its prime-time programming that brought national stars to a huge national audience, was all but gone.

But radio was not dead; its programming changed, which again produced new kinds of celebrities, especially pop and rock stars, and disc jockeys who also became famous in their own right. In 1948, there had been 1,621 AM stations in America; by 1960 that number had more than doubled to 3,458.[100] By 1954, 70 percent of American households had two or more radios, and 33 percent had three or more.[101] Each year in the 1950s and 1960s showed increased advertising revenues from the year before, and sales of radio sets—especially portables and sets inside cars, made possible by the invention of the transistor—continued to increase. Unlike the 1930s and '40s, listeners now tuned in to stations better known for their local, rather than national, identification. It was still, in the 1950s and early 1960s, the major source of news for most people. So, for millions of Americans, radio still mattered.

Two major demographic changes reshaped, yet again, who could become a celebrity via radio. One of course was the baby boom, the seventy-six million people born between 1946 and 1964 that produced a huge youth market. The other was yet another wartime mass migration of approximately 1.2 million African Americans from the rural South to cities like Detroit, Los Angeles, and Mobile, Alabama to work in wartime industries. Membership in the NAACP soared from 50,000 in 1940 to 450,000 in 1946.[102] And advertisers and station owners began "discovering" them as a market.

With the increased availability of radio licenses for small local stations, the networks' gradual abandonment of radio in favor of television, and the discovery that African Americans were an important new niche market, certain independent stations began courting the black audience. They featured black DJs—and white DJs who tried to sound black—and they played rhythm and blues and then what became rock 'n' roll. Because some of these stations had powerful transmitters that crossed state and regional lines, white listeners could and did tune in as well. Many of them were young people; by the late 1950s, teenagers were buying more records than adults, bringing huge new profits to the industry: record sales nearly tripled in five years, from $213 million in

1954 to $613 million in 1959.[103] In addition, and increasingly, teenagers' music was written or performed by African Americans.

While television, in its early years, first reactivated minstrelsy, with *Beulah* (a black maid) and *Amos 'n' Andy*, and then, after protests against such stereotypes, ignored African Americans altogether (with the exception of a few singers like Nat "King" Cole), many radio stations provided a cultural trading zone between the two cultures. This was made possible by the proliferation of the small, independent station that, by 1948, was more numerous than any other kind in the country.[104] These smaller stations became outlets for the 400 new recording companies started during the 1940s.[105] Now local stations could produce regional, even national, hits.

While clean-cut white singers like Pat Boone became teen idols by "covering" songs initially performed by black artists, African American singers and groups started getting major radio play and also became widely known singing stars, who also performed in highly publicized rock 'n' roll concerts featuring multiple black stars. Chuck Berry, Fats Domino, Bo Diddley, the Platters, LaVern Baker, Eartha Kitt, and Sam Cooke, to name a few, had multiple hit records in the 1950s and found white fans. So, as with jazz in the 1920s, music and radio listening once again became highly politicized. The reason was simple—this technology's reliance on sound but not image made it an agent of desegregation. Radio—more so than films, television, advertising, or magazines in the 1950s—was *the* media outlet where cultural and industrial battles over just how much influence black culture was going to have on white culture were staged and fought. It wasn't so much that now, in the postwar period, there were more radio outlets featuring black music, which panicked many older white Americans. It was that whites themselves—the DJs, the performers, and their fans—embraced a racial hybridity that confounded and defied the existing racial order between blacks and whites. There was a renewed form of interracial male-bonding on the air as white men, through their voices, assumed a black self.[106] Anxiety about increased infusions of black culture into the white mainstream escalated after 1956, when increasing numbers of white boys like Elvis Presley and Jerry Lee Lewis took on black performing styles. No one embodied this appeal and this threat more than Elvis Presley.

Figure 4.6. Elvis Presley performs, 1956. Photograph by Jay B. Leviton, National Portrait Gallery, Smithsonian Institution.

Elvis

Presley was rock 'n' roll's first star, made so via radio, and the 45 RPM single records young fans could then buy. And he was a sensation. Presley fused country music with the blues, gospel, rhythm and blues, and boogie-woogie, bringing together American music "from both sides of the color line and performed it with a natural sexuality that made him a teen idol." He began recording at Sam Phillips's Sun Records studio; when Memphis DJ Dewey Phillips (no relation) got a copy of "That's All Right," he played it over and over as the phones lit up. People hadn't heard anything quite like it. As Sam Phillips put it, he had found "a white man with the Negro sound and the Negro feel."[107] The combination of Presley's good looks, baritone voice, vocal energy, and hip-thrusting sexual display onstage made him a phenomenon, especially with female fans. Photos of these girls and women show them in near rapturous delight, holding their hands up to their faces, screaming, dancing in the aisles, or extending their arms toward him on stage, desperately trying to connect with him. But there were male fans too and they swarmed venues to see him.

In an era of even greater opportunities for cross-promotion, Presley appeared on television and starred in movies like *Love Me Tender*, which recouped its $1 million cost in three days.[108] His appearance on *The Ed Sullivan Show* in 1956 was seen by 82 percent of the television audience. When he sang "Hound Dog" and bounced on the stage, standing on his toes and twisting his legs and hips, the audience screamed in ecstasy. By his third appearance, the cameras only shot him from the waist up.[109] Prior to Presley's success, virtually all of the R&B music that white listeners heard on the radio was performed by black artists. But once white performers began imitating blacks in their music, and performing with greater physicality on stage, it was clear that black music constituted the identities of a significant group of white teens. Presley and other rock 'n' roll stars represented—and evoked—emotional and physical excess, "pleasure without connection to morality," and a rebellion against conformist codes around gender, race, and sexuality. Because of his onstage display and the emotionality and sexuality of his voice, Elvis was no manufactured safe star like Pat Boone—Elvis was authentic, the real deal. In some performances, a shock of Elvis's pompadoured hair hung suggestively over his forehead. As P. David Marshall notes, "a recurring technique for establishing authenticity in popular music performance is the breaking of codes and the creation of new or transformed codes of style." This style—of dress and hair, onstage performance—is an emphatic statement of difference, but also one of solidarity with the audience, which fans identify with and embrace.[110]

Once again, this time in the form of rhythm and blues and then rock 'n' roll, it was African American music that spoke to the cultural alienation, rebellion, and sexual energy of the younger generation. One teenage-dance promoter reported that rhythm and blues was, especially among the young, "a potent force in breaking down racial barriers."[111] And just like jazz, the music was condemned as lewd and dangerous, and many stations actively censored certain records or banned the music entirely.[112] A predictable coalition of religious leaders, schoolteachers, more conservative disc jockeys, politicians, and newspaper editors denounced the music as utterly corrupting trash. Members of the southern White Citizens Councils staged bonfires where rock records were torched and denounced rock as "a means by which the white man and his children can be driven to the level with the Negro." Not that the

North was any more progressive. Boston's Very Reverend John Carroll warned that rock inflamed teenagers "like jungle tom-toms readying warriors for battle." By 1955, authorities in Bridgeport and Hartford, Connecticut, and Washington, DC either banned or tried to ban rock 'n' roll concerts and dance parties.[113] Nonetheless, between 1955 and 1963, the number of black artists with Top Ten pop hits on the air increased by more than 50 percent.[114] Radio brought teenage listeners Maurice Williams, the Shirelles, Jackie Wilson, Otis Redding, the Ronettes, James Brown, and the Marvelettes, to name a few, and with Berry Gordy's Motown, founded in 1960, even more African American stars.

So Elvis was a threat. Like many sensational stars, he represented, as the civil rights movement was gaining momentum, and as sexual mores were beginning to relax, a collective expression of cultural change. When he was drafted into the military in 1958, record companies tried to create alternative teen idols, safer ones like Frankie Avalon (who especially gained fame in the various "Beach Blanket" movies) and Paul Anka. These singers did have their fans, but Elvis left a hole that would be filled by other hugely popular megastars.

What began to emerge in the 1950s and led to the invention of the "Top 40" format was "programming by the charts"—basing what you would play on the air on record sales and jukebox plays. By 1956, the year Elvis burst onto the national music scene, Top 40 and tight playlists were becoming more common, a programming breakthrough that brought huge profits to many stations. It foregrounded rock 'n' roll, and it meant that you would hear artists as different as Fats Domino, Connie Francis, and the Beach Boys all on the same station. Top 40's talent for making the national—even the international—seem local reached its apogee with Beatlemania, which would be fanned by radio, but also by the new star-making technology, television.

5

TV and the Need for Familiarity

It's 1955. Edward R. Murrow sits in an easy chair smoking a cigarette, looking directly at us, as he introduces the subject of today's interview. The camera, closely framing his face, pans around to show a window, its curtains opened. Outside, we see the exterior of a house in western Connecticut, its siding and yard. It is a house, Murrow tells us, which belongs to the vice president of Marilyn Monroe Productions, Inc., Milton Greene. As Murrow continues to describe the house and its features, the camera zooms through the window, transporting us across time and space, into that pastoral yard, and we approach the house. Greene's studio, as Murrow points out, is filled with *Look* magazine covers of famous movie stars, all of whom Greene had photographed, documenting how much celebrity profiles now dominated certain publications and, indeed, popular culture. Back in the studio, Murrow turns to look through his window, and then we see Marilyn Monroe sitting across from us at a kitchen table. As the camera frames Monroe's face in close-up—her iconic wispy blonde hair, blackened lashes, the beauty mark—the star appears disarming, funny, and honest as she jokes and flirts with the camera. Through Murrow's questions about what kind of a houseguest Monroe is, we learn that she knows her way around the kitchen and even (gasp!) makes her own bed. She confesses that one magazine cover she'd like to be featured on is *Ladies' Home Journal* (though, she teases, she's been featured in plenty of men's magazines). Through the magic of television, we gain access to Monroe, her private residence, and her personal thoughts.

The CBS television program *Person to Person* pioneered the televised home tour of the famous, later made ubiquitous on shows like *Lifestyles of the Rich and Famous* and *MTV's Cribs*. These programs provide a live action, conversational, behind-the-scenes look into the intimate spaces of celebrity life. On *Person to Person*, Murrow, a well-known and highly respected journalist, served as our trusted guide, interviewing a glittering roster of icons from film, politics, and pop culture from 1953 to 1959. One

Figure 5.1. Edward R. Murrow on the set of *Person to Person*, with Marilyn Monroe, 1955. Getty Images. Reprinted with permission.

of the first and most admired radio news reporters, Murrow had built his reputation as a CBS correspondent during World War II, especially through his coverage of the bombing of London and then his graphic description of the liberation of Nazi concentration camps. This often very dangerous reporting had made him a celebrity in his own right, albeit one with gravitas. Yet now here he was, to the horror of some of his journalistic colleagues, chitchatting about domestic matters with movie stars.

Murrow's lead role on *Person to Person* sent a clear message: celebrities were newsworthy, and political figures were becoming celebrities. Murrow brought us into the homes of Bobby Kennedy, Groucho Marx, and Marlon Brando, using techniques that were groundbreaking for the time. Dynamic cameras led us down hallways and across dining rooms while the invisibility of wireless microphones made it seem like the stars were speaking directly to us. As Ellis Cashmore argues, these kinds of intimate peeks into celebrity life gave the thrill of "peering surreptitiously through peepholes or eavesdropping," while simultaneously reassuring us that "the talented, rich, and famous had home lives just like everyone else."[1]

Murrow sought to take viewers into the back stages of celebrities' lives. But while *Person to Person* transported audiences into the apartments and townhouses of the stars, it also brought celebrities into dens and family rooms across America. So television allowed celebrity culture to further penetrate our daily routines and imaginations, and brought to life the "just like us" discourse around stars that had begun with fan magazines and newspapers back in the 1920s. To watch a show, to glimpse a favorite actress or catch up with a beloved character, people now didn't even need to leave the house. Simply press a button and, presto, they appear. Like radio programs, which made characters, singers, and hosts familiar voices in the American home, television now made famous figures visible. So the real revolution of television was that it allowed us to see the stars—their faces, their mannerisms, their interactions with one another, and with us—all through the eye of the camera, and within the comfort and informality of the domestic sphere.

Television gave further impetus to the trend of making celebrities part of everyday life. Unlike film, where in the darkened movie theater stars appeared larger than life, projected onto the supersized screen, television as a medium shrunk them down, compacted them, and beamed them, conveniently, into our world in "physically manageable size."[2] "Whereas the film celebrity plays with aura through the construction of distance, the television celebrity," as P. David Marshall writes, "is configured around conceptions of familiarity" because television brought stars visually right into the home.[3] Given this unprecedented visual proximity, and that these performers were indeed in your living room or den, the glamour and mystique of the remote movie star didn't match the medium. The television celebrity had to be much more like a regular person—maybe funnier or more attractive—but also approachable, less intimidating, not elevated on the movie star pedestal.

Ordinary and Extraordinary: TV, Stars, and Postwar America

By the time Marilyn Monroe appeared on *Person to Person* in 1955, 90 percent of American households had a television set and prime-time radio listening and moviegoing were in decline.[4] But initially, television ownership was slow to catch on. It took decades of technological innovation, beginning in the 1920s, to identify and refine the building blocks of the TV set, early versions of which were simply too expensive and too unreliable. In the late 1940s, wartime advances in technologies brought a parade of new gadgets into the American household and department and appliance store windows began showcasing televisions, but these were still clunky and unaffordable. While radio execs and television investors scrambled to popularize the technology, it was Earl "Madman" Muntz, a self-taught electrical engineer and used-car salesman, who, in 1947, brought to market a pared-down TV, the first to cost less than $100.[5]

That same year, David Sarnoff of NBC teamed up with the DuMont television network to broadcast the World Series battle between the Brooklyn Dodgers and the New York Yankees. Up and down the East Coast, crowds watched, transfixed by sets in store displays, bars, and restaurants.[6] Not only did the broadcast help pave the way for national sports coverage, and for the further celebrification of athletes, but it also fueled consumers' fascination with the technology. As a growing number of television stations began broadcasting across the nation, rising salaries propelled workers into an expanding middle class, and television ownership became a part of everyday life. By the end of 1952, one in three American households owned a TV;[7] it became a marker of middle-class success. In Levittown, New York, for example, where assembly-line style housing was built at a rate of up to thirty-six homes per day, "some models had a 12-inch Admiral Television set built into the staircase."[8] The television became a fixture of domestic life, a symbol of success in the new American scene.

Early television was limited in its channels and programming, which meant that content had to appeal to the whole family. Following the template established with radio, different times of the day were set aside for specific viewers—soap operas for women at home in the afternoon, Saturday mornings for children home from school, and after-work news and sports for men.[9] Overall, programming, especially during "prime time," was designed to attract the largest possible share of viewers, and so TV stars had to be widely relatable and engaging. In order to be successful, a show—and its stars—had to appeal to grandma, dad, and the kids, as well as to what came to be called "the lowest common denominator," the least sophisticated, least discriminating viewers. Advertisers, which had played a central role in the production of radio shows, and needing a national market, were loath to offend any sector of the white, middle-class population. Thus, with some exceptions, television produced shows and stars that were seen as "safe" and had broad and inoffensive appeal. Television in its early years then functioned as a mediated gathering space, a site of relaxation at the center of the home. As a "TV hearth," as Cecelia Tichi writes, the medium was associated with "friendliness and familial cohesiveness"; it functioned as a symbol of unity and tranquility, a point of access to the nation, and a vehicle through which our collective fantasies and desires could be displayed.[10]

What kind of stars did such a medium, reliant on advertising and dependent on ratings, require? As P. David Marshall emphasizes succinctly, "Compared with the film industry, the institution of television has positioned its celebrities in a much different way." The television celebrity, particularly in the network era with only three channels, had to embody familiarity and "mass acceptability."[11] Unlike the movie star, whom we might idolize or admire from afar, the TV star needed to be someone seemingly familiar with whom we could relate to and identify. This applied especially to talk show hosts, news anchors and reporters, hosts of variety and quiz shows—two staples of 1950s and '60s television—and to comic and dramatic actors.

Moreover, as John Langer notes, television programming is personality-driven. Virtually all televisual genres "are organized around a central persona or sometimes personae—the news 'reader', the current affairs 'anchorman', the talk show 'host', the variety programme 'headliner', the quiz show 'master of ceremonies'—each of whom appears to be essential to the programme's unfolding action, pace and thematic directions, as well as providing his/her 'on-air personality' as a crucial aspect of the programme's televisual identity."[12] To construct a sense of intimacy, TV personalities often use direct address, acknowledging the viewing audience in order to create the requisite sense of familiarity. Even when this mode of address is not present, the spectator remains "the focus of television's attention."[13] In many nonfictional programs, such as news, documentaries, and talk shows, the host serves as a mediating figure, whom the audiences comes to know and trust, and through whose personality the vantage point of the narrative unfolds. But even fictional shows guide the viewer in their own way, establishing points of identification with protagonists and reinforcing specific ideologies and perspectives. Thus, in some ways, these TV personae, much more than film stars, can and are required to bring viewers to a middle ground "common sense" about what is transpiring on the small screen.

Langer calls this phenomenon "Television's Personality System," an extension of the celebrity culture that grew out of cinema. Yet unlike movie stars, television stars, whether playing a role or simply being themselves as a show host, came into the home on a weekly or even daily basis. As such, TV stars were still seen as special, but they also had to seem, and became, knowable, regular, and predictable. "The personality system is cultivated almost exclusively as 'part of life'," as Langer notes. "Whereas the star system always has the ability to place distance between itself and its audiences through its insistence on 'the exceptional,' the personality system works directly to construct and foreground intimacy and immediacy."[14] In the late twentieth and early twenty-first centuries, we could point to Oprah, Jimmy Fallon, or Ellen DeGeneres, to name a few, who personify this kind of accessible, engaging, comforting television personality.

This sense of personal connection is reinforced by the domestic setting of television viewing. Whereas film requires audiences to leave the comfort of the home, to make a plan, television is always there, ready when you are, and requires no advance planning. Cinema going was an outing; television viewing is a part of everyday life, and often the TV was on in the background with people moving in and out of viewing. In addition, the repetitious nature of TV viewing, with its ongoing serial sagas, regularly scheduled programs, and recurring characters and plotlines meant that audiences could form a kind of ongoing, parasocial relationship with televisual characters and celebrities. In sum, TV personalities become a regularly scheduled, taken-for-granted part of our lives too.

All of these shifts toward familiarity have the effect, Marshall argues, of breaking down the aura of the star. "The domestic nature of television viewing, the close affinity of the celebrity with the organization and perpetuation of consumer capitalism, and the shattering of continuity and integrity of character that takes place through the interspersal of commercials in any program" work to reduce the remove of stardom that had helped bolster the image of the film star.[15] But what television stars lacked in aura, they made up for in charisma and the ability to connect with viewers, and a host of them quickly attracted a following. These qualities became increasingly central to the ways in which audiences recognize and relate to famous figures.

Three factors powerfully shaped the nature of television celebrity: its roots in radio, its reliance (unlike film) on advertising, and (like film) its emphasis on the visual, albeit on a much smaller and, in its early years, black and white screen. Radio influenced the forms and features of television, and much of the new content was, in both style and organization, lifted directly from radio. As Susan Murray writes of this era, "early television borrowed many of radio's cultural signifiers and narrative strategies."[16] From soap operas to quiz shows to variety programs, television borrowed heavily from its predecessor, a practice that reintroduced existing stars to the public while also generating a new crop of on-air talent.

Very early television, in the late 1940s and early 1950s, featured programs like *I Remember Mama*, *The Goldbergs*, *Life with Luigi*, and *The Honeymooners*, with ethnic, immigrant, or working-class families. But as the industry, and advertising's grip on and comfort with it consolidated, sitcoms became more "aspirational," with white, mostly Anglo-Saxon seeming characters living in upscale, picket-fence-surrounded homes. So TV stars embodied advertisers' aspirational vision for the future, as visions of people and families possibly more financially comfortable than you were meant to encourage viewers to buy products that would allow them to inhabit that lifestyle as well. Fictional, serial programs like *Leave It to Beaver*, *Lassie*, and *Father Knows Best* were a kind of American reassuring reverie, a collective daydream where life was simple, people were financially comfortable, and problems were solved by the end of an episode. Not surprisingly, these narratives were extremely limited in their representations, focusing primarily on white, middle- to upper-middle-class nuclear families, untouched by poverty, racism, inequalities, or injustice.

Most importantly, not only did on-screen personalities represent the values and personality of the networks, they were also increasingly used to sell consumer goods to television's national audience, often as part of the show. Thus, in their presentation of self, they had to come across as genuine and sincere, that what you were seeing was their true, core self.[17] This posed a challenge to stars tasked with "represent[ing] the sometimes competing commercial aims of both the sponsor (who wanted its star to be associated with its specific product) and the network (who used the star's persona to represent the character of the network as well as to attract a mass audience)."[18] Meanwhile, TV personalities were also used to promote and sell a range of household products, including television sets and branded merchandise, and to publicize on-air content.[19] Unlike the Hollywood star system, which emphasized a consistent vision of the star devoted to the aims of a single entity, the studio, television stars had to be commercially viable "for at least two very different products."[20] Film companies are, of course, commercial entities, but it was the advertising-driven nature of American television—first, with wholly sponsored programs, then with advertising breaks featuring different products, and now with subscription-based models—that necessarily enmeshed stars in the representation and promotion of commercial goods.

From the late 1940s through the 1960s, television enjoyed a "golden age." The big three networks—NBC, ABC, and CBS—dominated the market, attracting large-scale viewership by reinventing proven entertainment formulas. The tropes and actors that grew up on the vaudeville circuit, for instance (many of which had been popularized on radio), were once again retooled, this time for TV. But now there was a big difference, especially for comedy: gags based on verbal jokes or puns or wordplay were no longer enough. Television comedy and variety shows needed sight gags, pratfalls, costumes, facial expressions, and body language to produce laughs on the small, often low definition TV screen. Live vaudeville performance was a thing of the past; however, the community provided a talent pool, and a point of reference for, televised comedy and variety shows. Indeed, with the early success of variety shows on TV, in which a host introduced a variety of acts with the "something for everyone" format, "vaudeville-trained performers became the most sought-after personalities in television."[21] Experienced in appearing on stage before live audiences, vaudeville stars' performance styles "emphasized the visuality, spontaneity, immediacy and intimacy of the television medium."[22]

Early Television Stars

Milton Berle became one of the medium's first breakout stars. He had earned a name for himself on the vaudeville circuit before landing roles in film and radio, where he became a popular performer on *The Rudy Vallee Hour* and the *Texaco Star Theatre*. By 1948, Berle brought his vaudeville stylings to the small screen, transitioning the *Texaco Star Theatre* to television. Berle created a powerful and intimate connection with the television audience through his interaction with the studio audience, through his mugging, self-deprecating humor, willingness to make a fool out of himself, and often laughing uncontrollably at his own jokes or those made at his expense. During skits, Berle would interrupt the performance by making asides and jokes to the studio audience that often came across as inside jokes between him and his viewers. So popular was the show, with its comedic sketches, visually dramatic slapstick humor, and costume gags, that it earned massive ratings for NBC, decimated movie ticket sales on Tuesday nights when the show aired, and was even thought to have driven the sale of television sets.[23] In the process, Berle himself became a beloved figure and TV icon, earning the nicknames "Uncle Miltie" and "Mr. Television."

Soon, a host of other performers culled from the ranks of vaudeville and radio would appear on television. Imogene Coca, who began her career as a dancer, Broadway chorus girl, and comedian, brought her quirky humor and, like Berle, her talent for facial mugging and physical comedy to television on sketch comedy shows like *The Admiral Broadway Review* and *Your Show of Shows*, and would go on to win Emmy and Peabody Awards for her work. Jack Benny's career took a similar trajectory, as his early stage work led him to star in *The Jack Benny Program*, a hit for NBC on radio, which was then picked up for television by CBS. Unlike glamorous movie stars, the appeal of Berle, Benny, and other comic performers lay not in conventional good looks or allure, but in a specifically delineated personality and relatability that captured audience attention. Jackie Gleason and Ed Sullivan each hosted popular variety shows for which they themselves became celebrities. Such shows often had movie stars or famous singers as guests, providing an additional platform of exposure for those in the film industry while allowing the glamour of the stars to dust off on the hosts. But at heart, the charm of the host lay in his ability to connect with the audience, being relatable, funny, and down to earth. Week after week, the host was the reliable, familiar anchor, with whom we could identify.

The star who most successfully navigated the transition from radio to television was Lucille Ball. More to the point, she and her husband invented syndication, or the rerun, which eventually meant that television stars could be seen and celebrated long after their death. In the late '40s, Ball gained an audience and honed her comedic timing on the radio program *My Favorite Husband*. She married her real life partner, the Cuban American bandleader Desi Arnaz, and in 1950 CBS asked Ball to adapt *My Favorite Husband* for television. But when Ball proposed her real-life Cuban husband, instead of her radio costar Richard Denning, the network hesitated, unsure about featuring what they saw as an interracial couple on television.

To prove the show could work, the couple founded Desilu Productions and then produced their own pilot, something that was typically done (and then owned by) the network or an ad agency. With NBC also competing for the series, CBS eventually acquiesced to the casting. At the time, most television programs were broadcast live, which meant that shows had to be shot in New York, the center of broadcast production, some with prerecorded laugh tracks. However, Ball and Arnaz lived in Hollywood and wouldn't move. Over CBS's objections, they insisted on shooting in Hollywood, on film, in front of a live audience despite the expense involved in doing so; to cover the extra costs they agreed to cut their initial salaries, on condition that Desilu retain all rights to the show. This may have been one of the shrewdest deals in television history, because the filmed episodes could be rerun endlessly, earning residuals and ongoing fame for decades.[24]

I Love Lucy, which debuted in 1951, quickly became one of the top-rated shows on television, and Ball became a superstar.[25] The show became known for its high-quality visuals, which film made possible, and for how funny it was. Ball's enormous talent as one of the greatest physical comedians ever played to the studio audience; she fed off the energy of the crowd, heightening her ditziness and pratfalls for laughs. In contradistinction to glamorous movie stars, Ball's character was often clumsy, unsophisticated, and constantly in the midst of some self-created fiasco. We laughed at her, but also identified with her and her situations. In an era of increased conformity (especially for women), she tapped into people's anxieties about embarrassing themselves, about getting into situations that would expose their ineptitude. While she may have played a scatterbrained fool, she also broke boundaries by using defiant language and physical humor—distorting her face and contorting her body—to challenge her husband, the confines of domesticity, and stereotypes of femininity. The live, on-set laughter that ensued especially created a sense of camaraderie between the studio audience and the viewers at home.

Lucille Ball's transition from radio to television star made her a cross-platform success, a quality that would become de rigueur in the television, film, and recording industries in the decades that followed. Ball also proved that women could act as star, producer, and titular character, carrying a leading role both in front of and behind the camera. In 1962, when Ball bought Arnaz out of Desilu Productions, she became the first woman to head her own studio.

I Love Lucy also confronted the question of fame in all its ironies. Lucy and Ricky played aspiring celebrities on the show, with Lucy constantly looking to break into show business and Ricky performing as a bandleader, but the couple was, of course, already famous in real life. Lucy plays with audiences' awareness of this fact, poking fun at the bizarreness of fame and people's hunger for it throughout the series. In an episode entitled "Harpo Marx" (May 9, 1955), Lucy brags to her out-of-town pal, Carolyn, claiming she has loads of famous friends, which we know to be a lie. So when Carolyn shows up in Hollywood, Lucy and best-friend Ethel hide Carolyn's glasses and then parade before her a group of "stars." Carolyn blindly fawns over Clark Gable, Bing Crosby, and Gary Cooper, who are all just Lucy dressed in ridiculous costumes, performing wacky imitations with cheap rubber masks. Her shtick allows us to laugh at poor Carolyn, who plays the fool for gleefully thinking she's encountered genuine stars. Though the episode reassures us of our own superior judgment (surely we'd never be taken in by such a ruse), it also slyly pokes fun at the glorification of fame and at our reverence toward the stars. By the end of the episode, when the real Harpo Marx shows up, much to the surprise of Lucy (by then in Harpo garb), celebrity has been shown to be a performance, one that can trick us, amuse us, yet endear us to the stars.

Contestants as Stars

Television was changing industry practices for established stars but, like radio before it with its talent shows, was also launching everyday folks onto the small screen. While somewhat of a generalization, there were two kinds of everyday, nonfamous people television sought out, primarily as contestants on game or talent shows: those who were knowledgeable enough to participate in information-based competitions or had some other kind of talent, or those willing to expose or humiliate themselves in exchange for getting on the small screen and enjoying a fleeting moment of fame. This latter trade-off—personal debasement in exchange for often momentary stardom—TV demanded from the start, and it is a bargain that has carried through to the present in talent, quiz, and reality TV shows.

In 1956, ABC debuted a televised version of the popular radio program *Queen for a Day* (1956–60), in which women would often tearfully divulge their intimate, personal hardships in order to gain sympathy, applause, the royal title, and an array of consumer goods (which served as product placement ads). Not only did the show allow ordinary women the opportunity to tell their private stories to the world, but the prize on offer also reinforced television's power to coronate a star—here, a lady lacking royal blood could still earn the crown, if only she were willing to reveal her personal travails on national television. Other shows, like *Twenty-One* and *The $64,000 Question*, presented contestants with challenging trivia questions; to win required both skill and luck. Meanwhile, programs like *What's My Line?* and *To Tell the Truth* put celebrities in the hot seat, testing their ability to suss out information about the identity of mystery contestants.

With an ever-revolving cast of contestants, game shows promised that anyone could earn fame and cash by clinching a spot on the small screen, and certain contestants did become celebrities for a while. But this fantasy was soon tarnished by a successful contestant on NBC's *Twenty-One*, the clean-cut Columbia professor Charles Van Doren, who gained national attention for his winning streak—earning over $129,000—so impressive that it landed him on the cover of *Time* magazine in 1957, and a hosting role on *The Today Show*. Van Doren was eventually found to have been fed answers by the show's producers in an attempt to boost ratings, stoking the audience's interest in seeing whether he would win again this week. Thus he was revealed to be a fraud; it was a huge national scandal, as it emerged that fixing had occurred on other game shows as well. (Van Doren lost his job at Columbia and his gig with *The Today Show*.) Even President Dwight Eisenhower condemned the cheating, and new laws made it illegal for game shows to intentionally deceive the audience. Yet the damage was already done. Van Doren's deception—combined with the fact that he was an educated, pedigreed fraud to boot—challenged the American public's faith in the meritocracy that such shows sought to sell. Because many of these shows had been controlled by a single sponsor with a vested interest in boosting ratings, after the scandals the networks moved away from single sponsorship, moving to fifteen- to sixty-second "spot ads" featuring a variety of products.

While most prime-time quiz shows were cancelled in 1958 in the wake of the scandal, game shows, especially during the daytime schedule, rebounded in the 1960s, with NBC dominating the genre. Trivia shows were replaced by new formats, which blended prizes, audience participation, and campy banter. Shows like *Hollywood Squares* and *Match Game* cast celebrities as foils to the housewives and businessmen contestants. Famous and flamboyant figures offered pun-filled quips to help fill in the blanks, aiding contestants in their quest for success. Meanwhile, *Let's Make a Deal* promised members of the studio audience a chance to "trade" with celebrity host Monty Hall, if only they dressed in a costume ridiculous enough to catch his attention.

All these shows brought ordinary people into contact with stars in a relaxed, comical format. In an important twist on the cultivation of identification, they promised players—and the viewers at home—that the stars would be our teammates and helpers in our quest to win gleaming new appliances or a vacation to Maui. But regardless of which contestant claimed the grand prize, the real winners were the shows' hosts and celebrity guests. While the names and faces of individual contestants were quickly forgotten, audiences grew to know and love the shows' celebrity fixtures, like Joan Rivers, Florence Henderson, and Paul Lynde, who appeared each week to dish out quirky one-liners and winking sexual innuendos.

Award Shows and Celebrity

Television, by broadcasting an ever-increasing number of awards shows, also brought "A-list" celebrities, especially movie stars, and the glitz and glamour of the industry into our homes, providing access to gatherings previously reserved for elites—and fans lucky enough to be nearby. In 1953, NBC hosted the first television broadcast of the Academy Awards ceremony; Bob Hope was the evening's emcee. Though the event had previously aired on radio, television brought viewers into the theater where we could transport ourselves as invited guests, up close and in on the drama of who would win. As *Time* magazine reported:

> For the first time, some 34 million televiewers got a look at Hollywood's most ballyhooed annual event. . . . All the cinema queens, some appearing for the first time on TV, looked as gorgeous as they ever did, but a few seemed to miss the careful direction they get in films. The cameras might have been less rigid (the losers in the audience were ignored, even though Bob Hope had advised watching them: "You'll see great understanding, great sportsmanship—great acting"). But the show was still fascinating in an unrehearsed, star-studded way.[26]

Suddenly, we could be there as they were bestowed with the highest honors of their careers. We could see their dresses, their jewels, their interactions with one another. Television brought audiences into an event previously reserved for the stars and Hollywood insiders to see.

Award shows would go on to become a staple of network television, and a way to further bring celebrity culture into our homes. In 1958, the Oscars were being broadcast live from Hollywood and, three years later, a red carpet was introduced (though the show was still broadcast in black and white).[27] By 1964, producers had decided to air footage of the stars as they exited their vehicles, walking up to the venue as announcers heralded their arrival.[28] Two years later, the event would be broadcast for the first time in color. The annual celebration had become a television tradition, what Daniel Dayan and Elihu Katz call *media events*, the "high holidays of mass communication," which employ "the unique potential of the electronic media to command attention universally and simultaneously in order to tell a primordial story about current affairs."[29] Media events can occur in times of serious national affairs—as in the case of President Kennedy's funeral service—or when there's a competitive sporting event—like the en masse viewing of the Super Bowl. Similarly, award shows necessitate live, collective engagement and, in doing so, weave us into a broader community of film fans and viewers, all of whom are experiencing the event in unison.

The year 1960 also saw the first stars being constructed on the Hollywood Walk of Fame, a path of markers laid in honor of celebrities along Hollywood Boulevard and Vine Street in downtown Los Angeles. Not only did the stars celebrate famous industry icons, but also they functioned as sites of worship, as Chris Rojek has noted about the religious aspects of celebrity culture, to which fans could flock to commune with, or remember, their favorite idols. The pathway, which is continually updated and extended with new stars, provided an opportunity for fans to "visit with," and thereby feel physically close to, famous figures.

TV and Political Celebrity

Comedians, actors, and contestants were not the only ones who needed to appear more accessible on TV. In the 1940s, radio and newsreels had made politicians less remote and more familiar, their voices and words giving a sense of sobriety and, at times, comfort to a wartime listening public. But television, with its emphasis on appearance and style, further humanized—and celebrified—political figures, making them more enfolded into everyday life for many Americans. And while Harry Truman would become the first president to have his nomination speech televised (and to treat the public to a televised tour of the White House), it was Dwight D. Eisenhower who fully embraced the medium, appearing on *The Ed Sullivan Show*, palling around with Abbott and Costello, and inaugurating the first use of political ads on TV. In his "I Like Ike" TV spots, Eisenhower encouraged Americans to call a president by his nickname, bolstering his appeal with catchy jingles and smiling self-portraits.[30] He also held televised news conferences that were, however, taped, not live, and he appeared on air in fireside chats. Eisenhower's embrace of television was recognized in 1956, when he was presented with an Emmy Award for his use and encouragement of the medium.

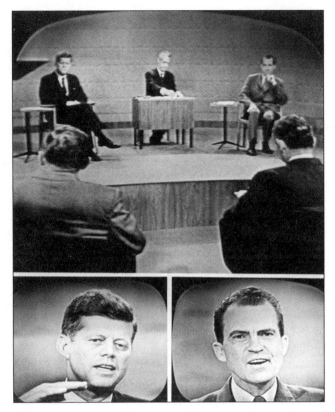

Figure 5.2. Kennedy-Nixon debate, 1960. Getty Images. Reprinted with permission.

By the time the junior senator from Massachusetts, John F. Kennedy, debated Vice President Richard Nixon in the fall of 1960, political and media figures had become one and the same. But it was this, the first live televised presidential debate, that would illustrate the visual power of the medium to influence public opinion. Leading up to the debate, Nixon suffered from a knee injury that resulted in hospitalization and notable weight loss, and, as the debate wore on, his noteworthy political experience was eclipsed by his frail appearance. Nixon appeared nervous, especially when the camera caught him listening to Kennedy's answers, marked by his eyes shifting back and forth, pursed lips, and, perhaps most remarkably, sweating. As Goffman reminds us, these were ungovernable acts, that Nixon did not or could not control, seeming to reveal his true self. Meanwhile, the youthful and handsome Kennedy was tanned and poised. Instead of speaking to the moderator, Kennedy addressed his remarks directly to the camera, telegraphing his message into the homes of the American viewing public with steady eye contact and a Massachusetts accent. It was famously reported that those who listened to the debate on radio felt that Nixon had won it; however, by a "broad margin" the seventy million viewers watching TV at home felt Kennedy had.[31] The face-off highlighted the importance of visual self-presentation and the cultivation of a likeable and trustworthy televisual persona. JFK understood this, using the medium to help shape the public image of his presidency, his family, and his administration. He inaugurated the live, televised press conference, which showed off, in part, his quick wit and sense of humor.

First Lady Jaqueline Kennedy, young, slim and classically beautiful compared to recent previous first ladies, seemed more like a movie star than a politician's wife, and captivated the media, with photos of her appearing on the cover of fan magazines like *Photoplay* (sample headline: "America's Newest Star"). The streamlined Oleg Cassini coat and Halston pillbox hat that Mrs. Kennedy donned at her husband's inaugural swearing in sparked public attention; her appearance symbolized a new kind of White House, one where youth, glamour, and a willingness to defy tradition were on display. In 1962, she led the public through an at-home-with-the-Kennedys style tour in the special *A Tour of the White House with Mrs. John F. Kennedy*. Like the celebrity home tours of Murrow's *Person to Person*, the special allowed viewers to feel a sense of personal connection with the First Lady, and with the institutions of American democracy. Carefully staged elegant events and images, of White House galas featuring renowned artists like Pablo Casals or Leonard Bernstein, to which the media were invited, were exemplars of the new marriage between television and public relations for the presidency. JFK also made sure that photographs of his small children playing in the Oval Office were released to the press, to cement the image of the administration's youthful energy. Jacqueline Kennedy became a groundbreaking First Lady, who gave so many interviews with newspaper, magazine, and television reporters that she became the first presidential wife to have her own press secretary. She became an icon for her beauty, fashions, and poise and, quickly, one of the most famous women in the world.

Early TV news was limited to fifteen-minute broadcasts—it was not until September 1963 that the networks expanded coverage to a half hour. Two months later, the assassination of JFK would push the boundaries of television news, challenging industry standards as anchors sought to keep a stunned American public informed and calm. In the days that followed the shooting, broadcast journalism would overshadow print coverage, and reporters like Chet Huntley and Walter Cronkite would become the trusted faces who helped lead viewers through a collective, real-time grieving process. According to Nielsen, 93 percent of U.S. homes watched the networks' coverage of the assassination—more than half of them for thirteen or more straight hours.[32] In the days to come, the public saw images of Jackie, her pink suit stained with her husband's blood and, later, the veiled widow standing beside her children, Caroline and John Jr., as her small son saluted his father. Viewers mourned along with Jackie. Television, which had allowed the public to get to know her in the early days of the Kennedy administration, had held her and her family up as a shining example, and was now providing a window into a tragedy that was both deeply personal and publicly enacted.

Throughout the 1960s, political figures would continue to appear on television, exemplifying the visual power of the medium and its ability to influence politics and pop. The social movements of the era—from civil rights to women's liberation to the peace movement—were fueled in part by a sense of collective engagement made possible by Americans' common televisual viewing experiences. Influential, charismatic leaders in government, social justice, and the culture industries came to represent a new kind of fame, driven not by some individual desire for success, celebrity, or wealth, but by a desire to realize social change and advocate for progressive agendas. Yet like traditional stars, the power of these leaders lay in their ability to attract and persuade audiences, and the new visual medium helped them to do just that.

When Martin Luther King Jr. stood on the steps of the Lincoln Memorial in August 1963 and outlined his dream for America, his baritone voice, call-and-response style, and allegorical language coupled with his appearance—commanding, powerful, energized—transported viewers across the country to the mall, into the crowd, alongside 250,000 other Americans, young and old, black and white, who had gathered together in solidarity. When King spoke of white men and women banding

together with black men and women, viewers saw that very dream realized in the march itself. Sweeping images showed the Washington mall,
filled with a massive crowd, responding to King's words, clapping and
cheering together, as one. The camera also panned across the Lincoln
Memorial, visually recalling the nation's history of slavery and eventual
progress. In all of these ways, television brought King, and his dreams,
into American households while also visually connecting him to American history, situating his message alongside national monuments, persistent sentinels of those influential leaders who had come before.

Meanwhile, television politicized, and celebrified, members of the
American space program. Throughout the 1960s, the United States
engaged in an ongoing effort to advance space exploration, a mission
fueled in large part by a Cold War desire to complete with the Soviet
Union's 1957 success in placing the first artificial satellite into Earth's
orbit.[33] The ongoing efforts of NASA (the National Aeronautics and
Space Administration) were well documented in the press, and audiences followed closely as each new mission, flown by daring astronauts,
brought with it the risk of life-ending failure or stunning achievement.
Television narratives about the space program cast the race between the
United States and the Soviet Union as a nationalistic horse race and the
crew members as heroes. John Glenn, the first man to orbit the Earth in
1962, and an extremely gregarious and media-savvy astronaut, became
so famous that he easily converted his NASA stardom into a long-lived
political career in the Senate, carrying all eighty-eight counties in Ohio
when he ran in 1974.[34] When the Apollo 11 completed the first lunar
landing on July 20, 1969, TV coverage was nonstop, and the event was
viewed by 528 million people around the world (though not in the Soviet
Union).[35] Special cameras were designed to give the audience a clear
view of the sharp contrast between the surface of the moon and the
black sky. So when Neil Armstrong took his "giant leap for mankind," he
and his comrade "Buzz" Aldrin became American heroes, and national
celebrities.[36]

Fame and politics have been intertwined since ancient times,[37] but
television made this relationship highly visible. As the nightly news
rolled into the evening's entertainment, politicians and performers no
longer seemed to occupy distinct worlds. Their faces and expressions,

their interviews and speeches, appeared alongside one another. Soon celebrities from the worlds of music, film, and art would publicly express their political views, influence public opinion, and run for office. Meanwhile, political figures were increasingly being covered, and judged by the public, for their appearance, personal affairs, and charisma—media narratives formerly reserved for movie stars. Richard Nixon, having lost both the presidency in 1960 and his bid for governor of California in 1962, turned to public relations (PR) men and television specialists to rebrand himself as "the New Nixon" in 1968. Television, and expanded news coverage, especially of the various social movements of the late 1960s and early 1970s, also meant that leaders of those movements like Abbie Hoffman and Jerry Rubin of the Yippies, or Betty Friedan and Gloria Steinem of the women's movement, also became political celebrities.

With the increasing impact of television news in the 1970s and beyond, the proliferation of political talk shows, and the televising of political conventions, politicians had even more opportunities to be seen—and make a splash or a gaffe—before a national audience. Speeches at political conventions—California governor Ronald Reagan in 1976, New York governor Mario Cuomo's keynote speech in 1984 (which made many delegates wish that he, and not Walter Mondale, was the nominee), then Senator Barack Obama's keynote speech at the 2004 Democratic convention, propelled all these men to political stardom. Performing well on television (and relying on media coaches to help one do so) has now become absolutely essential to political success. And with the election of reality TV star Donald Trump as president, we have seen how celebrity power in the televisual realm can be converted to power in the political realm.

Chatting with the Stars: The Expansion of Audience Discourse

Talk television shows also worked to further diminish the divide that separated celebrities from audiences and to enhance identification with certain stars. Where early variety shows brought celebrities on as performers or to engage them in scripted repartee with the host, now they were sitting down for interviews, divulging details about their professional and personal interests. Steve Allen (1954–57) and then Jack Paar (1957–62) pioneered in hosting the late night talk show, in which an unassuming but quick-witted host, sometimes seeming to be starstruck himself, served as a stand-in for audience admiration of and curiosity about celebrities. They also had routines that involved going into the audience for interviews or banter, breaking the proscenium boundary that typically separated the famous host from everyday people.

In 1962, Johnny Carson, having starred in his own successful variety show on CBS, took over hosting duties at *The Tonight Show*, where he seemed to perfect the late-night talk show format. Carson showcased sketch comedy and especially ingratiated himself to viewers through his monologues, which sometimes required studio audience interaction, and when a gambit bombed, evoked self-deprecating jokes and zingers. He became especially known for his reaction shots, his resigned or faux-embarrassed facial expressions when a comedy bit or interview was going south; these intimate and disarming displays were especially funny and endearing to his fans. Carson became famous for his interviews—he did about 21,000 of them over thirty years—with all kinds of stars, ranging from Groucho Marx, to Barbara Streisand, Betty White, Dolly Parton, and Jimmy Stewart, as well as a rotating roster of musical acts and even everyday people who were quirky or had done something noteworthy.

Carson's dominance over the late night slot and his emergence as one of the most powerful men in television meant that appearing on *The Tonight Show* indicated you had arrived. Carson thus played a key role in making various comics, like Jay Leno and Roseanne Barr, stars in their own right after they appeared on his show. Carson's charm, along with the new, more casual interview format, engaged both audience and guest in what came across as a kind of public conversation between friends. Today, so many interviews with stars on late night programs seem highly orchestrated as they tell some preplanned anecdote or two and then promote their latest "project." But Carson succeeded in having genuine and often surprising conversations with stars, many of whom later reported that they forgot the viewing audience was there and felt like they were talking just to him. As a result, viewers often felt they got a new and different glimpse into the personality and life of that celebrity.[38]

Figure 5.3. *The Tonight Show* starring Johnny Carson, 1982, NBC. Getty Images. Reprinted with permission.

Carson's relaxed, conversational interview format would soon be adopted within and beyond the network nighttime circuit, influencing the content and style of morning news shows and daytime talk programs for decades to come. Over the years, the structure of the talk show evolved, as some hosts traded desks for couches, encouraged participation from the studio audience, and hailed viewers with their casual style, humorous banter, and direct address to viewers at home. Talk shows celebrate famous figures, showcasing their personalities and highlighting their achievements, but they also present celebrities as accessible, relatable individuals. So many of these hosts became stars that by the 1970s a not uncommon fantasy was to aspire to have your own talk show.

As P. David Marshall points out, television hosts are treated as people whom "everyone has a right to know fully," so "the construction of sincerity and conviction is supposed to be part of the authentic host. There is little mystery."[39] Their job is to be personable, to be a conduit for our engagement with their guests. As they walk among members of the studio audience and speak directly to the camera, to the viewers at home, talk show hosts become our allies, likeable mediators who bridge

Figure 5.4. Oprah Winfrey, 1978. Getty Images.
Reprinted with permission.

the gap between celebrities and audiences. Over time, we bond with the
host, come to trust him or her; in turn, our fandom celebrifies them.
So trusted was Oprah Winfrey by her fans, who knew and called her
only by her first name, and so vast was her audience that she became a
lifestyle guru; her endorsement of a book or product meant that it was
certain to fly off the shelves.

Sports Celebrities and Television

At the height of radio, sports figures who gained favorable press and
celebrity status were those whose achievements were outsized, but who
also knew how to present themselves as deserving heroes. On their front
stage they needed to appear cooperative and modest with the press,
appreciative of and flattering to their fans, boosters of their team and
the city in which they played. But now being telegenic, performing well
on camera and during televised interviews also mattered to an athlete's
fortunes. Some worked assiduously to establish their own distinctive
brands as athletes, which made them very attractive as endorsers of

various products. Interacting with television coverage was the ongoing power of sports journalism, which writer Danny Peary argues began to change in the late 1950s. A new breed of sportswriters was less reverential toward famous athletes, more brash, and less interested in statistics than in asking personal questions and probing one's private life.[40] Thus, increasingly, sports celebrities had to further hone the art of public relations in their pregame and postgame interviews, as well as in personal profiles. Sports heroes, especially in the age of television, have faced enormous pressure to be "role models." And with the rise first of the civil rights movement and then the women's movement, the political and social context of the 1960s and 1970s also shaped who would and would not gain celebrity status as an athlete.

In the early days of television, the networks were desperate to fill time and often turned to sports programming to do so. By the early and mid-1950s, television increasingly became the way that most audiences consumed sports. Baseball, well established on radio, led the way, and by the mid-1950s baseball was a staple of TV, and the medium turned players like Mickey Mantle, Willie Mays, Roger Maris, and Don Drysdale into national celebrities. Los Angeles Dodgers power pitcher Drysdale appeared as himself—a sports celebrity—on various television shows, including *Leave It to Beaver*. The Yankees' Mickey Mantle was already a sports hero by the late 1950s thanks to television and cross-promotional appearances on entertainment programs like *The Ed Sullivan Show*, and he and fellow Yankee Roger Maris (dubbed the M&M boys) saw their fame soar in 1961 when the two were engaged in a race to break Babe Ruth's homerun record, which Maris did when he hit his sixty-first homer on October 1, 1961. In an interview with Yankee sportscaster Mel Allen earlier that fall, the clean-cut, self-effacing, and reserved Maris talked about being swarmed by photographers and journalists every day and embodied the humility still expected from sports heroes when he bemoaned the fact that except for Mantle his teammates were not also getting the attention they deserved.

But despite his record-breaking feat, Maris was the victim of negative coverage. A small-town guy from Fargo, North Dakota, Maris was not used to playing on a national stage and having his privacy probed. His first mistake, when it was rumored that he would be traded from Kansas City to the Yankees, was when he said he didn't want to go, which the New York press interpreted as Maris feeling he was "too good for New York" rather than his concern about how the Yankees allegedly treated their players. Thus Maris was tagged with the worst slam an athlete could get: that he had a "bad attitude." *Sports Illustrated* in 1961 noted that Maris was probably at the time the most relentlessly covered athlete and reporters asked him all kinds of personal, often ridiculous questions. Maris was married yet was asked "Do you play around on the road?" Another asked who his favorite female singer was, and when Maris said he didn't have one, the writer said, "Would it be alright if I wrote Doris Day," to which Maris responded testily, "How could you write Doris Day when I tell you I don't have a favorite?" But when asked if he truly wanted to beat Babe Ruth's record, Maris would say "Damn right" without including the obligatory paeans to what a great player Ruth was. As he pursued the home run record in September 1961, Maris made three crucial public relations errors for a sports celebrity: he criticized the fans at Yankee Stadium, the calls of an umpire, and refused to meet with reporters after a doubleheader.[41]

Legendary slugger Mantle, meanwhile, brought in to replace legend Joe DiMaggio in 1951, early on told an interviewer he didn't think anyone could fill DiMaggio's shoes, fulfilling the modesty requirement. The city's press also favored Mantle, who had been with the team for ten years, for his more gregarious personal style, and hoped he, not Maris, would break Ruth's record (injury prevented him from finishing the 1961 season). The press heightened interest in the home-run race by promoting a rivalry between the two men, who were actually friends, and urged readers to choose sides. Most chose Mantle.

And then came football, whose popularity on television eventually hurt baseball. Unlike the leisurely pace of baseball, which was not dependent on time constraints, football was well suited to television broadcast because its breaks more easily allowed for networks to show commercials. Although initially not profitable for the teams, by the mid-1950s the commercial potential of televised football was clear. In 1959, NFL commissioner Pete Rozelle convinced football franchise holders to negotiate as a group, and this was hugely lucrative; by 1963, CBS was paying $14 million a year for the broadcasting rights to NFL games.[42]

The man who revolutionized sports on television, and thus the proliferation of sports celebrities, was Roone Arledge at ABC, who brought

Monday Night Football (1970), *Wide World of Sports* (1961), and the Olympics to the airwaves, making athletes, as well as sports announcers like Jim McKay and Howard Cosell, celebrities as well. Arledge pledged to use a variety of technologies—cameras mounted on jeeps, on helicopters—to "add show business to sports!"[43] He pioneered in using production staples we take for granted today—instant replays, slow motion, freeze-frames, split screens, handheld cameras, end-zone cameras—all of which glorified the athlete and his or her feats. *Wide World of Sports* (with its instantly famous tagline "the thrill of victory, the agony of defeat") rested on the premise that you could make viewers interested in athletic events previously not televised and in which most viewers did not already have an interest: track and field, pole vaulting, cliff diving, skiing, gymnastics, ice skating. By the mid-1970s, the gold medalist in skating Dorothy Hamill (whose short haircut started a fad), gymnast Nadia Comăneci, and boxer Sugar Ray Leonard became national and even international stars, with Hamill becoming a celebrity spokesperson for a variety of products over the years.

Monday Night Football also became a sensation—its first broadcast in 1970 garnered 33 percent of the viewing audience—and was another celebrity production machine. The show was anchored by the often pompous Howard Cosell (both the most-loved and most-hated sportscaster at the time and a ratings generator), former Dallas quarterback Don Meredith, and Keith Jackson. The Jets, with their chisel-faced star quarterback Joe Namath, played in the first broadcast. Namath (known as "Broadway Joe") became one the of the first football pop culture icons, wearing a fur coat on the sidelines and promoting himself as a sex symbol. (This was the height of the sexual revolution, and it was becoming easier and more acceptable for those athletes who fit the role to present themselves in a more sexualized fashion.) Namath easily converted his sports stardom into endorsement deals, acting in television shows and movies, and famously in television commercials, including one for Noxzema shaving cream where he was provocatively shaved by then unknown star Farrah Fawcett ("You've got a great pair of hands," he tells her) and in an ad wearing pantyhose, telling women if they could make his legs look good, think of what they would do for yours.

Heisman Trophy winner and star running back O. J. "The Juice" Simpson also converted his sports celebrity status into television and movie roles (*Roots, The Towering Inferno*), as a commentator on *Monday Night Football*, and, famously, as a celebrity endorser for Hertz rental cars, where he was seen running through airports to get his car with the tagline "The Superstar in rental car." It was this clean-cut and heroic image that made the subsequent murder charges so enormously shocking. Television had made football one of the most popular sports in the country; National Football League commissioner Pete Rozelle admitted in the 1960s that, without television, half of its teams would not exist and the rest would be struggling.[44]

With the increasingly rapid racial integration of American sports in the 1960s and beyond, interacting with growing TV news coverage of the civil rights movement, television also accelerated the production of African American sports heroes. One of the most dynamic, controversial, and icon breaking was Cassius Clay, who in 1964 changed his name to Muhammad Ali, dismissing Clay as "a slave name. I didn't choose it and I don't want it." Unlike the deferential and humble Joe Louis in the 1930s and 1940s, or Jackie Robinson in the late 1940s who endured racial slurs and threats with a quiet dignity, Ali (then Clay) was two things a sports hero was not supposed to be: a totally cocky braggart, and one vocally derisive of and blisteringly insulting to his opponents. For this alone he gained the visibility he needed to become a contender.

He was also hugely charismatic, and became an international star because of his incredible speed and skill as a boxer, but also because he upturned the athlete's rules of self-presentation. What he introduced to sports stardom was unpredictability and the drama of defying the accepted rules of athletic comportment. This element of sports stardom—anticipation, what would he do or say next—affected other sports as well, including tennis and basketball. Prior to his match against Sonny Liston for the heavyweight boxing championship in 1964, Ali predicted his win, proclaimed to reporters on TV "I am the greatest" and "If he falls in eight, I'll prove I'm great, and if he keeps talking jive, I'm gonna turn it to five." He boasted that he would "float like a butterfly and sting like a bee." No one had spoken to sports reporters like this before, and when Liston—the 8–1 favorite to win—failed to return to the ring after the seventh round, Ali proclaimed to the stunned reporters that he was indeed the greatest and chastised them for not believing his predictions.

Ali and sportscaster Howard Cosell further enhanced their visibility through their interviews and banter with each other. They embodied a team performance in which they would, by turns, buttress and undermine each other. Cosell, a Jew who had been blacklisted in the 1950s, caught the attention of Roone Arledge because of a 1962 interview with Ali. He was one of the first sportscasters to address Ali by his new chosen name, and his biographer reports that Cosell was one of the few white sportscasters to gain the trust of African American athletes. Overall, Cosell's attitude toward his subjects, sports stars, and his relationship with Ali helped to establish a more human-interest, celebrity-focused side to sports journalism and was mutually beneficial to both their careers. The interviews were characterized by their chemistry and became "an iconic fixture of American broadcasting." Ali would razz Cosell that he followed Ali everywhere just so he could keep his name in the papers, while Cosell would counter that "you'd still be stealing bikes in Louisville" if it wasn't for Cosell.[45] Ali's subsequent matches, the 1974 "Rumble in the Jungle" against Joe Frazier and the 1975 rematch the "Thrilla in Manilla," were must-see media spectacles.

Tennis was another sport transformed by television, vastly increasing the visibility of the sport and its players. The U.S. Open was first broadcast in 1968, and by 1969 NBC began airing taped coverage of the men's finals at Wimbledon. In 1979, NBC's "breakfast at Wimbledon" carried the men's and women's finals live. Television challenged the tradition-bound sport, especially by the 1970s, when more brash, "bad boy" players—Jimmy Conners, John McEnroe, Ilie Nastase (nicknamed "nasty") —outraged traditionalists but also increased ratings—and their brand as stars—by yelling at the linesmen, having mini tantrums on court, and throwing their racquets to the ground. At the same time, because there were now televised pre- and postgame interviews, players also had to develop their PR skills, thanking and flattering the fans ("New York fans are the best!") and being complimentary to those they defeated. The rules were different for women. Tennis was one of the few televised sports outside of the Olympics that featured female athletes, and feminine codes of behavior meant they could not act out in the same way that the men players did. Increased coverage made many players—women as well—international stars, which led to increased advertising support and product endorsements.

Billie Jean King, by 1967 the top-ranked women's player in the world, and an outspoken advocate for equal prize money for women, threatened to boycott the U.S. Open in 1973 if the tournament's pay inequality was not addressed; it was. That same year, the 1939 Wimbledon champion, Bobby Riggs, a provocative sexist (and self-promoter) who baited women players by claiming they could never be as good as the men, challenged King to a match. Labeled the "Battle of the Sexes" and set in the Houston Astrodome, the televised match attracted an estimated fifty million viewers. Remember that this was during the height of the women's movement, when women were challenging their second-class citizenship through massive demonstrations and lawsuits, so the match became symbolic of these very immediate battles. Both players embraced the televisual spectacle, with Riggs rolling in on a rickshaw pulled by a team of women called "Bobby's Bosom Buddies" and King carried onto the court in a gold litter carried by four beefy men. Riggs had promoted the match for weeks by bragging about how handily he would beat King, but she defeated him in straight sets to the delight of women all across the country. She later acknowledged the pressure she felt as a role model and exemplar for all women: "I thought it would set us back 50 years if I didn't win that match."[46] With the arrival of the Williams sisters, Venus and Serena, in the early twenty-first century and their domination of the sport, which led to endorsements and appearing in fashion spreads, African American women had become international sports celebrities as well.

Television also increased attention to basketball and its players. The sport was minimally covered in the press in the 1950s, so TV was crucial to its economic fortunes. Coaches and players criticized the early coverage in the 1950s, feeling it was too crude, that there were not enough close-ups of players during the game (especially when they scored or missed a shot), and not enough interviews with players and coaches.[47] Basketball posed opportunities and challenges to television. Its fast pace was well suited to the medium but the constant play left little or no time for commercial breaks; hence the need for more "time-outs." But Roone Arledge argued that "[p]hysically, professional basketball is an excellent sport for television; it's played in a confined area and the cameras can be placed to show the agility, finesse, and contact." The ball was large and easy to see, there could be increasingly dramatic shots, and the games were never rained out. Yet Arledge also felt that, unlike football, the commentators were not doing enough to explain the strategies involved in the game.

In the mid-1960s, Arledge's ABC began airing National Basketball Association (NBA) games during prime time, and ratings started to increase. Popularity stalled in the 1970s, attributed to poor announcing, the hiring and firing of too many sportscasters and thus no personalities to attach to, and boring halftime presentations. In addition, some of the teams in major cities were deemed weak, as well as "dull and faceless."[48]

What changed the game's fortunes was Larry Bird joining the Boston Celtics and Magic Johnson joining the Los Angeles Lakers in 1979. The two had faced off in the NCAA (National College Athletic Association) championships, generating the highest ratings for a championship game, and what came to be known as the Bird-Johnson era began. Both players had spectacular first seasons, with Bird named Rookie of the Year and Johnson named Most Valuable Player in the NBA finals. By now there were superstars who played great basketball and embodied different styles of play and personality types. Julius Erving—"Dr. J"—known for his dramatic leaping style of shooting baskets, was "a symbol of grace and dignity"; Kareem Abdul-Jabbar, known for his trademark "skyhook" shot, the symbol of "consistency"; Larry Bird, regarded by some as one of the greatest players ever, personified tenacity and a determined work ethic on the court; and Magic Johnson "personified a person having fun with his job." This "divergence of personalities" brought the NBA into its "golden age."[49] By the mid-1980s, the NBA was the fastest growing and most financially successful league in team sports, with Johnson and Bird the two best-known athletes in the country, and when Michael Jordan (also regarded as one of the best players ever) eclipsed both of them, he replaced Muhammad Ali as the most famous athlete in the world.[50]

The television cameras with their freeze-frames, instant slow-motion replays, and repeated airing of certain shots, in addition to close-ups of the players, served to visually enhance the seemingly superhuman status of these stars. At the same time, these technologies allowed us to scrutinize, memorize, and imitate every move, providing a game plan for wishful identification that allowed viewers to imagine that sports stardom could one day be in their future, or reminisce about their own glory days.

When Jordan joined the Chicago Bulls in 1984, his performances doubled game attendance. He entertained crowds with his incredibly high scoring and slam dunks that earned him the name "Air Jordan," later, of course, marketed as athletic shoes. A media-savvy star who came across as likeable and a hard worker on the court, he became one of the most marketed athletes in sports history, endorsing Nike, of course, Coca-Cola, and McDonald's, to name a few. As Barry Smart observes in his book on sports celebrities, "There was a synergy between the ability, skill, bravery and competitive drive and will to win displayed on the basketball court by Jordan and the myth-making television advertising campaigns created by Nike." Both the Bulls and Nike "were beneficiaries of the circuits of cross-promotion that were created."[51]

Such perceived synergy could of course go wrong, as the O. J. Simpson case powerfully demonstrated. Tiger Woods, an enormously talented golfer, burst on the scene in 1996 and also became an international celebrity, in part because of his seeming embodiment—as a "multicultural ideal"—of the myth that America was transcending racial barriers. Part of his appeal came from the fact that he was breaking the barriers of a predominantly white sport. Several daring Nike ads, including "I am Tiger Woods," nearly deified him as the agent of a new "postracial" and multicultural future. He was "encoded as an antidote to an outdated race discrimination" and also as a clean-cut sports hero and, after his 2003 marriage, as a family man.[52] He became the world's most marketable athlete, signing endorsement deals with American Express, General Motors, Accenture, and a five-year, $105 million deal with Nike, the largest package ever signed by a sports hero. When his infidelities with multiple women came out in 2009, tarnishing his clean-cut image (and, sadly, reinforcing the image that men of color were sexuality promiscuous), he lost most of his endorsements. Tabloid journalism, beginning with revelations in the *National Enquirer*, revealed a huge gap between Woods' front stage and back stage personas, tarnishing his reputation, his performance, and his economic value.

Tabloidization: News and Infotainment

We see, then, that the media landscape was shifting throughout the 1950s and '60s, away from a model of celebrity that relied upon the audiences' sense of reverence and distance, and toward a model that celebrated access, knowability, and authenticity. The intimate and immediate nature of television played a critical role in facilitating this evolving attitude toward stardom. By the 1970s, this shift had expanded beyond the world of entertainment, infiltrating news coverage. Personality journalism was on the rise. Some of the public sought escape from the increasingly negative news surrounding the Vietnam War and the various social upheavals of the 1960s and early 1970s. Coverage of the Nixon administration and the breaking Watergate scandal may have been, as Anne Helen Peterson contends, "the final disillusionment" for a public suffering from "serious issue fatigue." Established publications like *Life* magazine and *Photoplay* were folding, but infotainment was taking off.

Time magazine's market research in the early 1970s revealed that the very first part most people turned to when they opened the magazine was its "People" section featuring brief tidbits about recent celebrity marriages, divorces, scandals, or accomplishments. So in March 1974, Time Inc. launched *People* magazine, with an emphasis on human interest stories, large photos, short, easily digestible stories, and, of course, celebrities. The production team behind the new title had honed their skills at nationally recognized publications like *Life* and *Time*. *People* was pitched as "a new magazine based on the old journalistic precept that names make news." In an interview with *Time* magazine, Managing Editor Richard Stolley put it this way: "We're getting back to the people who are causing the news and who are caught up in it, or deserve to be in it. Our focus is on people, not issues."[53] The premiere issue featured actress Mia Farrow, starring in *The Great Gatsby*, on the cover; designer and socialite Gloria Vanderbilt ("A fourth marriage that really works"); and a story about the wives of U.S. Vietnam veterans who were missing in action ("Demanding answers that nobody has"). Here, stories about world news appeared beside celebrity featurettes; tales of ordinary people were laid out across from those of the well-heeled and well-to-do.

On August 16, 1977, Elvis Presley died suddenly at the age of forty-two, shocking the nation. "For more than a decade," as Janice and Neal Gregory write in their account of the day, "CBS Evening News with Walter Cronkite had led the [evening news] ratings." But on that date, "the opening CBS headlines did not mention the story from Memphis. Millions of viewers, not finding the information they sought, immediately tuned out the video eye and switched to one of the other networks." NBC and ABC did lead with the story of Elvis's death, followed up that evening with late-night special coverage.[54] The network coverage showed not only that celebrity and hard news coverage were no longer relegated to separate journalistic worlds, but also that a failure to adequately cover a celebrity story that resonated with public interest could be devastating to mainstream news' ability to hold its audience.

In December of that same year, veteran journalist Barbara Walters premiered a show called *Specials*; in it, she conducted interviews with celebrity guests, asking very personal and sometimes ridiculous questions (Walters famously asked Katherine Hepburn what kind of tree she would like to be). Walters went into celebrities' homes herself with her cameras and would do whatever it took to manufacture intimacy, even if it meant, as it later did, lying with all the looseness of a driftwood log on a mattress with basketball star Dennis Rodman. Because such programs were ratings bait, and those chosen to be in them seen as stars above the others, there was a mutual interest between network and celebrity to abet the metastasizing of celebrity culture on television. In addition, closely guarded boundaries between "hard" and entertainment news, celebrity and politics, public and private, were shown to be flimsy and tenuous constructions.

The regulatory environment governing television also changed in the early 1980s, providing a much more welcoming climate for celebrity-based programming. Back in the 1940s, the Federal Communications Commission set forth policies that required local radio stations to include "discussions of public issues, programs covering religious, educational and civic matters" and local news in its programming. No quantity of time was specified, except that it had to be "adequate" and during "the good listening hours." The FCC reiterated these principles in 1960, which now of course applied to television as well. Then in 1973, the FCC stipulated that at least 10 percent of a station's programming had to be "non-entertainment," and in 1976 further specified that 5 percent of programming had to be local programming, and 5 percent news and public affairs.[55] Many stations devoted the 7:00 to 8:00 p.m. time slot to news and public affairs shows to meet these requirements.

But under the Ronald Reagan–Mark Fowler FCC in the early 1980s, the requirement to offer a certain percentage of nonentertainment programming—locally produced documentaries, talk and public affairs programs—was eliminated, although stations were still expected to "provide programming responsive to community issues."[56] Also in the 1980s the practice of stations' and networks' entertainment divisions "carrying" (covering the costs of) the news divisions changed; now news divisions were expected to generate their own profits. At many local stations this led to more sensationalism, "news you can use," and "if it bleeds, it leads" journalism, instead of in-depth reporting about their communities. It also led to the replacement of public affairs programming with celebrity journalism, like CBS's newly syndicated *Entertainment Tonight* (1981), which introduced viewers to a nightly rundown of "breaking news," all of which revolved around celebrity culture, and *Lifestyles of the Rich and Famous* (1984), with its tours of the most opulent homes in the world, especially those of showbiz celebrities.

The advent of cable news shattered any remaining barriers between these two worlds. The rise of cable television in the 1980s expanded the viewing field by offering audiences a broader array of channels. Prior to the popularization of cable stations, television viewing was limited to the three networks—ABC, NBC, and CBS—or to public broadcast television. These stations aimed to appeal to the broadest possible audience, and therefore produced specific types of content that would be accessible to viewers of many ages and backgrounds. Cable ushered in the era of more: more stations, eventually hundreds of them, more shows, more choices, all of it more targeted. The collective viewing practices of the "national market," wherein one or two shows might attract a third of the entire viewing public, was made possible by the limited choices of network TV. More choices meant increased market segmentation; niche viewing replaced mass viewing, affording audiences a wide range of viewing options suited to their interests and tastes. Channels now needed to "brand" themselves and to produce shows that would attract specific demographic niches of interest to advertisers. Cable news needed an endless stream of content to fill the twenty-four-hours-a-day, seven-days-a-week airtime. Celebrity news helped meet those needs.

Cable television allowed for the creation and promotion of new types of celebrities, sometimes eccentric individuals whose specific interests and expertise were targeted to increasingly diffuse demographic groups—the quirky sexual therapist Dr. Ruth on Lifetime (television for women), sports announcers like ESPN's George Grande, even child stars like the cast of Nickelodeon's *You Can't Do That on Television*—who spoke to audiences about their particular interests and desires. The act of watching television was becoming one of active selection, identification, and participation on the part of the viewer, not just a mode of entertainment but a way of making a claim about one's individual personality and self-concept. Through television, actors, singers, comedians, talk show hosts, athletes, politicians, and newscasters became celebrities. And as the number of channels expanded in the 1980s and beyond, there was a greater need for recognizable personalities to launch shows, and greater opportunities for everyday people to become stars.

From its inception, the technological affordances of television, especially its proximity to the viewer and its locus within the home, both benefitted from and supported celebrities whose appeal was based in friendliness and relatability. As the television market continued to grow with new cable stations and subscription-based platforms like HBO and Showtime, the amount of airtime that needed to be filled expanded. So, too, did the number and types of opportunities to launch individuals into television stardom. Though the medium remains dynamic—its content, distribution mechanisms, and modes of audience engagement have all continued to evolve over the past fifteen years—television still produces stars with whom the audience can interact and feel akin. Television celebrities function as examples of Hermes's extended family; whether we watched our *Friends*, Rachel and Joey, or tuned in weekly to swoon over McDreamy on *Grey's Anatomy*, or, more recently, even following the sometimes jaw-dropping machinations in the mythological world of *Game of Thrones*, we have a sense that these characters (and the stars who play them) are part of our experience of everyday life.

By the early 2000s, these modes of interaction would no longer be purely parasocial, as new programming models would increasingly call upon the public to participate by casting a vote, or by *actually casting* ordinary viewers in the role of TV star in a new wave of "reality-based" programming that would come to dominate television content and launch a new celebrity media frenzy in the twenty-first century. Soon, it would become clear, anything, or anyone, could serve as the center point of a television series, as a new crop of fashion designers, aspiring chefs, singers, competitive dancers, and makeup artists would find their place alongside more traditional television celebrities.

6

Musical Celebrity

Why is it, when we want to emphasize that someone is highly acclaimed in his or her field, we say they're "a rock star"? Successful movie and TV stars have fame, wealth, and widespread visibility, but they don't have what the rock, pop, country, or rap star has: being worshipped by thousands of live fans at your feet. You are elevated on a stage, dazzling lights dramatizing your moves, sometimes being suspended above the crowd by wires, Jumbotrons making you larger than life, a stadium full of adoring fans screaming, cheering, applauding your every move. In the realm of celebrity, especially in the late twentieth and early twenty-first centuries, it has been music stars who have been especially deified. Why is that, what role do they play in our lives, and what technologies of production have enabled this phenomenon?

What makes someone a rock, pop, country, or hip-hop star? Why do some remain stars for decades while others do not? And why is our fandom of musical performers—whether it's Beyoncé, the Beatles, Bruce Springsteen, Jay Z, Taylor Swift, Kendrick Lamar, or One Direction—often so powerful, often stronger than our attachment to film or television stars? Of course, there are different audiences for different styles of music (although many fans embrace multiple genres), and various of these styles produce their own stars who are tied to and build on particular taste cultures marked by age, race, gender, sexuality, and geography. But it is when the individual or the group, through their music, articulate our own fears, our hopes, our desires, our deepest feelings, and provide us with an "emotionally intensified sense of self"[1] that we connect with them.

The personal intensity of the performer is often crucial here to our bonding with the star. As fans we enter the personal and private realm of the singer and his or her feelings; the relationship between the performer and listener is deeply personal. We look for the symbolic significance of the music—what does the song mean to me, what does the singer express about me, my passions, my relationships, my hurts and losses? How does it capture my daily cares? This has been called "associative identification" when, through the music, the barriers between star and listener are broken down; it feels like they know us and we know them; we are actively participating in the meaning of the song to us.[2] For each of us a certain star's voice is sexy, evocative, haunting, and we connect with them when they express our passions, and "celebrate the inarticulate" feelings we have had but couldn't quite put into words.[3] Often through the language of confession, the use of metaphors, but also everyday phrases, the musical star helps us see things differently, or more clearly, and makes ordinary language "intense and vital."[4] So another element of fan-star identification is the "sheer pleasure of interpreting lyrics."[5] And certain stars and their music are tied to very particular moments in our lives.

The medium for these stars is, of course, music, which affects us physiologically. We hear music not only with our ears, but also feel it with our entire bodies—our bones, our innards vibrate, too, to music. In addition, the brain's musical networks and emotional circuits are connected: the auditory system of the brain feeds into the limbic system, the part of the brain from which we derive emotions and memory. The limbic system then generates a host of associations and emotional states, which is why certain songs and their performers are so powerfully tied into our memories and feelings.[6]

The technologies of listening, and the mechanical and then electronic reproduction of sound, from the gramophone to the stereo to the Walkman and then the iPod, have also transformed our relationship to the musical celebrity. All these devices privatized listening, furthering the intertwining of our personal experience with the meaning of the music, intensifying our sense of a "personal possession of the song and performer."[7]

Then there is the element to musical stardom that forcefully enhances it: the concert. We all know the rush of seeing our favorite band or performer up on stage, of becoming caught up in the moment, of hearing our voice echoed through the crowd as we sing the lyrics that we know by heart. Here, along with hundreds or, more typically, thousands of other like-minded fans, we are actually feeling similar sensations in our bodies at exactly the same time, which feels like a "collective celebration, a celebration of a community."[8] It is here, with fans stretching their arms toward the performers on stage, or collectively waving candles or lights in the air, singing along simultaneously—often at the performer's command—to the words of a song, that this form of celebrity culture can seem most like religion. And singing along with the star and the crowd is a version of "enunciative productivity," in which the audience adds further collective and individual meaning to the music. The concert is an enactment of the solidarity, the communion, between star and fan, and fans and each other. Over the years, various technologies—those in concert venues and those in our homes and cars—have enhanced this sense of communion.

Beatlemania

When the Beatles appeared on *The Ed Sullivan Show* in February 1964, the broadcast was viewed live by seventy-three million people—the largest audience for an entertainment program to date.[9] In front of a live studio audience of 700 screaming fans, mostly teenage girls (culled out of over 50,000 requests for seats), the band sparked a cultural phenomenon that produced its own moniker—Beatlemania. At the time, the Beatles were already a success in England; in December 1963, several American DJs had begun playing "I Want to Hold Your Hand,"[10] and by January 1964 the record had soared to the top of the charts, selling 1.5 million copies. In rapid succession, the Beatles released a series of hit songs and by April 1964 the band held the top five slots on *Billboard's* charts.

The Beatles may have been the most significant pop culture phenomenon of the mid-twentieth century. Why did they become such a sensation? It was a combination of talent, charisma, and promotion that intertwined with an emerging sense of youthful solidarity among baby boomers. Beatlemania is a perfect example of how heartfelt, bottom-up fandom merges with top-down celebrity craftsmanship to produce stars. First, like other achieved celebrities, they were extremely good as songwriters and performers, and they took their audience, especially their female audience, seriously. They did not pander or condescend to them; indeed, they conveyed that they understood and respected them. Their sheer joy of performing onstage was obvious and infectious. And like

Figure 6.1. Ed Sullivan and the Beatles, 1964. National Portrait Gallery, Smithsonian Institution.

Elvis before them, the Beatles reconfigured pop music, male performative styles, and the look of male pop stars, all of which spoke powerfully to baby boomers coming of age. Unlike Frankie Avalon or most other early 1960s white male pop stars, the Beatles wrote most of their own music, a sign of a new authenticity in rock, and played their own instruments; when they covered the songs of others, it was typically R&B hits like "Mr. Postman." They also embodied a less threatening sexuality than the often hypermasculinity of Elvis's performances. Onstage they exuded a kind of sexual energy that came across as completely genuine yet nonaggressive. As P. David Marshall observed, while Elvis, being white, may have given rock 'n' roll a more palatable image, he embodied an "African-American creative-though-culturally-threatening" star while the Beatles seemed so much more like the "boys-next-door."[11]

Brian Epstein, the Beatles' manager, also cultivated the American press to aggressively promote them prior to the band's U.S. arrival. Working with Capitol Records, which had released "I Want to Hold Your

Hand" and pushed DJs to play it, Epstein hired publicity agents to drive up interest in the group. New York City lampposts suddenly had "The Beatles Are Coming" stickers affixed to them; DJs in major markets got promotional material about the band; and, as anticipation grew, radio stations in New York vied to be *the* Beatles station as they hyped the band's imminent arrival at Kennedy airport. (WABC radio in New York started billing itself WA-Beatles-C.) When they landed, thousands of screaming fans greeted them.[12]

Historical context matters too. The Beatles arrived in the United States a mere eleven weeks after the assassination of President Kennedy, a traumatic shock to the nation. Kennedy was the youngest president since Theodore Roosevelt took office in 1901; his youthful exuberance, his faith in progress, and his quick wit with reporters especially captivated young people, who now felt bereft. The Beatles were highly irreverent and loved to joke with reporters, but in a way that both made fun of established norms without being negative or hostile. Asked why they had become so phenomenally successful, John quipped, "We have a press agent," mocking the rank commercialism of the industry. They tweaked pretension every chance they got, including making fun of themselves; "the Beatles' wit was contagious," noted the *New York Times*.[13] Through their clowning and mugging for reporters, they captured many young people's emerging contempt for middle-class conventionalism and for authority figures. The Beatles' joyful energy reaffirmed the vitality and spirit of what Kennedy had hailed as "a new generation" and that this spirit was alive and well.

Fans had their "own" Beatle—you were a "Paul" girl or a "John" girl and so forth. Girls chose the Beatle that they felt they most resembled, either physically or as a personality type, or the one they most wanted to be like, or, of course, the one they were most attracted to. Like a form of transportation, in which fans, through narratives or celebrities, can "try on" different personas, the identification with the Beatles, individually or together, brought many girls a feeling of completion. At a time when the aspirations of baby boom girls were being stoked by increased attendance at college and emergent social and political movements, the Beatles—with their long hair, Edwardian suits, boots with heels—acknowledged that there was masculinity and femininity in all of us. The Beatles' look signaled a shift in the era's ideals, a new willingness to embrace gender fluidity and androgyny.

These rock 'n' roll fans, screaming in ecstasy and pulling their hair, signaled the arrival of the teenaged baby boomer fan, powerful in their numbers, frenetically expressing the depth of their fandom and the power of that adoration. For the viewer at home, the impact of *The Ed Sullivan Show* performance lay not only in the ability to see, up close, the faces and demeanors of musicians previously only heard on radio and records, but also in seeing the uninhibited reactions of other fans, which signaled the power of this generation's collective expression and the extent to which pop idols could influence youth culture. Thus, the Beatles were also harbingers of a new wave of pop fandom, a cultural sea change buoyed by the baby boom, who were now growing into young adulthood, challenging the trappings of often conformist middle-class Americana of the 1950s and the bland, safe, deliberately inoffensive cultural offerings that went with it, especially on television. In their sheer numbers, baby boomers constituted a new phenomenon—youth culture—that would come to define a new economically and politically powerful segment of the media market audience.

The Beatles also embodied the crucial fault line that had come to divide musical celebrity: that between performers seen as "authentic" and those seen as cynically manufactured just to sell records. As Simon Frith has noted, the "struggle between music and commerce is [at] the core of rock ideology" and has played a central role in demarcating, for different fans, who is and is not a legitimate object of musical fandom. Hence the derision typically heaped upon "teenybopper" music and boy bands, seen as produced with almost assembly-line precision to extract money from preteen girls. Authenticity—typically characterized as writing your own music that expresses your genuine feelings, experiences, and attitudes; emotional honesty and artistic intensity; musical or lyrical complexity, or both; instrumental or vocal virtuosity; and cultural, social, or political critique and rebellion—became by the mid-1960s the gold standard for identifying which music was art versus which music was commercial trash. Whether an individual star or group seemed authentic determined their critical success and the nature of their fandom. And while some female musical stars—Janis Joplin, Joni Mitchell, Pat Benatar, Beyoncé—earned the mantle of being "authentic," the discourse around authenticity and the dividing lines it polices are riddled with gender bias.

Once Elvis Presley—who was certainly seen as authentic by his fans—was drafted in 1958, music impresarios sought to produce replacements. These included Frankie Avalon (subsequently paired with ex-Mousketeer Annette Funicello in "Beach Blanket" movies), a blandly handsome dark-haired guy whose first song was "so perfectly made up and synthetic that it had to be a hit" and who was ceaselessly plugged on the after-school TV show *American Bandstand*. Another was Fabian, also dark-haired with a slight resemblance to Elvis, who "couldn't sing" and "knew it" but with enough promotion also had some hits.[14] The main counterpoint to such vapid and constructed pop idols were R&B groups and singers like the Silhouettes ("Get a Job," #1 hit, 1958), Sam Cooke ("You Send Me," #1 hit, 1957; "Chain Gang," #2 hit, 1961), the Shirelles ("Will You Love Me Tomorrow," #1 hit, 1960) and other mostly African American performers. Even though they usually did not write their own songs, they, by contrast, seemed genuine.

It was into this vacuum that the Beatles stepped. While manager Brian Epstein certainly produced their look—leather jackets and jeans gave way to matched suits and ties, and of course the identical "mop top" haircuts—the Beatles also met nearly all of the criteria of authenticity. And they did so during the height of the folk music revival, the embodiment of protest music and grass-roots authenticity.

From Rock 'n' roll to Rock

The 1960s was a period defined by rapid and tumultuous social change. Young people, frustrated by the injustices of segregation, the failings of capitalism, lack of equality in education and the workforce, restrictions on voting rights, and the ravages of the Vietnam War, were engaging in collective action to try to shape a new world, one which they would be proud to call their own. The earliest music to capture this disaffection was folk music. Bob Dylan and Joan Baez (whose 1961 album went gold) were noteworthy participants in the March on Washington in the summer of 1963 when Martin Luther King gave his "I Have a Dream" speech. When Dylan released his third album, *The Times They Are a-Changin'*, the following year, it was a clarion call, with lyrics (from the title song) like "The order is rapidly fadin'/ And the first one now will later be last / Cause the times they are a-changin'." Peter, Paul, and Mary became the most popular acoustic group of the 1960s, as well as the most overtly activist, and "brought protest music firmly into the mainstream."[15] Songs like "We Shall Overcome" and Sam Cooke's "A Change Is Gonna Come" served as spirit-lifting anthems for progressive activists and supporters working to end segregation.

By the mid-1960s rock 'n' roll, which had referred to a heterogeneous array of music from Elvis to girl group music, gave way to "rock," a more self-conscious and often politically informed music dominated by white guys with guitars. Most performers wrote their own songs and met most of the other criteria of "authenticity." At the same time, the audience for this music was seen as appreciating musical complexity and exceptional instrumental skill, as being independent minded, and thus able to distinguish between good, authentic music and bad, commercially contrived music.[16] Thus there was a strong sense of "kinship" between fans and performers, that "the stars weren't being imposed from above but had sprung up from out of our ranks."[17] In addition to the Beatles and then the Rolling Stones, a host of bands and performers—including Led Zeppelin, the Who, Pink Floyd, Jefferson Airplane, Jimi Hendrix, and Janis Joplin—became international stars, known for their musical virtuosity, creativity, and passion.

As with other modes of celebrity, technological developments enhanced rock stars' connections to their fans. Indeed, the late 1960s and early 1970s witnessed a complete auditory revolution that shaped musical stardom. The rise of the counterculture in America included a readiness and desire among young people to hear more challenging and complex music; there was an intensified quest for deeper, richer, more nuanced listening. The promotion of albums, as opposed to 45 rpm singles, to young people began with *Meet the Beatles* in 1964, which topped the charts by February. The year 1966 was the last year that singles outsold LPs.[18] Increasingly, these albums were being recorded with the new stereo technology, which produced a richer, deeper, layered sound that intensified appreciation of the performers' vocal and especially instrumental virtuosity. Single-unit record players gave way to stereo systems with separate components—amplifier, turntable, and the biggest speakers you could afford.

Music produced in stereo could increasingly be heard on a new radio band, FM. FM—frequency modulation—used a much wider band of frequencies for radio transmissions, providing a higher signal-to-noise ratio, which allowed for high fidelity sound reproduction and a greater suppression of static. This new system achieved a whole new level of clarity and lack of static interference unattainable with AM. In 1962, according to the FCC, there were 983 commercial FM stations on the air; in 1972, their number stood at 2,328. Four years later, there were nearly 3,700 FM stations on the air.[19] By 1972, in cities such as Chicago and Boston, it was estimated that 95 percent of households had FM sets.[20] FM radio, and the new stereo systems that showcased it, separated sounds, highlighted how they were layered, made the components of music more distinct and pure. When young people tuned to certain FM stations in the late 1960s, they entered a brand-new auditory, political, and cultural world. And they went there specifically to indulge in a newly heightened, much more concentrated mode of listening.[21] By the early 1970s, with the introduction of in-car stereos that played cassette tapes, drivers could listen to and blast stereo music while driving.

Musical stars determined to be seen as authentic and meriting stardom had to play to this technology, take it into account, and push it to its limits. This made certain songs—the Beatles' "A Day in the Life," the Chambers Brothers' "Time Has Come Today," Cream's "Sunshine of Your Love"—legendary for their play with instruments and sounds. Increasingly "live" concert recordings were produced to bring listeners to a performance they were unable to attend in person.

Just as the movie industry had spawned the fan magazine, this revolution in music produced publications dedicated to assessing and promoting the news stars. *Rolling Stone* in particular, launched in 1967, cast itself in opposition to typical fan magazines with their gushy, saccharine profiles of the stars. It was tied to the values of the counterculture and focused on musical criticism and political reporting, but did also take one "behind the scenes" of tours and the offstage lives of performers.

In the summer of 1969, nearly half a million concertgoers flocked to a farm in upstate New York, the Woodstock festival, forever linking popular music with youthful exuberance and counterculture rebellion. The festival is remembered not only for performances by rock pioneers like the Grateful Dead, Jefferson Airplane, Creedence Clearwater Revival, and Sly and the Family Stone, but also for the way in which it spoke to a new ethos of "free love," experimental drug use, and anticapitalist communalism. The musicians embodied these new ideals—in Jimi Hendrix's revolutionary electric guitar or the powerful vocals of Grace Slick, for example—but perhaps even more consequential was the festival experience, which showed that popular artists could come together to create a landmark cultural moment in which participants could connect not only with the music, but with one another. Here the musician was no longer just a pop idol, but a conduit for broader social change. Woodstock set the stage for an entire music festival industry, one that would spawn Lollapalooza, Glastonbury, Coachella, and dozens of others, which cater to (and monetize) audiences' desire to participate in this kind of collective experience.

Though the Beatles broke records in the mid-1960s when they played to huge crowds in massive venues like the Hollywood Bowl and Shea Stadium (which drew a live audience of 55,600 in 1965),[22] it was Led Zeppelin that would set the stage for the move to massive stadium rock. They broke the Beatles record with their 1973 performance at Tampa Stadium in Florida, which boasted a crowd of 56,800 fans and followed it up with a string of sold-out shows at New York's Madison Square Garden.[23] New, large-scale sound systems projected the band's experimental solos, pulling the audience in. But, as music scholar Simon Frith notes, stadium tours are not only about the rock gods on stage: "To experience heavy metal is to experience the power of the concert as a whole— the musicians are one aspect of this, the amplification system another, the audience a third. The individual fans get their kicks from being a necessary part of the overall process—which is why heavy metal videos always have to contain moments of live performance."[24] Such huge stadium performances, with their massive sound systems, light shows, and, later, Jumbotrons, began to transform country music celebrity and fandom as well.

Stardom, at least in rock, was now melded to virtuosity, but with few exceptions, it was a male-defined virtuosity based on mastery of the electric guitar or, to a lesser extent, drums. Eventually this came to be known (and criticized as) "cock rock," exemplified by superstar bands like Led Zeppelin, and then the "hair metal" bands of the late '70s and early '80s—from Van Halen and Motley Crüe to Whitesnake, Poison, and Bon Jovi, with their pleather pants, wild sexuality, and often very big hair. This new batch of bands embraced a hypermasculine persona (including overtly sexual lyrics) but also played with androgyny, with teased-out tresses, skintight clothes, and guyliner. The performers were "aggressive" and 'boastful" on stage, drawing attention to their musical prowess and instrumental control, turning their microphone stands and guitars into phallic symbols, or caressing them as if they were female bodies. Yet for some fans, such a performance style was alienating and threatening, and these fans, typically younger and female, were a market for music as well.

Heartthrobs and "Bubblegum"

It would be a mistake, then, to see the rise of the counterculture and the rock star as the only form of musical celebrity in the 1960s and '70s. In fact, it was the enormous success—and profits of—rock music that made various entrepreneurs and producers, totally unconcerned with "authenticity," interested in cashing in on musical fandom. What they sought was to manufacture and promote the latest "phenomenon."[25] Their stars could have all the markers of illegitimacy—not writing their own music, not playing their own instruments, trafficking in simply structured music and sappy love songs, appealing to preteens, chosen by producers or in a talent search, thus total and obvious products of a calculating music industry—and still become international stars.[26] They also become brands.

Take, for example, the TV show *The Partridge Family* (1970–74), depicting a fictional clan of musicians (based loosely on the popular, real-life family band the Cowsills). The show was so upbeat and exuberantly optimistic, even its poppy theme song urged us all to "Come on Get Happy." The fictional Partridge Family may have been acting on TV, and the show never ranked higher than #16 in the Nielsen ratings, but their success quickly translated into real world fame. The cast produced popular studio albums, generating hit songs like "I Think I Love You" that shot to the top of the Billboard charts, but more importantly the show featured Keith Partridge, played by David Cassidy, whose feathered hair, boyish, even androgynous good looks, slight build, and squeaky clean image embodied prepubescent, unthreatening maleness and made him the ultimate American heartthrob. His real life tours played to sell-out crowds of hysterical young girls. Thus, even when "authenticity" was the

Figure 6.2. David Cassidy, promotion photo for *The Partridge Family*, c.1972.

sine qua non of rock star fame, and maybe even because of that, an obviously manufactured pop idol could also become a major celebrity for a very different audience.

Cassidy tapped into what came to be dismissively called "teenybopper" culture, consisting primarily of preteen and early teen girls with a preference for simply constructed music and lyrics known, also derisively, as "bubblegum." It is seen as music based on a mass production, planned obsolescence model producing cookie-cutter, interchangeable stars—the pseudoindividuation criticized by Adorno and Horkheimer. The songs sung by these primarily smooth-faced, androgynous boys typically involve vulnerability, even self-pity, with the needy singer wanting someone to love.[27] As Simon Frith notes, these idols are much more tied in to merchandise: magazines, posters, notebooks, lunchboxes, with "the sight of the star [being] more significant than his sound." David Cassidy's records, for example, accounted for only about one-fifth of his earnings.[28]

Cassidy's fame was magnified by a new cohort of fan magazines, obsessed with showcasing a poppy blend of bright colors, frenetic text, and, of course, loads of photos and posters of the dreamiest stars, ready to be ripped out and taped to your bedroom wall. These magazines, which featured idols from Mick Jagger to the Monkees, also manufactured for a TV show of the same name, were also targeted to teens. In 1957, 16 debuted, branding itself "the magazine for smart girls," with its chatty style, pinup images, and random details about pop idols, from Paul McCartney's favorite color (blue) to Elvis Presley's advice on how to enjoy a date. Then came *Tiger Beat*, *Teen Beat*, and *Flip*, promising insider access to musical idols like Donny Osmond, the Beach Boys, and Herman's Hermits. Fans could even write in for a chance to meet their favorites. These publications reflected, and propelled, "teenybopper" culture, where adolescent girls, presumed to be obsessed with television, fashion, and music, projected their desires and identities onto the increasingly feminized male stars sold back to them. It's during this period where the idea of the celebrity fanatic came to life in the crowds of screaming, hysterical thirteen-year-old girls, who were passing out, as if in the throes of rapture, at the mere sound of John Lennon's voice. And these fans were typically pathologized by cultural critics and musical snobs.

We might dismiss this version of engagement with celebrity culture as trivial, juvenile, and excessive, a kind of trashy, disposable cultural by-product. But "teenyboppers" were not simply engaged in a kind of mindless scream-fest. The new teen culture of the late '50s, '60s, and beyond was a meaningful response by baby boomers, coming into their own, collectively expressing their aspirations and their sense of community with one another. For girls, as Angela McRobbie writes, there existed fewer outlets for this type of emotional and collective expression, so fan culture provided a cheap, easy to access social engagement, with few barriers to entry and low personal risks. Girls could attend concerts without a date, and the lyrics on offer by the likes of Donny Osmond were light and fun, not sexually explicit. Best of all, fandom offered the opportunity to bond with other girls in a fantasy of celebrity reverie and generational—and gendered—solidarity.

As P. David Marshall notes, the youth of such stars or groups is essential to their success. The teen idol, designed to appeal to the young teen pop audience, often serves as initiation into fandom and the buying of music; he is "the conduit for the move from the toy market of childhood into the market of youth." Teen idols thus cannot be (like Elvis was) threatening to their young fans or to their parents. They have to embody a harmless form of sexuality; more to the point, because they are "over-coded to have a baby face" with no facial hair, and often have feminized hair, there is a play with sexuality in which they embody both maleness yet nonmasculinity at the same time.[29]

With the record industry constantly trying to cash in on the way music taps into the emotive side of existence, so strongly felt especially in adolescence, the production and packaging of singers and groups geared to preteen and teenaged girls accelerated right along with the parallel success of rock. With each new "mania" or craze, the popular press usually casts the latest phenomenon as a spontaneous response emanating from the will of the people and the power of the audience, which helps validate the legitimacy of the latest idols. But, of course, groups seen as potentially "bankable," for however short a period of time, were and are intensely promoted with ads, fan magazine profiles, tour support, and, at the height of MTV's video days in the 1980s and early 1990s, music videos. This doesn't mean such groups have no talent or appeal, but their look and sound are carefully and deliberately crafted. The Bay City Rollers, a Scottish band of five cute teenage boys with poufy, blow-dried hair clad in tartan pants and scarves, became worldwide teen idols in the mid-1970s. As was typical of these kinds of groups, the height of their success lasted for just a few years. Thus the teen idol—especially the "one-hit wonder"—is the personification of another key aspect of celebrity culture: the obsolescence of the once worshipped star.

By the mid-'90s, similar performers proliferated whose appeal, whose very existence, was precisely crafted and edited by talent managers like Simon Cowell, Lou Pearlman, and Heat Management. These celebrities functioned as branded commodities whose identities were crafted for and marketed to particular niches. By now, this was a tried and tested process. In the wake of the Monkees, the Jackson 5, and the Osmonds, we got New Kids on the Block, who rose to fame in the late '80s thanks to their boyish charm and falsetto vocal stylings (the appeal to young girls was once again undeniable). Like the boy bands that would follow, and unlike "authentic" rock stars, the New Kids on the Block did not play their own instruments or write their own music, but they did have choreographed moves onstage. Despite their roughly similar features, each boy was distinguished from the other and given a typecast personality—the rebel, the shy introvert, the cute one—so girls would have a choice about who to identify with and who to love. In 1989, New Kids sold more than fourteen million records in North America, and their album *Hangin' Tough* was the second-best-selling album of the year.[30]

Like David Cassidy, the New Kids' success was quickly parlayed into consumer goods, as Marshall outlines in his analysis of their fame. "The marketing of New Kids," he writes, "produced a plethora of products aimed at school-aged children. Folders for school notes, lunch pails, T-shirts, dolls (which came in several sizes and materials), concert videos, television shows, games, and comic books." By 1989, 100,000 fans a week were calling a 900 number to hear their favorite band member reveal a "secret." Sales estimates for the band's merchandise in 1990 hit $400 million.[31] The New Kids had shown how pop stardom could be distilled and commodified for a new generation. And they also exemplified the often short shelf life of such groups; by 1992, there was a backlash against what was seen as the fabrications of their music and image, and in 1994 they disbanded.

But this was hardly the end of boy bands or other groups created to appeal to young teenaged girls. Enter the Spice Girls, NSYNC, Backstreet Boys, LFO, Savage Garden, 98 Degrees, Boyz II Men, S Club 7, and the Pussycat Dolls, to name just a few. Members of these groups were selected and styled to represent, and appeal to, different types of listeners (sporty, or posh as in the Spice Girls, dreamy or tough in the boy bands). These "types" helped distinguish individual acts from one another and create a semblance of individuality, even as similar bands flooded the market. And then there were the new young idols, Britney Spears, Christina Aguilera, and Justin Timberlake, pulled up through the ranks of the Mickey Mouse Club, groomed, from childhood, for what seemed like inevitable breakout stardom. Through publicity and marketing, these individuals were transformed into celebrity products, designed to generate economic capital, the real mark of success. As Joshua Gamson points out, "the marketing model of celebrity has moved from random 'discovery' and refinement to deliberate 'breeding'" and manufacture.[32] In the 1990s, we see an increasingly hyper-regimented celebrity culture produced through a growing number of intricate, inter-connected, multifaceted industries whose specialists—agents, promot-ers, public relations experts, personal trainers, private chefs, and plastic surgeons—are required to control and manage the public's impression of their protégés. It is an elaborated process that, as Gamson and Mc-Donald have emphasized, often looks like mass production. Once a star is pressed and polished, each corporate mastodon has multiple outlets through which to promote its product and to synergize, or coordinate, that promotion to produce maximum fame for the stars, and maximum profitability for the shareholders.

Musical Celebrity and Cross-Platform Promotion

The 1960s, with the metastasizing of pop culture forms and outlets so powerfully riveted to youth culture, saw the exponential growth of cross-platform fame, and thus extensions of their brand, as stars from the worlds of music, television, and popular culture appeared across the media landscape. Musical stars continued to transcend the confines of radio and records, launching such cheeky films on the big screen as *Viva Las Vegas*, *A Hard Day's Night*, and *Don't Knock the Twist* that featured, respectively, Elvis, the Beatles, and Chubby Checker. These were films about music, starring musicians, that attempted to propel pop idols into the ranks of movie stardom. On television, *Hootenanny* (1963–64) show-cased folk singers and briefly became ABC's second most popular show. *Shindig!* (1964–66), a rock 'n' roll variety show, brought the Beach Boys, the Supremes, the Rolling Stones, and the Beatles to TV viewers, and its success spawned an imitator, *Hullabaloo* (1965–66). *Soul Train* (1971–2006) brought funk, soul, and disco tunes into the American living room. As they shimmied their way down the "Soul Train Line," dancers freestyled, showcasing (and inventing) popular moves. The show was also noteworthy for its representation of African American performers including host Don Cornelius and artists like Chaka Khan and Kool and the Gang, along with a host of young dancers, mostly black, some of whom became recognizable in their own right simply by performing their freshest moves for the camera.

But it was *The Sonny and Cher Comedy Hour* (1971–74) that truly high-lighted the new pop idols' cross-platform appeal. The variety show, whose episodes ended with the duo (and real life couple) singing their hit tune, "I Got You Babe," featured comedy sketches and wisecracking banter, and a host of comedic talent from Phyllis Diller to Carol Burnett to Betty White.

Cher embodied the new synergistic pop diva. A carefully styled icon, she launched her musical career with a string of chart-topping hits— from "Baby Don't Go" to "The Beat Goes On" with then-husband Sony Bono. She also cultivated her own solo career, with albums like *All I Really Want to Do* and *Gypsies, Tramps, and Thieves*, which won critical acclaim and spots near the top of the pop charts. After splitting with Sonny, she also starred in films, including *Silkwood* (1983), for which she was nominated for Best Supporting Actress; *Mask* (1985); and *Moonstruck* (1987), for which she won an Academy Award for best actress. Cher would go on to star on Broadway and headline shows on the Vegas Strip. She worked as a model, became a '70s fashion icon, and, with her strong features, exuberant personality, and penchant for drama, showed how a female musician could cross multiple pop culture platforms.

Musical celebrity on television was further bolstered in 1971, when the Grammy Awards aired live for the first time on ABC. The award show (previously a prerecorded affair) brought musical artists into the red carpet circuit and iconography. No longer were fancy dresses and golden statues reserved for film stars; now pop idols could also participate in these kinds of top-shelf media spectacles. As with film and television awards, the institutional and industrial recognition they offer, and the television viewer's ability to access the event live from their living rooms bolstered the legitimacy and influence of the music industry while making its stars ever more visible to the public. Adding music stars to the ritual of the red carpet and the televised awards show further enlarged the visibility and reach of celebrity culture.

Then in the mid-1970s came disco, with its exuberance, dance moves, and glitter. Disco was a reaction, in part, to the straight male domination of rock with its dismissal of dance music and fetishizing of "authenticity" that excluded many musicians, especially women and people of color. This—the "breaking of codes" musically and stylistically, the creation of new codes of music and performative styles—opened the door for new kinds of performers and new kinds of musical venues and fandom. Gays, blacks, and women found in disco music and the disco scene a more simpatico environment. Artists like Abba, the Bee Gees, and the

Village People mixed dance beats with funk rhythms and synthesizers and became major stars. Disco became a pop culture phenomenon— John Travolta's hip thrusts and white leisure suit brought the new sound and especially its dance moves to the big screen with the hit film *Saturday Night Fever* and its accompanying soundtrack by the Bee Gees, which topped the charts for twenty-four weeks straight in 1978, producing a record four number-one singles.[33]

Disco indeed created major stars like Donna Summer, but given the discourse of authenticity, the genre was also critically reviled and despised. As rock historian Ed Ward noted in 1986, "No other pop musical form has ever attracted such rabid partisans and fanatical foes, dividing audiences along racial and sexual lines."[34] Disco especially evoked an "us versus them" identification of rock fans, who insisted on a hierarchy of music with rock at the top. Various DJs, rock critics, and fans participated in an antidisco crusade, which was undergirded by racism, sexism, and homophobia. Nonetheless, the genre was enormously popular in the late 1970s.

As inspired fans flocked to the dance floor, a Manhattan nightclub called Studio 54, dubbed the "citadel of disco," became a magnet for celebrities and celebrity sightings. Media coverage of what went on there came to connect the music to decadence, power, and drugs. Now "being seen" on your own and with other famous people further glamorized and added to the visibility of musical stardom. The club gained a reputation for attracting a heterogeneous mix of celebrities and ordinary people; Andy Warhol, Truman Capote, Elizabeth Taylor, Grace Jones, and Salvador Dalí drank and socialized with drag performers, wealthy tycoons, and the young and beautiful people of New York. In 1977, Bianca Jagger rode in on a white horse to celebrate her thirtieth birthday. Four tons of glitter were reportedly trucked onto the dance floor for New Year's Eve parties.[35] Thus, it was the perfect playground for existing stars looking to rub shoulders, to be seen (and photographed) in the middle of it all. As Loretta Charlton wrote for the *New Yorker*, it was a place where ordinary people could reinvent themselves, and feel like a star, if only for one night.[36] "Thousands of nobodies," wrote Ed Ward, "clamored to get in" so they could mix and been seen with the famous. Beefy bodyguards manned velvet ropes where only selected everyday people got in after the "Disco Select" were granted entry.[37]

By the later part of the decade, some of the exuberance of the disco era was giving way to a new type of pop stardom, one that was more aggressive, more hypermasculine, and more given to studded leather jackets, torn jeans, and spiked out hair. In New York and the United Kingdom, the punk movement emerged out of a resistance to the commercialism of the early '70s, especially huge, overproduced stadium shows, rock's financial success, and the "preening excesses of big-name rock stars."[38] Punk rejected capitalism and mainstream appeal in favor of a do it yourself (DIY) aesthetic, youthful rebelliousness, an antiauthoritarian stance, and an embrace of that which middle-class consumers would find offensive. Bands like the Ramones, the New York Dolls, and the Sex Pistols proved that you didn't have to be technically skilled at an instrument to become an idol. Antagonistic stage performances, the skillful use of symbolic gestures and fashions, and the adoption of pseudonyms (Sex Pistol's front man John Lydon adopted the moniker "Johnny Rotten" and cast himself as an antihero) attracted audiences who, frustrated by rock's overblown complacency and disco's "inauthenticity," eschewed stylized disco moves in favor of pugnacious fist pumps and flailing, at times violent, moshing. Ironically, punk groups became famous by breaking the model of celebrity as an idealized social type, but, over time, the ideological core of the punk movement would be co-opted as studded clothes, Mohawk hairstyles, and safety pin piercings became adopted as fashion status symbols, hollowed out of their meaning.

Video Killed the Radio Star

A grainy, black and white image of Trevor Horn singing into an old-fashioned stand microphone fades away, replaced by a futuristic scene, complete with synths, wires, and televisions, a bundle of unspecified technological innovation. It was August 1, 1981 and so began the first music video, the Buggles' "Video Killed the Radio Star," to air on an innovative cable music channel, MTV. Singing lyrics like "I heard you on the wireless back in '52," and "it seems so long ago" in robotic vocals, band members donned lab coats and funky goggles. A dancer in a galactic spandex bodysuit slid around in a giant plastic test tube. In true meta-fashion, backup singers appeared on television screens, as we watched them on *our* screens, through *our* TVs. So when a TV burst through a mountain of paper cut radios, the message was clear. Radio was passé. Music was no longer simply something you listened to, it was something you watched.

This new music experience was grounded in the image. The visual nature of television viewing transformed the music world; now, an artist or band couldn't just have a sound, they needed an image. So rock and pop stars had to deal with video technology, and move beyond simply performing on stage to having to match images and visual stories to their songs. This meant that singers or groups needed video producers to promote them and their music, so yet another new and now necessary profession emerged in the music celebrity production industry. What we saw in many videos was a new kind of surrealism, where odd visual juxtapositions and weird dreamlike sequences (some of which made no sense) demanded one's attention to figure out the relationship between sound and image. Up rose a cohort of one-hit wonders, whose catchy lyrics and bizarre visuals captivated viewers' imaginations; Flock of Seagulls performed "I Ran" in a spaced out hall of mirrors and tinfoil while the Human League's "Don't You Want Me" cut between Hollywood style close-ups and stalkerish behavior. Robert Palmer's deliberately campy "Addicted to Love" video had the singer backed up by five mannequin-like female models, nearly identical in appearance, wearing skintight black dresses, flame red lipstick, and serious expressions playing white electric guitars as his backup posse, which created a new visual iconography that simultaneously satirized and reinforced MTV's objectification of women and the often assembly-line style of music production.

MTV in its early years featured a contradictory lineup of stars, from new wave bands like Devo, Tears for Fears, and the Talking Heads to arena bands like Loverboy, hard rock groups like Kiss, to female singers, including Blondie, Cyndi Lauper, and Pat Benatar. And few women exploited this new visual medium of musical stardom more brilliantly than Madonna. Madonna launched herself into the spotlight in 1983 by using the music video as a platform for ongoing, evolving, and often highly controversial image creation and storytelling. A first-name-only celeb, Madonna combined her singing and dancing ability with an idiosyncratic personal style—lace, fishnet stockings, bleached and teased-out hair, and crucifix jewelry.[39] She adopted and subverted the image of the blonde bombshell; no longer one to be looked at, it was now she who was doing the looking. With her "Boy Toy" belt, and her video performances, Madonna sought to have it both ways: to indeed be an object of male desire but also to ridicule the rampant objectification of women (especially in way too many music videos) and to claim her own sexual agency. In video after hit video, Madonna rolled around in a white wedding gown while a lion strolled by ("Like a Virgin"), imitated Marilyn Monroe's performance in *Gentlemen Prefer Blondes* of "Diamonds Are a Girl's Best Friend" ("Material Girl"), and explored sexuality in interracial relationships ("Borderline," "Like a Prayer"), and the gay nightlife scene ("Vogue").

Her serial, defiant images were intentionally rebellious and in your face, designed to shock the establishment and, in doing so, solidify her status as the most fashionable provocateur. Again, she was recrafting the codes of female pop performance to become a star, and it worked. Young women, labeled "Madonna wanna-bes," especially found Madonna's message, and look, totally compelling, and legions of fans flocked to her concerts, dressed in their own versions of the stars' signature mishmash ensembles. Her message—that female sexuality was healthy, that if it was threatening to men, too bad, and that owning that desire was liberating—resonated with young women confronting mixed messages about female display and sexual liberation in the 1980s. By the early 1990s, Madonna was an international megastar and one of the richest women in show business, and regarded as the best-selling female rock artist of the twentieth century.[40]

While Madonna encouraged girls to push the boundaries of conventional femininity, a new crop of male musicians made it cool to be campy, and queer, on TV. Because it was a visual medium, MTV required distinctive, branded looks from male stars as well. Groups like Duran Duran sported guyliner, elaborate costumes, neckerchiefs, and coiffed hair. In 1982, Culture Club's androgynous front man Boy George became a sensation when he appeared in the video for the group's hit song, "Do You Really Want to Hurt Me?" Boy George's personal style—long hair with extensions, gold or lavender eye shadow and double-flick eyeliner, and free-form dance moves—made him an icon of gender play. Prince, too, would ignore preconceived ideas about gender norms with his sultry, come-on looks,

Figure 6.3. Madonna at MTV Music Awards, 1984.
Photograph by David McGough, Getty Images.
Reprinted with permission.

sexual lyrics and performance style, ruffled shirts, eyeliner, penchant for purple, and bondage-inspired costumes.

In its early years especially, MTV aired highly experimental, even surreal videos, many of which could be regarded as video art. And particularly with new wave and world music, MTV featured performers who would never get on rock-oriented radio. But there was a serious problem with MTV: it featured virtually no African American artists, which David Bowie, in a 1983 interview on the channel, said "floored" him.[41] Other artists spoke up as well.

The performer who changed this was Michael Jackson. His 1982 album *Thriller* became a massive hit, yet MTV would not play Jackson's videos, claiming it was strictly a rock channel. Walter Yetnikoff, then president of CBS Records, reportedly threatened to pull the videos of all CBS artists unless MTV played Jackson's videos. "Billie Jean" aired in 1983, a song that topped the Billboard charts for seven weeks, and was the first video by a black artist to go into heavy rotation. It also opened the door for other artists of color to appear on the channel.[42] Following a string of successes with "Billie Jean," the sensational choreography of "Beat It," and "Rock with You," it was the fourteen-minute-long "Thriller" that defied music video conventions with its storytelling and zombie dance sequences. *Thriller* helped transform Jackson's image from Jackson 5 child star to industry innovator. His moonwalk skills and leather jackets became iconic. Jackson blended a kind of street tough persona with smooth dance moves and a high falsetto, introducing a new kind of masculinity to TV, one that was young, ambiguous, and black. His mastery of the format catapulted him to international superstardom, with devoted fans regarding him as the "King of Pop."

Figure 6.4. Michael Jackson, 1995. Photograph by Kevin Mazur, Getty Images. Reprinted with permission.

Pressed further to open its doors to African American music and performers, in 1988 a new program, *Yo! MTV Raps*, would introduce the growing hip-hop scene and its primarily black artists, like Run-D.M.C., DJ Jazzy Jeff and the Fresh Prince, and Dr. Dre, to the mainstream cable market. Through the power and reach of cable, hip hop and rap would introduce themes, styles, and musicality of black artists to white kids in Middle America. This, the "golden age" of hip hop, was characterized by innovation and a diversity of styles, as KRS-One and Chuck D rapped about black activism, Public Enemy led a call to "Fight the Power," and groups like De La Soul blended wordplay, jazz influence, and sampled tracks. These provided what the scholar Tricia Rose has called "hidden transcripts," stories and videos about police brutality, racial profiling, and inner city poverty rarely discussed in the mainstream media.[43]

MTV provided a platform for experimentation, and the pop stars who succeeded there were image savvy and cutting edge. As they pushed the boundaries of self-presentation, experimented with the intersection of image and sound, they not only promoted their music and personal brand but also sparked conversations around sexuality, race relations, and gang violence. Unlike music stars of yesteryear, who crafted and worked to maintain a consistent public image, the new crop of stars embraced the idea that image was something to be adopted and then cast aside, to be tried on and traded in for a newer model. Stars like Cyndi Lauper, Michael Jackson, Madonna, and David Bowie engaged in flamboyant and serial self-reinventions, playing with fashion, gender, and narrative, morphing from character to character. They made it almost de rigueur to test the boundaries and embrace nonconformity as a path to breakout musical stardom.

But it wasn't just the artists who became stars. MTV's hosts, the scrappy band of so-called VJs—Mark Goodman, Martha Quinn, and J. J. Jackson—also became household names, channeling a sense of youthful cool, and humor, as they spoke directly to the camera. Personalities like Downtown Julie Brown and Carson Daly used their MTV fame to launch careers in film and as hosts of celebrity, entertainment, and gossip programs. These weren't the typical white male buttoned-up, cookie-cutter hosts. They were young, cheeky, irreverent, and each with their own signature appeal, yet they also embodied the relatability so

Figure 6.5. MTV's original VJs, 1983. Photograph by Mark Weiss, Getty Images. Reprinted with permission.

necessary for successful TV hosts. MTV crafted for itself and its artists a place in the new cable television landscape. It carved out a kind of experimental laboratory, where new modes of expression—and new kinds of celebrity—could be tested out. It was the specificity of the network, its brand, in both content and audience, which allowed it to become, in the 1980s, a musical celebrity production machine.

MTV helped transform previously unknown talented musicians into pop culture idols, and despite its notorious sexual objectification of women, as documented in Sut Jhally's *Dreamworlds* documentaries, it provided an especially powerful space for female artists. For Debbie Harry, the group Heart, Whitney Houston, Chrissie Hynde of the Pretenders, and Tina Turner, music videos allowed them to defy conventions and stake their claim in a historically male rock and roll arena, while also solidifying their status as bona fide pop stars. By the early '90s, Gwen Stefani was fronting the frenetic ska group No Doubt (whose music videos featured the lead singer aggressively moshing and confronting the camera while donning track pants). Soon, Alanis Morissette was taking viewers along on an angsty, ironic sing-along car ride in her album *Jagged Little Pill*, which sold thirty-three million copies; Björk was crafting futuristic video odysseys; and Sinéad O'Connor was breaking music video iconography in her stark, extreme close-up rendition of "Nothing Compares 2 U." Meanwhile, hip-hop artists like Missy Elliott, Erykah Badu, Lauryn Hill, and Queen Latifah were breaking into the male-dominated rap scene (a media mogul, Latifah would go on to earn cross-platform fame, with roles in TV shows, hit movies, and a Broadway play; she is a spokesperson for Cover Girl, where she sponsors a line of cosmetics designed for women of color). By 1997, when the first all-female touring music festival, Lilith Fair, grossed $16 million, it seemed the musical boys' club of yesteryear at least had been infiltrated.[44] Nonetheless, with a few exceptions—Tracy Chapman, for example—many female pop and rock stars still had to be conventionally slim, pretty (even beautiful), feminine, and often scantily clad to succeed in the business.

The New Synergy and Cross-Promotion

While the proliferation of cable networks opened up new opportunities for innovation, it also put financial pressure on producers and executives who were competing for viewership in an increasingly crowded and diffuse marketplace. And while the growing number of channels suggested diversification, the television industry—in fact, the entire mainstream media landscape—was actually contracting. The Telecommunications Act of 1996 dramatically loosened previous restrictions on the number and types of media platforms a single company could own and operate. The resulting consolidation of ownership in six major conglomerates produced a kind of celebrity echo chamber. These octopi corporations bought up publishing houses, news outlets, movie theaters, amusement parks, record companies, television stations, cable systems, and billboards. Thanks to this multiplatform ownership, media companies could now cross-promote, or create *synergy* between, their holdings.

Celebrities were the threads of connectivity within this new synergistic web and in this competitive media world, and this type of synergistic cross-promotion and brand extension was expanding. One exemplar was the 1997 film *Spice World*. A critical bomb, the film became a marketing juggernaut. *Spice World* followed the girl power adventures of the Spice Girls as they cavorted around London, occasionally lamenting the burdens of fame (*Rolling Stone* noted the obvious similarities to the Beatles' *Hard Day's Night*).[45] A manufactured UK-based girl group, the Spice Girls were assembled by Heart Management in 1994 and signed to Virgin Records. Following the 1996 U.S. release of their debut album, *Spice*, which would go on to sell thirty-one million copies worldwide, the group produced a book and "manifesto," entitled *Girl Power!*, which was not surprisingly launched at record label Virgin's Megastore. It sold 200,000 copies on its first day of issue.[46] *Spice World* was strategically released a few short months later, in October 1997, just one month prior to the debut of the group's second album, not coincidentally named *Spice World*, which sold more than twenty million albums worldwide. Just as the film was coming to the box office, the girls signed contracts with Pepsi Cola, Chupa Chups, Galoob Toys (which gave us Spice Girls dolls), Domino Sugar, Target, and PlayStation, which released a video game based on the film in 1998. For a while the girls became inescapable; they were on radio, in the movies, at the toy store, and even in the candy aisle of your local supermarket. And though some feared they risked overexposure, this type of synergistic windfall would become a new model for celebrity promotion in the 1990s and beyond.

But while celebrity was being increasingly manufactured, more and more we the audience were being told that we were the ones who were actually in control. In 1998, MTV debuted a millennial version of the chart-topper countdown *Total Request Live* (*TRL*). Within its voyeurism-inviting picture-windowed studio above Times Square, or the breezy, summer space in Seaside Heights, New Jersey, host Carson Daly (who became a star in his own right) invited viewers to call or log in to request their favorite songs. The most requested videos would then air, in order of popularity, until the top song of the day was revealed. *TRL* not only showcased the videos themselves, it was a fan-flattering microcosm of the celebrity/audience dynamic. Screaming fans lined up outside the New York City studio, often brandishing homemade signs in hopes of scoring a seat inside. The lucky few who landed a ticket not only got to sit beside Daly as he announced the lineup, but they also won a front-row seat to celebrity appearances. Top requested artists like Britney Spears, Kid Rock, Usher, and NSYNC would regularly stop by the set to chat with Daly, promote their latest projects, and schmooze with fans. A ticket to *TRL* was a direct pass to up-close and personal contact with the top pop stars, not to mention a chance to appear on TV yourself.

The top played artists on *TRL* were very much a part of the new industrial celebrity of the late '90s. Boy bands NSYNC, 98 Degrees, Hanson, and Backstreet Boys made regular appearances, as did Disney-stars-turned-sex-symbols Britney Spears and Christina Aguilera. Even the edgier stars—Kid Rock, Eminem, and Korn—were mainstream-approved, their songs playing on top 40 radio, their controversial lyrics and aggressive videos designed to prompt a reaction. At the same time the celebrity image was becoming more and more managed, and the industrial production of stardom ever more regimented, the audience was being told we were actually more in control than ever. We were given the opportunity to call and log in, to make our voices heard, and to decide which videos made it on TV. We were being flattered that the driver of celebrity influence rested not with the publicists, the agents, or even the media, but with us, the voting audience. This was of course only partially true.

Music Celebrity in the Twenty-First Century

By the late 1990s, a number of simultaneous developments were putting pressure on the mainstream music industry, which was, at the time, driven primarily by the sale of compact discs. These developments would change the nature of the production of musical celebrity as well. The expansion of home computing hardware and CD-ROM drives meant that consumers who purchased a CD could upload its contents to a personal computer in minutes, and the growth of high-speed Internet access meant that uploaded songs could be shared. In 1999, Shawn Fanning and his partners launched a peer-to-peer file sharing service called Napster, which provided a user-friendly interface for audiences seeking to share and download MP3 music files. The platform also provided a clever work-around for the creators, who were not providing the content and therefore were not (so they thought) responsible for violating copyright law. Napster became a massive success, boasting eighty million registered users at its peak and accounting for some 60 percent of file downloads on college campuses during its brief time in operation.[47] But as mainstream musicians became aware of the potential financial implications of the file sharing, they sued. Metallica and Dr. Dre filed litigation against Napster, claiming copyright violation. Following multiple appeals and legal defeats, Napster was forced to terminate its service in July 2001.

But the genie was out of the bottle. Numerous peer-to-peer sharing services sprung up in Napster's wake. Though none were as popular, reliable, or noteworthy, users now understood that music files could be shared online for free. Such services had become popular because many of the established labels were overproducing CDs that might have one or two good songs on them and were thus overpriced. It was no longer necessary to run out to Tower Records or Virgin Records to spend $19 on your favorite artist's new CD—with a minor amount of know-how, it could be downloaded online, in seconds, at no cost. In 1999, total revenue for CD sales and licensing topped $14.6 billion; by 2009 that number had plunged to 6.3 billion.[48]

Stunned, the major labels were slow to respond. Apple, however, was waiting in the wings, debuting its iTunes platform just as Napster was shuttering. With it came the iPod players, whose sleek design and portability further pushed consumers away from compact disc technologies. The iTunes store is now ubiquitous, accessible via laptop, smartphone, and other WiFi connected devices, and it sells most songs for 99 cents. In 2015, downloaded music generated $2.33 billion in U.S. digital sales, but even downloads are quickly being replaced by streaming services, such as Pandora and Spotify, which in the same year generated $2.41 billion, outpacing download sales for the first time.[49] The decline in the sales of CDs and the rise of streaming services, which pay often miniscule amounts every time a song is played, means that, with the possible exception of superstar performers, musicians now must generate additional revenue from touring and ancillary sales in order to support their music and actually earn some money. MTV is no longer the star maker it once was, but sometimes social media is. Services like Spotify, which do feature entire albums, have nonetheless revived the prominence of the single. Thus, many more performers can be featured on such services, but it also takes more to break out of the musical clutter. Yet there's also been an increased ability to follow music and stars from other countries, like various of the K-pop (Korean pop) bands, some of whom embody the next stage of boy bands and heartthrobs.

In 2007, a Canadian twelve year old, Justin Bieber, was discovered when a manager at So So Def Recordings happened upon a YouTube video of the preteen singing. He was quickly signed to a label and his brand of catchy, flirty pop songs shot to the top of the charts. Introduced and initially mentored by R&B star Usher, Bieber became a sensation in the classic teenybop style, his androgynous, baby-faced good looks and wispy hairdo generating "Bieber fever," massive adoration and excitement from female fans. But unlike the pop idols of yesteryear, Bieber and his team were savvy in their understanding of and ability to activate social media in support of his success. In 2012, Bieber told *Forbes*, "Social media helped launch my career. . . . Without the Internet and without YouTube, I wouldn't have gotten the chance to put my music out there and have people hear it."[50] Today, Bieber has 98.8 million followers on Twitter alone.

While his presence on social platforms has certainly earned him publicity, it has also contributed to his notoriety. Like many child stars growing into adulthood under the public eye, Bieber has been criticized for disorderly and illegal behavior—he was banned from China in 2017 for allegedly driving drunk and drag racing and had previously been arrested on charges of DUI (driving under the influence) and resisting arrest in Miami in 2012. He's also gained media attention for allegedly smoking marijuana in public, assaulting photographers, and egging a neighbor's house. Inevitably, these incidents have been blasted across social media, accompanied by paparazzi photos and videos. Though the young pop star continues to use his online influence to connect with fans and explain his side of the story, his image as a squeaky clean singing sensation has been undercut.

Another musical star who has successfully navigated the shifting shoals of musical distribution and platforms is Taylor Swift, a country-pop darling who has used her glossy music videos, Facebook page, and Instagram to promote herself as a bubbly blonde girl next door whose lyrics revolve around fairy tale romances, friendships, breakups, and perseverance. Her first album (2006) went platinum, *Fearless* was the best-selling album of 2009, and by 2017 her net worth was estimated at

$380 million. She regularly interacts with her fans, known as "Swifties," across social media, and she has gained a reputation for surprising her most ardent supporters with visits, personal sing-alongs, and even appearances at their weddings.

Taylor Swift is not only adept at generating loyal followers. She is also keenly aware of the machinations of a changing music industry. Thanks to digital technologies, the musical economy has become more diffuse. Content streaming on YouTube, Vevo, iTunes, Bandcamp, and even artists' Facebook pages have generated dynamic opportunities for artists to have their music discovered, but also to have it exploited and undervalued compared to the CD era. So these new venues also create a space for mainstream stars to flex their muscle outside the bounds of an industry historically dominated by the major labels.

In 2015, Taylor Swift posted an open letter on her Tumblr account and shared it with her fifty-four million Twitter followers.[51] Entitled "To Apple, Love Taylor," she announced that she would be "holding back my album, *1989*, from the new streaming service, Apple Music" because it was offering a free three-month trial. Apple, in turn, would not be paying writers, producers, or artists for those three months, meaning they would be expected to "work for nothing." Apple quickly responded with assurance (also posted to social media) that artists would be paid, even during the free trial promotion. The dustup demonstrated that successful musicians, especially those with a dedicated following, could use their online presence to exert influence, not only over their image but also over the industry's distribution and payment structures. Swift achieved all this via an online "love letter," a move that allowed her to maintain her sweetheart image while publicly negotiating her own payday. On the other hand, some artists have successfully used Apple Music, as when Chance the Rapper released his third album, *Coloring Book*, exclusively as a two-week stream, and saw it open in *Billboard*'s Top Ten list. It was also the first streaming-only album to win a Grammy, affirming the viability of this latest form of distribution.[52]

And then there's Beyoncé who, rather than negotiate terms, has taken control over the system of production itself. In 2010, the megastar who rose to fame in the hip-hop group Destiny's Child and then went on to launch successful solo careers in music, film, and fashion, founded her own management company, Parkwood Entertainment, through which she launched a series of projects and fashion collaborations. When, in February 2016, Beyoncé was ready to release her new album, *Lemonade*, she launched the first single, "Formation," exclusively on Tidal Music's streaming platform, which just so happened to be owned by her husband, Jay-Z. The next day, she performed the song at the Super Bowl XLIX halftime show, to an audience of 115.5 million viewers.[53] Two months later, she released *Lemonade*'s "visual album," a kind of long-form, conceptual music video, on HBO; that same day, *Lemonade* (produced by Columbia and Parkwood Entertainment) dropped exclusively on Tidal. The move sent all twelve tracks from the album shooting to the top of the Billboard Hot 100 chart, making Queen Bey the first female act to ever have so many songs on the list at one time. Within one month, *Lemonade* had been streamed 115 million times.[54]

Clearly the release of *Lemonade* was expertly choreographed, but its commercial success was also made possible by Beyoncé's existing social networks and digital media presence (she has more than sixty million followers on Facebook and more than 105 million on Instagram). Unlike the Kardashians and other social media self-promoters, Beyoncé does not post aggressively on social media, nor does she use the platform to sell products (except her own). Instead, she is known for her simple, personal messages and images, which she offers to her "Bey Hive" of fans with little comment or embellishment. She's adept at squashing or fueling rumors with a single post, and she gives followers just enough—a carefully curated glimpse into her private world, her family, her marriage, her forthcoming projects—to keep them wanting more. Her aura is further bolstered by her limiting the number of media interviews she is willing to give, a fact that makes the diva's personal posts all the more compelling.[55]

Some elements of musical stardom have not changed. We continue to connect with—even adulate—some musical performers. We look to them as conduits who express our joy, our pain, and our hopes for the future. We also look to them as icons of style and exuberant personality. Sometimes, we look to them as markers of social change, rebels who push the boundaries and, in doing so, move audiences toward an aspirational future. Yet our expectations for musicians have, in some ways, been exaggerated. Thanks to streaming and social media platforms, we no longer have to wait for MTV to play our favorite videos; we can listen to or watch them on demand, as often as we like. We also expect musicians to be ever-more available to us, to not only connect with fans at concerts but to also share with us the details of their daily lives. As opportunities for online interaction have expanded, so too has the need for musical celebrities to manage their presentation of self. Indeed, this is a challenge that all celebrities face in the twenty-first century media economy.

7

Everyone's a Star

Everyone knows that furtive moment, belting out our favorite song in the shower, or singing along with the car radio blasting, or going all out in a committed karaoke session, when for a fleeting (sometimes embarrassing) moment, we can imagine ourselves as a pop star, achieving pop idol glory. It is a fantasy of having talent (especially for those of us who can't sing), and expressing powerful emotions to others, for which they in turn express adulatory gratitude. And it turns out to be a widely shared dream. In the first two decades of the twenty-first century, proliferating digital platforms opened up vast new virtual realms for celebrity production—and self-branding as a star.

In 2002, a new television show premiered, one based on the promise of turning hopefuls into singing sensations. *American Idol*[1] plucked unknown singers from cities and small towns across the country, paraded them before a panel of music industry stars, and had them sing their hearts out on stage for a chance at a record contract—and the adoration of the American public. Each season, thousands of hopefuls auditioned, willing to expose their life stories and vocal abilities, sometimes while donning humiliating costumes, all for a chance at *Idol* fame. The twist? Viewers were empowered judges too: they could anoint the winner from the comfort of their living room, calling and logging in to vote for their favorites.

The show's emphasis on audience participation helped propel *Idol* to a spot atop the ratings for eight consecutive years (2003–11).[2] *Idol* would mint a new pop sensation for fifteen consecutive seasons, but importantly, it also pioneered new techniques for audience interactivity, encouraging fans to vote via text message, Facebook, and even the show's own AT&T-sponsored mobile app. Season one champ Kelly Clarkson has gone on to win three Grammy awards, but even contestants who didn't win, like Fantasia Barrino and Jennifer Hudson, would become top-selling recording, film, and Broadway stars, a testament to the

Figure 7.1. *American Idol*, 2005. Photograph by Kevin Winter, Getty Images. Reprinted with permission.

show's influence. Sponsorships—from Coca-Cola, Ford, and iTunes, to name just a few—turned *Idol* into a synergistic juggernaut; video packages showed the idols riding around in F-150 trucks while judges sipped from large red cups emblazoned with Coca-Cola logos. The sponsorship deals not only worked to link the emerging singers to big-name brands, bolstering their celebrity status, they also netted the show up to $60 million per sponsor, per season, cementing the genre's legitimacy and profitability.[3]

American Idol was part of a wave of new televisual content that would further reshape the nature of celebrity as we knew it. It promoted and intensified the quest for self-branding and visibility above the masses. It also embodied and extended the model of audience participation and control modeled by shows like MTV's *Total Request Live* in the '90s, while also pointing to a broader shift in celebrity culture at the turn of the twenty-first century. Celebrities were now in a constant state of creation, of coming into being, live, on air, right before our eyes. And this was not just happening on television. Online, thanks to the affordances of digital technologies and high-speed Internet, new stars were popping up and grabbing the spotlight. Not only were these technologies making it easier to produce fame, but they were also allowing audiences ever greater access to, and control over, celebrities themselves. The fantasy that now almost anyone could become a star had much more credence. Plus the best venue wasn't only through the talent show; there were now increasing opportunities through reality TV as well.

Celebrified Reality

The industrial production of celebrity that we saw throughout the 1980s and 1990s, coupled with the proliferation of cable channels, produced a bizarre dilemma: there weren't enough true "A-list" actors, pop stars, or supermodels to fill the need for 24–7 TV programming. But creating new stars required time and the support of advertising dollars that could no longer be justified in an increasingly segmented marketplace, one that lacked the kind of mass viewership network television enjoyed. To address this gap, and save cash, producers sought alternatives to union actors and writers, who, though necessary for the production of scripted shows, commanded high salaries.[4] The ideal content was cheap, easy to shoot, and formulaic enough to reproduce. Reality television provided a creative solution to fill this need.

In 1992 *The Real World* debuted on MTV and famously told "the true story of seven strangers picked to live in a house . . . to find out what happens when people stop being polite and start getting real." Despite mostly negative reviews, the show was a hit with young audiences, perhaps in part because it reimagined for television a trope previously on display in cinema and radio—the ordinary person, plucked from obscurity, thrust into the spotlight. The housemates/cast members were quickly catapulted to fame. This was especially true during season three, in San Francisco, when the show featured Pedro Zamora, a young, openly gay AIDS activist living with the disease. Zamora gained widespread media attention as the first such person to appear on television, which was further amplified after his death in 1994, just a few hours after the final episode of the series aired. Clearly reality TV could attract and hold audience attention, produce its own celebrities, and even generate awareness about social issues through the human interest lens of the genre.

Meanwhile, cable news stations were creating drama out of real world headlines, transporting us into the courthouse and turning national news into entertainment. In 1991, Pamela Smart, a twenty-five-year-old high school employee, stood accused of seducing a fifteen-year-old male student into killing her husband. In this era of increased sensationalism, the murder scandal was a boon for the news; the case would be the first trial to be televised gavel to gavel. The media frenzy and public outcry whipped up by the Smart case would pave the way for comparable constant coverage of the trial of O. J. Simpson. The infamous Simpson case, the latest in the "trial of the century," became the television event of the year in 1995, as network and cable stations alike cancelled regularly scheduled programming to broadcast every detail of the trial. Coverage of the star football player and actor, accused of murdering his ex-wife, Nicole Brown Simpson, and her friend, Ron Goldman, proved a ratings bonanza, as the *New York Times* reported in 1995:

> CNN's afternoon ratings for the first three weeks of the Simpson trial coverage were 5.1, 5.6 and 6.3—far above its 0.7 average for that time period. And the ratings for Court TV were even higher—as much as double those of CNN in the 20 million homes that receive both CNN and Court TV. At the same time, the evening news ratings for ABC, CBS and NBC have declined, collectively, nearly two ratings points from the period in 1994, to an average of 9.4 from 11.3 last year.[5]

The Simpson case made stars of its key players while further eroding the line between news and entertainment.

Public attention was riveted on some of the most notorious figures of the day, who were sensationalized even as they were condemned. While O. J. was on trial, Timothy McVeigh became a household name after detonating a truck bomb outside of a federal building in Oklahoma City, killing 168 people; Colin Ferguson was convicted of a brutal rampage, killing six passengers on the Long Island Rail Road; and Mexican pop sensation Selena was murdered. That same year—1995—a guest revealed a crush on his straight, male friend on the nationally televised *Jenny*

Jones show, only to be shot and killed by that very friend three days later. The 24/7 news cycle, made possible thanks to the existence of news-only cable channels, thrived on—and needed—every minute of it. Thanks to an expansion of the "variety and scale of media technologies," "the opportunities for publicizing criminals," individuals whom David Schmid dubs *idols of destruction*, multiplied.[6] Celebrity scandals and human interest stories proved irresistible to producers hoping to secure high ratings and advertising revenue at low cost. Network news programs, struggling to compete, could no longer afford to ignore celebrity content, including criminals who became household names through their often vicious crimes. For audiences, the line between so-called hard news and celebrity journalism crumbled even more.

By the early 2000s, an explosion of reality shows and their rapid-fire transformation of everyday people into celebrities started clogging the media pipeline, designed to further stoke both audiences' fascination and repugnance. In the spring and summer of 2000, America became transfixed by *Survivor: Borneo* (CBS 2000–present). Eight men and eight women volunteered to be marooned on a tropical island filled with palm trees, venomous snakes, rats, pulsating phalanxes of ants, and a series of contests, dares, and obstacle courses. Every three days at a "tribal council" someone was voted off the island. The contestant who could withstand the elements, and other tribe members' personalities, would be named "the sole survivor" and win a million bucks. When the show premiered in May, it reeled in 15.5 million viewers. By the time of the season finale on August 23, when Richard Hatch won (after island-mate Sue famously compared him to a snake), 51.7 million viewers tuned in, proving that a reality show could draw a larger audience than major live events, including the Academy Awards. *Survivor* even beat out the top watched scripted show of the time, its finale trumping *ER*'s most-watched episode by 12.3 million viewers.[7] Hatch instantly became a celebrity, although a widely hated one, and he was eventually found guilty of and imprisoned for tax evasion.

Some of these show turned unknowns into knowns, while others offered C-list or has-been celebrities a chance to reboot their visibility. We were then treated to, in rapid succession, the creepily surveilling *Big Brother*,[8] *The Amazing Race*,[9] *Newlyweds*,[10] *Laguna Beach*,[11] and *The Hills*,[12] to name only a fraction of the offerings. The key strands of the genre were also solidified—competition programs (*America's Next Top Model*,[13] *Project Runway*,[14] *The Apprentice*,[15] *Top Chef*[16]), makeover shows (*Queer Eye for the Straight Guy*,[17] *What Not to Wear*[18]), dating programs (*The Bachelor*,[19] *Joe Millionaire*[20]), and voyeuristic glimpses of how others "really" live (*The Simple Life*,[21] *The Osbournes*,[22] *Jersey Shore*[23]). Meanwhile, shows like *My Super Sweet Sixteen*,[24] about the over-the-top conspicuous consumption of wealthy teenagers, and *Here Comes Honey Boo Boo*,[25] featuring a child beauty contestant and her southern, backwoods family, nodded to their own self-reflexivity, implicitly ridiculing those in the show while reassuring audiences about their feelings of superiority. They were designed, in other words, to produce "enunciative productivity" among viewers, many of whom watched such shows in groups. While these programs took up various forms, themes, and aesthetics, they all provided access to a constantly evolving cohort of "real" people facing situations both ordinary and extraordinary.[26]

Some programs presented an unscripted chronicle of the lives of "normal" people, and so produced an ever-changing lineup of this-minute celebs who would compete with established stars for airtime and viewership. Each new cast of bachelors, models, fashion designers, and housewives, season after season, were a willing and often cut-rate gift to the celebrity culture industries, who could write stories about them, photograph them, and sell their discovery narrative. On the flip side, other shows gave the viewing public a peek into the lives of famous, gorgeous, or superwealthy people, presenting their worlds and habits as though they were typical. Either way, audiences could get to know, root for, or actively despise the cast. Established stars who took a gig on reality TV benefited from the sense of authenticity, approachability, and access that the shows celebrated. The result—a tiered system of celebrity culture in which the most established, glamorous (often film) stars sat atop the A-list, commanding audience attention and the paycheck to match, followed by B, C, even F list stars, culled from the ranks of club-going socialites, *Duck Dynasties*, and wannabe top models.

The reality stars who profited most, and who ingratiated themselves most thoroughly into mainstream celebrity culture, were those who managed to parlay their fifteen minutes of fame into sponsorships, book projects, fashion lines, and licensing deals. To remain in the limelight, especially if you got there via a reality TV show, you have to work hard to stay there. You need to both perform at "being yourself" while also becoming a brand. "Real housewife" Bethenny Frankel used her C-list status (and pin thin figure) to launch her own line of "Skinny girl" books and cocktails along with a quickly cancelled talk show. Others, like Lauren Conrad of *Laguna Beach* and *The Hills* and Nicole Richie of *The Simple Life*, launched mass-market and high-end fashion lines, respectively. While viewers might remember Jessica Simpson infamously mistaking the canned tuna Chicken of the Sea for, well, chicken, she's the one laughing now—her branded lines of shoes, fragrances, handbags, and beauty products have made her one of the wealthiest women in the business. Simpson presides over a retail empire worth an estimated $1 billion.

The effect of reality television on celebrity culture was immediate and potent. The line between star and audience, which had narrowed throughout the twentieth century, was erased completely—except for who was visible and who was not. Celebrities were shown to be flawed, and willing to expose their imperfections on camera. And so-called ordinary people were also willing to self-expose; the primary award for doing so was not the title of season champion, but the chance to launch oneself into the celebrity sphere. The often melodramatic nature of reality television—its celebrations and condemnations, fantasies of perfection and caricatures of evil, its participants' frequent comments about "so much drama"—cultivated in many viewers twin desires: to envy and even admire those on the screen, but also to make fun of and look down on them.

These shows pointed out the absurdity of what some people will do for fame—think of the heiress Paris Hilton trying to milk a cow on *The Simple Life*—and, in doing so, highlighted the inanity of celebrity as a phenomenon, allowing the audience to feel superior in our ironic viewership. Especially in the wake of the 9/11 attacks, reality narratives transported us away from the very real stresses of economic and military instability, administrative ineptitude, and social injustice, replacing them with the trivialities of stars' backbiting over boyfriends, sabotaging a red carpet look, or gossiping over $15 salads. Our ability to judge those in positions of cultural and economic power provided a morale boost to audiences who, in an age of terrorism and war, may have felt politically and economically impotent.

Celebrity Gossip Magazines

At the same time, a new crop of magazines was emerging that would mimic the gaze, and tone, of reality television, while helping to publicize the genre's stars. In 2001, the entertainment magazine *US* transformed itself into a celebrity-focused weekly and was quickly followed by a new cohort of freshly minted mags; *InTouch* (2002), *Life & Style* (2004), *Ok!* (2005), and the revamped *Star* (2004) all hit newsstands in the early 2000s. Soon, the *National Enquirer* and the *Globe*, formerly black and white tabloids, went glossy and turned their attention away from Elvis sightings and alien abductions and toward celebrities who were living on planet Earth.

The concept and appeal of these magazines was not, as we have seen, new. Like *Photoplay* and *Silver Screen* before them, celebrity weeklies promised "genuine" "behind the scenes" access to the top stars of the day, especially female celebs. And like the tabloids of the 1950s, these magazines were concerned especially with moral disorder—collapsing marriages, female train wrecks, men who punched paparazzi photographers—juxtaposed with the rituals of moral order—weddings, births. The reliance on unnamed sources—a "friend," "someone in the know"—usually involved the conflation of fact with fiction, thus stoking that "puzzle solving" pleasure (do I think this is true or not?) of following celebrity journalism.

When Canadian magazine makeover guru Bonnie Fuller took the helm at *US Weekly*, and later *Star*, she transformed the tabloids from sleepy also-rans to *People* by pioneering the genre's new look, content, and tone. Fuller's genius was in further reducing the distance between celebrity and fan through her "just like us" features and increasing reliance on paparazzi shots of stars out grocery shopping, walking their dogs, or playing with their kids. This further encouraged voyeurism of the famous, and marked an even greater push to get ever more into the stars' protected back stages. Such gambits both increased identification with the famous while also encouraging readers to be more judgmental, to feel a greater sense of discursive power over the stars.

And how the tone had changed. While the fan magazines of the mid-twentieth century relied on studio-sanctioned information, professional portraits and headshots, and aspirational narratives, millennial gossip magazines and blogs emphasized snarky, winking commentary and salacious tidbits about the celebs' personal lives, accompanied by a raucous blend of (often unflattering) paparazzi photographs. Celebrity gossip stories still treated readers to tales of stars living the good life, stoked readers' interest in and desire to emulate them, but they also served as a warning, holding that good life up to a discriminating light, showing its potential pitfalls—addiction, betrayal, cheating spouses, eating disorders. Thus, in addition to seeking to produce pleasurable escape and envy, central to the emotional pull of these publications was the production of disgust and outrage.[27]

Recurring features like "best and worst beach bodies," "thinner by dinner," and "destroyed by fame" ensured that the bodies, faces, and life choices of celebrity women in particular would not escape public scrutiny. Articles about actors' upcoming roles and professional lives were replaced by stories about Kirsten Cavellari's breakups and Lindsay Lohan's probation violations. The new mags revealed—in hot pink, bold-face detail—the highs and lows of life for famous women and, in doing so, made them available for public scrutiny and discussion. Here fame was laid bare, shown to be both a blessing and a curse and reminding us, reassuring us, that it might not be so bad to be ordinary after all.

If there is one story that most clearly embodies the ethos of celebrity magazines in the early twenty-first century media economy it is this: Team Jen vs. Team Angelina. In the early 2000s, girl-next-door and America's favorite friend Jennifer Aniston had recently married the actor Brad Pitt, fresh off his success playing darkly hunky characters in blockbuster films like *Seven* (1995) and *Fight Club* (1999). With their nearly perfectly matched beauty and blond hair, they embodied the ideal couple. But by 2005, they had announced that they would divorce, amid fierce speculation that Pitt was having an affair with his then costar, Angelina Jolie. Jolie was famous in her own right as the daughter of actor John Voight and for her edgy roles in *Gia* (1998) and *Girl, Interrupted* (1999). Jolie was also known for creepy red carpet appearances where she kissed her brother on the lips and wore then-boyfriend Billy Bob Thornton's blood in a vial around her neck. For the gossip press, the narrative was too good to be true—Pitt had left America's sweetheart, blonde innocent Anniston, for the dark-haired wild seductress Jolie. The story practically wrote itself.

The scandal and the threesome got its own name: Brangelina. "How Angelina Stole Brad" blared the cover of *Us Weekly* in May 2005.[28] Inside? "New details! Teasing, flirting, the lure of a family. What ANGELINA had that JEN didn't." In signature gossip mag style, the headlines used direct address, the stars' first names, and personal pronouns to insinuate readers into a close, personal relationship with the stars. We were hailed as if we truly knew them, as if they were part of our own *extended family*, as Joke Hermes observed in her study of gossip magazine readers.[29] We could talk about their drama, and judge their actions, as though they were our cousins or in-laws. That we were asked to identify with one of these women (and fiercely despise the other) went without question; to be part of the story, we had to claim a team and, by turn, a moral code. Sides taken, battle lines drawn, fans became critical participants in the narrative, a point fantastically illustrated by the parade of "Team Angie" and "Team Jen" T-shirts that followed. (In a moment of meta-celebrification, Paris and Nicky Hilton were photographed sporting dueling T's). As Fox News later reported, "Aside from being a way to pledge your allegiance to a star, the tabloid shirts have also become a way to say something about your own character."[30] Meanwhile, two women—each professional, influential, and financially successful in her own right—were pitted against one another in a perpetual feud.

Thanks to the Jen/Angie saga, and similarly sensational stories, celebrity gossip magazines became so successful and prolific that *Advertising Age* coined a word for the genre: "celeb-azines."[31] In the first half of 2005 alone, *US Weekly*'s paid circulation increased 24 percent to 1.7 million, the *Star*'s increased 21 percent to 1.4 million, while *People* led the pack at 3.7 million.[32] By 2005, entertainment or celebrity news consumed more space in magazines than any other topic.[33] And while there was an 8 percent drop, overall, in magazine ad sales in the first half of 2008 as the Great Recession hit, many celebrity magazines not only survived the downturn, but increased their sales.[34] Yet, by 2016, with so many more readers going to apps or online for their celebrity news, the circulation of the celebazines overall had fallen significantly: *US Weekly* was down to just over 300,000 circulation, *Life & Style* down to just under 200,000, and *People* down to just over 650,000.[35]

As early as 2004 these magazines faced competition from digital sites as often snarky celebrity gossip blogs and websites like PerezHilton.com,

Figure 7.2. Paris and Nicky Hilton declaring their allegiance, c. 2005. X17online.com. Reprinted with permission.

TMZ.com, Gawker.com, X17online.com, and Pink is the New Blog, also proliferated. They could post stories any time, day or night, leading to a frenetic pace of publication so up-to-the-minute that even weekly print sources seemed passé. These sites required a constant geyser of stories and images, further stoking the celebrity production industry, boosting gossip interest and sales, and giving rise to an ever-expanding roster of famous figures. In the process, the historic shift already in process further accelerated, with stars no longer elevated to the removed, protected pedestals they enjoyed during the Hollywood studio system. Actors—especially A-listers—who wanted to avoid this often moved away from Hollywood or simply did not frequent sites where the paparazzi were most likely to be.

The success of the genre and the inflamed competition to get candid, unguarded, "back stage" shots of celebrities also fueled the growth of the paparazzi, whom magazine editors relied upon for revealing shots of the stars. The noxious reputation of the so-called stalkerazzi was cemented in 1997 when their relentless pursuit of thirty-six-year-old Princess Diana resulted in a car crash that was widely attributed to her driver's efforts to steer the vehicle away from pursuing photographers. Nonetheless, the images they produced continued to generate big business, especially as new lightweight, telephoto lenses and digital cameras with high-powered, long-distance shooting abilities allowed photographers to capture images of the stars faster and from greater distances. Agencies sprang up to collect and archive these images, providing writers and editors instant access to a dizzying array of photos. On any given evening in 2007—the year she shaved her head in a manic fit—between thirty and forty-five paparazzi stalked Britney Spears. The X17 agency estimated it raked in $2.5 million on Britney-related photos alone (an amount estimated at nearly a third of the agency's total revenue).[36] The celebrity gossip magazines spent record-breaking sums to obtain rare

Figure 7.3. Britney Spears drives her car through a crowd of paparazzi, 2007. Photograph by Robyn Beck, Getty Images. Reprinted with permission.

and revealing shots, peddling new images to readers each week in an endless pursuit of Spears and her subsequent, sadly predictable, breakdown. The most important product of this cycle was not the individual image or even the headline, but us, the newly shame-free, avid audience, who simply did not exist to the same extent at all in the early 1990s.

Celebazines flipped the script on traditional fan magazines, reveling in a mixture of adoration and scorn, elevating celebrities up on a pedestal, but only just long enough to let us kick them in the proverbial shins a few weeks later. They put the personal lives of female celebrities in particular under intense scrutiny—their relationships, life choices, and especially their bodies—using a tone that was often critical, and sometimes gleeful, in the face of celebrity failure. The focus of the genre was no longer on the aura of the celebrity, but also on the rest of "us," how we were supposed to assess and judge them in their everyday lives. Celebazines laid bare all the ways in which celebrities are, paradoxically beautiful and insecure, talented and flawed, unique and ordinary. Their humanity, and fallibility, was on display each week, especially in the trademark "just like us" photo spreads, ripe with evidentiary paparazzi pics of stars cruising the supermarket, eating a sandwich, and having a bad hair day to prove it.[37] And if they could have it all, so could we: the magazines provided advice on how to shop, diet, date, even give birth like the stars, driving home the neoliberal ethos that consumer and lifestyle choices could be a central component of our own success.

The Celebrification of Self

The notion that anyone can become a star has long been a mantra of celebrity narratives, reinforcing the broader American myth that anyone can make it to the top—the version of this theme displayed on reality television and in getting the "look for less" pages of the latest gossip magazines was not particularly new. What *was* changing, however, was the means of self-celebrification that were now available to those seeking the public eye. At the turn of the twenty-first century, audiences' relationship to technologies was shifting rapidly. Personal computing and high-speed Internet became integral features of everyday life, while high-quality digital cameras, video equipment, and cameras in smartphones became cheaper, smaller, and ever more user-friendly. These developments allowed media users to become content creators, able to broadcast their identities and ideas across the Internet. These simultaneous developments multiplied and diversified the number and types of sites through which individuals could broadcast themselves and cultivate a following, thus transforming themselves into public figures, in hopes of earning celebrity status, which they could then monetize.

Paris Hilton epitomized this shifting media moment. As heiress to the Hilton hotel fortune, she had plenty of money but what she truly coveted was fame. She garnered public attention after a sex tape with ex-boyfriend Rick Salomon, *1 Night in Paris*, went viral. This helped attract thirteen million viewers to the premiere episode of Hilton's new reality show, *The Simple Life* (2003–7) in which she and another wealthy socialite, Nicole Richie, struggled to take on low-paying manual labor about which they knew nothing, like farm work and cleaning rooms. Hilton quickly became a tabloid fixture.[38] She leveraged her wealth, youth, looks, and notoriety to gain coverage in the gossip press and then monetized her fame, launching product lines, recording songs, appearing in low-budget films, hosting parties at nightclubs, and making herself endlessly available to be photographed. Her arrest for driving under the influence (possibly staged?) was a sensation. She even used her 2007 release from prison (for violating probation after her DUI conviction) to promote her fashion line, donning a pair of her branded jeans during her heavily publicized release.[39]

Paris Hilton represented a new kind of celebrity, one based on personality and self-promotion above all else. Hers was not the blushing fame that claims to shun the spotlight while actually embracing it; Paris Hilton worked the press, insinuating herself, her image, and her brand wherever and whenever she could. She came to learn exactly where the paparazzi were and when, and changed clothes multiple times a day and then appeared where they were, in a new outfit they would want to photograph. In this way she could remain constantly visible. She did so unapologetically, at once fascinating and dismaying in her wholehearted embrace of the motto that any publicity is good publicity. Though she may have played the role of the dumb blonde, she cunningly embodied the millennial media moment in which she flourished. The celebrity culture of the early twenty-first century was rooted in the self-promotion of personality, the public performance of one's private self, via digital technologies. The only talent needed to warrant fame was now the ability to attract attention.

Meanwhile, digital technologies were allowing people to create, post, and share content across the country and around the world in an instant. So media users could also become media stars. Perez Hilton, for instance, launched his celebrity gossip blog with a cheeky pseudonym, gaining his own following in the process. Launched in 2004, his blog included mocking comments or "doodles" scrawled over celebrities' photos, superimposing crude sketches and nasty catchphrases in white, hand-drawn text, literally defacing the celebrity image and inviting readers to post comments. Here he could focus on the most "minute observations of celebrity behavior," encouraging judgments of an increasing array of behaviors and appearances.[40] He prodded and enacted an invitation to judge and make moral appraisals, and to do so publicly. So his readers—and those of other blogs—could bond with or against each other as they articulated or rejected the sanctity of social norms flaunted by celebrities.

Interactivity on social media sites, in other words, only intensified the role of celebrity gossip as social glue and platform for collective moral judgment and outrage. Heralded for their alleged potential to democratize the media landscape, blogs provided a space for users to project their personal ideas and interests, removing barriers to entry that had previously limited the scope and authorship of print news and magazines and blurring the line between professional journalist and amateur author. Early influential bloggers became stars in their own right; gossip guru Perez and fashion bloggers Bryanboy and Tavi Gevinson appeared as pundits on talk shows (Perez, *The View*, Wendy Williams), starred as judges on reality competition shows (Bryanboy, *America's Next Top Model*), and gave TED talks (Gevinson). Bloggers were soon invited to participate in industry events, including red carpets and runway shows, premieres, and television dish sessions. They also drew large sums in advertising fees, sponsorships, and endorsements, converting their symbolic power into economic power.

Unlike writers and editors within established media networks, bloggers had no compunctions about posting an unflattering pic of a star experiencing a wardrobe malfunction or behaving badly after a long night of partying because, unlike traditional sources, they had no allegiance to the star or her publicists. Vloggers—amateur photographers and pros at TMZ alike—relished morning-after videos of stumbling stars, posting snide headlines in an effort to drive traffic to their sites. Where stars of the twentieth century could rely on careful handlers and savvy public relations firms to ensure public approval—or mitigate disasters—online's nonhierarchical structure, rapid content transmission, and lack of concern for privacy (or even accuracy) meant that it was even harder for stars to control the stories or images that would gain traction with online audiences.[41] If these developments were problematic for the pictured celebs, they were irresistible to readers. In 2007, Neilson estimated that PerezHilton.com had thirty-three million page views in a single month from visitors in the United States alone.[42] Whether crafting content in hopes of drawing the spotlight, or by checking out the latest blogosphere gossip, digital media drew us closer into the echo chamber of celebrity culture.

Social Media and the Side Stage: Revisiting Goffman in the Twenty-First Century

Soon, and in response to bloggers like Perez Hilton, the stars began using these same techniques to enhance their appeal to fans, bolster their image, and manage their digital profiles in the face of bloggers' efforts to rip off their cultivated veneer of glamour. This became especially pronounced with the proliferation of smartphones as one of the primary ways young people engage with the media, devices with us nearly all the time and in constant use, and devices everyday people can also use to photograph the famous. Goffman's concept of the presentation of self, therefore, is perhaps more relevant than ever, his schema helping us to unpack and appreciate a successful or unsuccessful performance of the persona we want to project. Across social media, we manage our back- and front-stage versions of self, posting extra-flattering profile pics, deleting embarrassing posts from hometown friends.

These practices have led to the application of a term previously used primarily for museum exhibits: to curate. Now, for celebrities and ordinary people alike, the front-stage version of self is produced through a dynamic and diffuse web of media outlets through which people carefully select, organize, and display what they will and will not present on social media while making the photos and comments they post seem genuine and spontaneous. The purpose is to further heighten a sense of intimacy between audience members and celebrities in what seems to be increasingly "unmediated" close-ups of their actually lived existences. As Sean Redmond notes, "It's as if one has unfettered access to their lifestyles, behaviors, hang-ups, material bodies and interior selves."[43] Fans can feel that they have entree to more regions of the celebrity's life and persona, which further cements identification and adds to the celebrity's symbolic and economic value. Social media thus further extends celebrity culture's purchase on our culture overall. Twitter, Facebook, Snapchat, and Instagram have placed more demands on celebrities, especially those not sitting on the secure perch of "A-list status," as they now have to be present on multiple platforms and seemingly available to and engaged with their fans 24/7.

Joshua Meyrowitz, updating Goffman's work, contends that there has been an expansion of the realms of personal performance.[44] There now exists a middle region, a side stage, which appears, for all intents and purposes, as an authentic back stage, honest and true, but which is, in actuality, a secondary performance zone. While this side stage may appear casual and unregulated, certainly less polished than the glittering front stage, the performance of self in this region is actually highly regulated and carefully curated as well. As Meyrowitz writes, "Whatever aspects of the rehearsal become visible to the audience must be integrated into the show itself. . . . When the dividing line between onstage and backstage behaviors moves in either direction, the nature of the drama changes accordingly. The more rehearsal space that is lost, the more the onstage drama comes to resemble an extemporaneous backstage rehearsal." Thus, "middle region behavior develops when audience members gain a 'sidestage' view.' That is, they see parts of the traditional backstage area along with parts of the traditional onstage area; they see the performer move from backstage to onstage to backstage."[45]

Consider as an example Gwyneth Paltrow's Facebook page. Here, Paltrow looks appropriately casual, hair tousled, posting about getaways in the Hamptons and green juices and the alleged challenges of sharing a bathroom with your mate, but all of the site's content is designed to bolster Paltrow's image as a crunchy, healthy, natural girl who just happens to spend thousands on her beauty routine. And to generate

synergy, exposure, and sales, most posts link to her lifestyle blog—goop
.com—or to brand extensions where followers can consume, and thereby
be, like Gwyn. On the one hand, we may view these digital performances
as simple extensions of Paltrow's front-stage self—they reflect her carefully controlled brand and performance of self. On the other hand, as
Meyrowitz points out, to view these performances simply as new front
regions would be to ignore the complex ways in which these new platforms challenge our assumptions about public and private, image and
authenticity, and seem to grant us access to the back stage, which of
course is carefully performed as well.[46]

With the public and private realms of self-presentation thus collid-
ing, audiences (and the bloggers and paparazzi of course) increasingly
seek out what Goffman terms *ungovernable acts*—those behaviors that
cannot be easily controlled or maintained: the subtle eye roll, bored
expression ("resting bitch face"), or truthful remark that slips out. The
paparazzi, the tabloids, and the derisive blogs take especial delight in
capturing celebrities in ungovernable moments, their faces contorted,
looking drunk or crazed or out of control in some other way. Because we
know that most people—and especially those in the public eye—seek to
present themselves in the most favorable light, we often use the ungovernable aspects of a person's expressive behavior "as a check upon the
validity of what is conveyed by the governable aspects."[47] It is these unguarded actions or gestures, as opposed to the performance the person
presents, which we feel are the true indices of what a person is really like.

These observational strategies provide audiences with a kind of lit-
mus test; we think we can determine how genuine, likeable, and "like
us" a star may be by observing them closely. In interviews, do their facial
expressions, body language, and gestures match what they are saying?
When they are out in public, if they can be caught doing something they
have failed to control or govern, that suggests their public image is a lie.
When stars slip up and reveal themselves to be suspect, the results can
be career ending.

Thus, the increased need to manage fans' access, in a way the stars can
control and curate. This involves protecting their back stage, to maintain
some privacy, while appearing to provide a more authentic interaction.
Celebrities are brands, and many have become determined to use social
media to control their brand identity and be their own publicists (with,

of course, help from a social media staff.) On "I.Am.Beyonce.com," the pop singer's personal blog, glossy photos of her at professional events— the Super Bowl, on the cover of *Vogue*, on the Metropolitan Museum's "Met Gala" red carpet—are posted beside intimate shots of the star with her husband and children, or behind the scenes at a concert, and with her eyes closed, in a moment of personal reflection. The blog allows Queen Bey to self-promote—her projects, products, and brand—while providing her beyhive with more, and more personal, access to her life. Taylor Swift's website hosts a tab called "Taylor Connect," which allows fans to share info with Swift and a community of other fans. The flexible, interactive, and customizable nature of digital content allows stars to craft and curate a version of themselves that is approachable, likable, and on-brand. Whether the content is generated by publicists and ghostwriters, or by the star herself, is often unknown, yet the resulting digital presentation nevertheless seeks to provide fans with a sense of the "genuine," unfiltered star.[48]

But blogs and websites are nothing compared to the reach of social media. Celebrities know we want access to their back stage and they provide it. They and their handlers appreciate that in this increasingly interconnected and interactive media environment, the public's demand for engagement and a seeming participation in the celebrity's world has amplified even more. So the opportunity to self-promote is greater than ever before, but so too is the pressure to do so. Facebook, Instagram, and Twitter allow us to "like" and "follow" celebrities quickly, constantly, even mindlessly. When we connect with stars in these virtual spaces— when we "like" or follow" their accounts—their photos, tweets, and ideas automatically appear in our newsfeeds, and become integrated into our social world. Celebrities use personal pronouns and casual, at times confessional, remarks to foster a sense of connection across these platforms. Like when Kim Kardashian West tweets, "If anyone is in San Diego make sure you stop by my grandma's kids clothing store Shannon & Company! I used to spend my summers there!"[49] They also post photos, especially of themselves, as when model Chrissy Teigen, known for her social media humor and relatability, posts makeup-free pics of herself with her daughter Luna on Instagram. Celebrity selfies—self-portraiture for the digital age—are shared across social media platforms, most notably Instagram. These images, sometimes funny, sometimes intimate, sometimes blatant marketing ploys, now take into account that fans have and want parasocial relationships with the stars.

Our engagement with celebrities on social media mirrors and inter-twines with our engagement with loved ones and friends. As we scroll along, updates from Rihanna and J-Lo appear alongside those of our close friends and neighbors, tweets from Laverne Cox and Katy Perry pop up beside posts from our moms. We may hope for a virtual interac-tion with our favorite stars in the form of a "like" or retweet. Some fans go even further, creating accounts inspired by, or parodying, favorite celebrities. On Twitter, for instance, fans have created accounts that echo the voice (and imagine the thoughts) of famous figures from Bill Clinton to the Queen of England. Even famous fictional celebs, whom Rojek has labeled *celeactors*, inspire their own handles: Harry Potter, Cersei Lannister, and Bart Simpson all have their own accounts. That fans are motivated not only to follow or communicate with celebrities on social media, but also to create their own content from the perspective of their favorite famous figures speaks to the platforms' personal appeal and cre-ative flexibility.

Celebrities recognize this potential too. And no star has mastered the art of cross-platform digital self-promotion better than Kim Kardashian, whose fame has resulted from her taking advantage of the reality TV craze and combining it with the affordances of Twitter, Instagram, and other platforms. While routinely dismissed as "famous for being famous," Kardashian works assiduously to maintain her visibility, and thus her financial worth. The lifestyle mogul, who initially rose to fame thanks to her father Robert, who defended O. J. Simpson, and a starring role in a widely distributed sex tape, now anchors a branding empire that includes beauty and fashion lines, skin care products, fragrances, corsets, books, diet products, video games, emojis, and the famous real-ity television show. Kim, along with the rest of the Kardashian family, ex-pertly uses social media to synergistically bolster multiple brands. Kim takes to her Twitter account (over forty-six million followers) to endorse her brands and other lifestyle products, for which she earns a kickback, all while posting selfies, musings, even her political perspectives.

All of it is a synergistic gold mine. A follower who notices a tweet about the star's reality show, *Keeping Up with the Kardashians*, tunes in to see Kim tweeting, to confirm that she, herself, is doing the tweeting and not some staff member, affirming her authenticity. Photos on Face-book show Kim's daughter modeling mom's very own children's fashion line. Likewise, with over sixty-four million followers, when sister Kylie posts about her newest line of lip kits on Instagram, it invariably sells out.[50] In this way, the Kardashians provide their followers with live, ap-parently unrestricted access—Kim's Twitter is "verified," meaning the account is actually hers—to their personal thoughts and everyday lives. As Scheiner McClean notes in her book about the Kardashian brand, "Social media . . . permits celebrities such as Kim Kardashian to sustain fame and fortune by building a portrayal of authenticity while simul-taneously intensely self-promoting."[51] This type of self-exposure and self-reflexivity is now taken for granted by audiences, accustomed to interacting with stars and consuming celebrity brands as a routine part of their online engagement.

Kim's mobile app—*Kim Kardashian's Hollywood*—further stitches the user into this digital relationship with the star. *Hollywood* is a mo-bile game, released in 2014, in which users take on a Kim avatar, com-plete with her most recognizable hair styles, fashion accessories, and family members, and move throughout Kim's virtual world to complete tasks, including working jobs and going on dates. Successful players earn fans and enhance their celebrity ranking (the goal is to make the A-list) all while earning virtual currency that can be used to purchase new clothing and accessories. Users act as Kim, interact with her real-life associates, and even style virtual characters after members of the Kardashian family. It is a hyperreflexive, arguably campy gameplay that nevertheless allows fans to enhance their relationship with the Kar-dashian clan by virtually embodying their identities while once again reinforcing the stars' renown and bankroll. In 2016, Kim tweeted that the game had netted her $80 million for the previous year. While some have questioned the accuracy of that sum, it is clear that Kim Kar-dashian has successfully managed to embed her persona across digital media platforms.[52]

Kim's success rests largely on her ability to foster a sense of inti-macy in ways that appear to be unmediated, like an extended running diary of her actual lived existence. Of course this access is highly con-trived, managed, and mediated with the star's symbolic and economic value in mind. But social media thus further extends and cements our

Figure 7.4. Kim Kardashian Hollywood game, 2017. Photograph by Andrew Harrer, Getty Images. Reprinted with permission.

identification with stars like the Kardashians even as it places greater demands on celebrities, now expected to be present on multiple platforms and seemingly available to and engaged with their fans 24/7.

Social Stardom: From Influencers to Instafame

While social media allows established stars to maintain and expand their brands, it also provides a platform for those seeking the spotlight, and has led to a new phenomenon, Instafame: having a great number of followers on one or more apps. This has been yet another major technological revolution in the production of celebrity. Social media "tacitly promises fame (and subsequent wealth) to 'ordinary' users" and thus encourages communicative techniques Terri Senft has labeled "microcelebrity."[53] This involves people—famous and not—seeking to boost their visibility and popularity via photo and video posts, blogs, podcasts, comments, and Tweets to create, maintain, and increase their audience.[54] Micro-celebrity "is a way of thinking of oneself as a celebrity, and acting accordingly"; thus practitioners strategically construct their presentation of self to appeal to others and regard those they perform for and interact with as fans. Those who follow YouTube stars or Instagram influencers can often see them as more authentic, because they have not emerged from the more established star-making system.[55]

The emergence of YouTube in 2005 allowed anyone to post video of, well, just about anything. Unlike Facebook, which directs users to content created by friends, family, and acquaintances, YouTube's audience is a global, loosely connected network with a vast pool of possible viewers. If your video is funny enough, ridiculous enough, or entertaining enough, it may go viral. When, in 2007, an overwrought, tearful Chris Crocker begged the public to "leave Britney [Spears] alone!," his video rant was viewed over 250 million times; Crocker's YouTube channel would become one of the platform's most viewed. Other breakout stars, such as the toddler whose little brother Charlie infamously bit his finger, drew close to a billion views.

Viral fame may come quickly to some, but other content creators work to establish their brand and grow their audience by posting regularly, interacting with and cultivating fans, and engaging followers across social media. Beauty vlogger Michelle Phan used her YouTube channel, which in early 2018 boasted over eight million subscribers, to launch a popular beauty subscription service, Ipsy, and her own line of cosmetics. Beauty vlogging is one slice of a popular YouTube genre—instructional videos. Want to learn how to knit? Practice guitar chords? Check out some yoga poses? Whatever you're interested in, chances are there are a dozen videos featuring vloggers ready to teach you, step by step, just how to do it. We can fast forward, rewind, and revisit at our own pace, all the while getting to know and trust the instructors. Phan has attributed her success to the community-focused nature of YouTube, which has allowed her to develop a brand that her followers see as "authentic" and "trustworthy."[56] In 2015, Ipsy was valued at $500 million.

Another influencer who has monetized his brand through social media is Tyler Oakley, who, as an openly gay teenager, began posting quirky, funny videos about his everyday life on YouTube in 2007. With vlogs like "How My Mom Knew I Was Gay," to "Stories of Queer Resilience," to "Becoming a Human-Sized Candy Bar," Tyler has attracted the attention of nearly eight million followers on YouTube alone. His cross-platform social media presence (he also posts regularly on Facebook,

Twitter, and Instagram, with more than twenty-four million followers across the sites) has attracted attention from mainstream media outlets. He has published with Gallery Books, hosted the Grammy's live red carpet coverage for CBS, and interviewed dozens of celebrities for his video blog posts, from members of the pop band One Direction to actress and activist Laverne Cox. In turn, Oakley has become a celebrity in his own right, appearing on talk shows, hosting media events, attending red carpet and fashion galas, and becoming an influential advocate for queer visibility and LGBTQA representation online.

Vlogging is a form of mass communication that *feels* intimate. Videos often have limited production value, using stationary cameras, basic sound and lighting techniques, and are shot from within the creator's personal space—her living room, den, or bedroom. Vloggers typically speak directly to the camera, placing them up-close-and-personal with the viewer, which further reinforces a sense of intimate conversation while contributing to the genre's DIY aesthetic. Unlike our parasocial relationships with blockbuster movie stars, our conversations with social influencers can actually be bidirectional; viewers can comment, and successful vloggers build their following by engaging directly with fans through these message boards. As social media scholar David Craig notes, these features allow content creators to engage their community of viewers "directly through the screen."[57] The challenge here, of course, with audiences having so many media platforms and outlets to choose from, is how to be distinctive enough to garner enough eyeballs. With thousands or millions of very different "followers," one has the old mass media problem, of constructing a persona and performance that will appeal to as many people as possible and alienate as few people as possible.[58]

These engagements now occur on a host of global networking platforms, including Twitter, Instagram, and Snapchat, which have produced a wide-ranging pool of "influencers," users whose content is regularly viewed millions—even billions—of times. Part of the allure of these sites is that they extend the myth of demotic fame; it's now commonly accepted that anyone can become "Instafamous," even though we know most people never gain widespread attention on social media.[59] Still, some social stars have emerged, and have even transitioned into mainstream media arenas. And with the success of the podcast "Serial" in 2014, other podcasts—such as *Pod Save America*, featuring former Obama administration staffers; *S-Town* by Brian Reed; and *My Favorite Murder* with Karen Kilgariff and Georgia Hardstark—have made their hosts famous as well, even if only among a niche audience.

Advertisers and established brands have come to understand that clicks and views can translate into significant revenue. High-school students turned Instagram stars have recently been commissioned to design a line of children's clothes for Target, Joy Cho (who has over 380,000 followers on Insta) now has her own line of Band-Aids, and beauty guru James Charles became the first male Cover Girl thanks to his social media following.[60] Now, cultural capital across social media translates into economic capital in the established media marketplace, as influencers serve as spokespeople and brand ambassadors whose taste and personalities speak directly to their community of viewers.

Thus, social influencers are increasingly moving into mainstream media spaces once reserved for traditional celebrities. Some, like Issa Rae, move from creators of shows on YouTube (*Awkward Girl*) to creators and stars of shows on HBO (*Insecure*). Social stars and viral video producers now regularly appear across the talk TV circuit on shows like *Ellen* and *The View* and popular news and entertainment websites cover their product lines and popular postings. MTV's *TRL* has recently tapped social media stars to serve as on-air hosts and red carpet correspondents.[61] Even reality TV has taken notice; the cast of the twenty-eighth season of CBS's *The Amazing Race* was comprised entirely of social media personalities from Instagram, Vine, and YouTube (including Oakley).

Curating Ourselves

Celebrities' digital influence, combined with the myriad avenues for self-promotion afforded by reality TV, gossip magazines, and digital platforms, has resulted in an amplification of the mantra that everyone can be a star. Celebrity culture has generated a pressure and a desire to be more visible, and to control that visibility. Graeme Turner calls this shift the *demotic turn*, a kind of democratization of fame resulting from "the multiplication of [media] outlets, of formats and of the numbers of people subject to the discursive processes of 'celebrification'" that results in "the opportunity of celebrity spreading beyond elites of one kind or another and into the expectations of the population in general."[62] "Ordinary people," David Schmid goes on, "have never been more visible in the media, nor have their own utterances ever been reproduced with the faithfulness, respect and accuracy that they are today."[63] The scripts for how to do so—how to present ourselves, to pose and perform—come from the visual and rhetorical tropes of celebrity culture. We can now broadcast the minutiae of our everyday lives on personal blogs, Twitter feeds, YouTube channels, even Pinterest pages. In this fame economy, merit and talent no longer matter particularly. Fame is now more accessible and more producible than ever before, but it is also more fleeting.

Whether we're seeking fame or not, social media platforms encourage users to self-expose, to publicize our inner thoughts, to share the highlight reels of our lives. Today's celebrities often make a living by doing just that, but even those who use these platforms casually may feel the pressure to keep up, to curate their image, to anticipate the public gaze. In order to succeed, socially, even professionally, requires that we consider our own audience. Even professional networking sites like LinkedIn call us to produce a digital dossier that will embody our personal brand. If we share an unflattering photo, or accidentally insult the wrong person, or fail to interact at all, we risk losing cultural capital, and can even face real-world punishment. In an age where anyone can be famous online, we must all be ready for our close-up.

The popularity of the selfie underlines this point. As we snap pics of ourselves with our mobile devices (sometimes with the aid of the ridiculous selfie stick) we create, as Jerry Saltz writes, "an instant visual communication of where we are, what we are doing, who we think we are, and who we think is watching."[64] Just as Renaissance self-portraits or Roman sculptures were used to establish a public face, selfies help us to define ourselves and bolster our social status. These new portraits can be produced instantaneously and shared globally by anyone with an inexpensive digital camera and an Instagram account. Just as celebrities must manage and protect their public persona, to appear authentic, genuine, and maybe just a bit enviable, so must we. Studies show that a major motive for active participation in social networking is impression management, our desire to control how others perceive us.[65] Fans now take, and share, selfies of themselves with celebrities, a kind of digital proof that marks the celebrity as an actual part of their online self-portrait, an active presence in their digital persona.

Increased fan interactivity (however curated) and the ability of audiences to respond to and, often, criticize celebrities, pose a challenge to stars. Gossip blogs in particular live to "undermine the often carefully crafted image that the entertainment industry works tirelessly to cultivate and maintain." As people have become more cognizant of and cynical about how much work goes into celebrity image-making, there has been more of an effort to try to knock them off their pedestals.[66] As Adrienne Lai has noted, given the voraciousness and increasing invasiveness of the paparazzi and tabloid press, "celebrities must negotiate some sort of working relationship" with them to keep them at bay, "providing them with material while still attempting to maintain some separation of their public and private lives."[67] But the blogs whose coin of the realm is circulating those often embarrassing "unguarded" moments, don't just rely on the paparazzi; they also urge everyday people to use their smartphones if they see a celebrity in action—especially behaving badly—and to then send the images in. In the age of more democratized celebrity, we want to have increased access to and intimacy with certain stars, and we also want to be part of the production and circulation process that produces and sustains their stardom.

The Burden of Celebrity

Given the enormous privilege celebrity provides—admiration, envy, deference, access to other famous people, wealth—it may be hard to have sympathy for the famous when they complain about wanting their privacy or about being hounded in public by photographers and fans. But unlike Paris Hilton or the Kardashians, who pursued fame and visibility for their own sake, some stars who went into acting or athletics or musical performance because they cared about the craft are unprepared for the relentless intrusions that are the consequences of success. As Julie Klam in *The Stars in Our Eyes* noted after interviewing some celebrities, "They didn't know how little control they would have over their own lives once they realized their dream."[68] The actor Timothy Hutton, who at the age of twenty won an Academy Award as Best Supporting Actor for his role in *Ordinary People* (1980), described what it's like to be at dinner, involved in a deep conversation with a family member or friend, and get interrupted by a fan seeking an autograph or a picture. Hutton reports that if he says, "I'm having dinner with my son right now. Do you mind if we do it later?," most people get offended. Some people just come to his table and sit down to talk without even asking permission. As a celebrity you have to be nice to people, no matter how rude they are to you. Because if you aren't, especially now in the world of social media, "they'll tell it ten more times than the story when you're just being nice. It multiplies like crazy if you're not nice to them." Hutton notes that even if you say as politely as possible "now isn't a good time," it can turn into "what a prick that guy was." "Politeness for you turns out to be impoliteness for them."[69]

Of course, the invasions can be much worse, also exacerbated by the expansion of the paparazzi and social media platforms. These are violations stars of the 1940s could not even imagine. Jennifer Lawrence, among others, had her iCloud account hacked into in 2014 and nude photos of her leaked onto the Internet. She acknowledged that most people feel that losing your privacy is the price you should willingly pay for stardom, that it is considered "part of my job." But most people fail to appreciate how stressful that is. "I knew the paparazzi were going to be a reality in my life. . . . But I didn't know that I would feel anxiety every time I open my front door, or that being chased by 10 men you don't know, or being surrounded, feels invasive and makes me feel scared and gets my adrenaline going every day."[70]

While Hilton or the Kardashians invite having their privacy violated in exchange for ongoing visibility (thus earning the moniker "media whores"), most celebrities have not, in fact, consented to have their privacy so constantly invaded. Yet celebrities in the United States have relatively limited privacy rights. Laws against trespassing, for example, do protect against paparazzi intruding on your property to take pictures, and in California also prohibit the use of a "visual or auditory enhancing device"—telephoto lenses, microphones—"regardless of whether there is a physical trespass . . . under circumstances in which the plaintiff has a reasonable expectation of privacy."[71] In other words, when out in public, at a restaurant, walking your dog, shopping, when so many of those "just like us" shots are taken, you can't have such an expectation, even though you might regard dinner with your husband as private. Paparazzi in California can also be charged with and penalized for "false imprisonment" if they swarm a celebrity in a way that prevents them from moving or driving away freely. By contrast, some courts in Europe have held that public figures could sue publications for publishing photographs taken of them in public against their will, and J. K. Rowling won a case in which she sought to protect her son from being photographed in public.[72]

In 2014 California enacted a law making it illegal to use drones to take celebrity photographs, which was enacted in part in response to various stars upset about what they labeled the "pedorazzi" stalking their children.[73] One paparazzo, for example, lurked outside the preschool of Halle Berry's four-year-old daughter to get a picture, and Suri Cruise took to putting a doll in front of her face to avoid being photographed.[74] Jennifer Garner, in testimony before the California legislature, reported that on any given day there could be "as many as 15 cars of photographers waiting outside our home." As she sought to take her kids to school or the doctor, they would be swarmed by "large aggressive men . . . causing a mob scene . . . yelling and crowding around the kids," making her seventeen month old "terrified."[75]

Thus, as visually driven blogs and social networking sites have proliferated, with some celebrities embracing them to post intimate images and commentary, they have also provided more methods for and platforms to violate celebrities' privacy. And those who willingly, even eagerly, encourage fans to enter their "side stage" views, help foster the expectation that all celebrities should accept and even provide such access.

More recently, social media has also begun to function as a space for public debate and disclosure around the moral, ethical, and legal failings of celebrities. Just as digital technologies may foster fan communities and enhance a star's public-facing brand, these spaces can also function as sites of public outcry, through which user-participants engage in celebrity bashing. At times, this shaming (sometimes generated by "trolls," users whose sole goal is to create controversy and feed online feuds) can be malicious, aimed at knocking celebrities off their pedestals— commentators expressed a deeply felt twinge of schadenfreude after Kim Kardashian was robbed at gunpoint in a Paris hotel in 2016. In these instances, Twitter may seem like a cliquey high school cafeteria, full of gossipers eager to launch the nastiest barbs.

Critical social discourse around famous figures also plays an important role in that it allows us to speak truth to the rich and powerful in a public forum. In early October 2017, the *New York Times*, and then the *New Yorker*, published stories detailing accusations of sexual harassment and assault by a number of women spanning several decades against Harvey Weinstein, influential film producer, executive, and cofounder of Miramax. While the stories laid the groundwork, it was the subsequent social media reaction that ignited a media firestorm. In rapid succession, a series of A-list celebrities, including Rose McGowan, Ashley Judd, Angelina Jolie, and Gwyneth Paltrow, spoke out against Weinstein on Twitter and across social media. Shortly thereafter, actress Alyssa Milano encouraged people to share their own stories of sexual abuse and harassment using the hashtag #MeToo. The call produced a viral catharsis, with millions of users, including celebrities, sharing their stories in an expression of solidarity.[76]

The discourse also prompted other survivors of assault to step forward; in the months that followed the Weinstein accusations, numerous politicians, actors, and businessmen were publicly accused. And while the debate may have been virtual, the consequences were quite real, with political commentator Mark Halpern, TV host Charlie Rose, *New York Times* reporter Glenn Thrush, comedian Louis C.K., and actors Ed Westwick and Kevin Spacey all resigning or being suspended from projects due to allegations against them. As of November 21, 2017, the *New York Times* reported thirty-four well-known men accused of sexual assault in the weeks following the Weinstein story.[77]

The relentlessness and ubiquity of twenty-first-century celebrity media has produced an environment in which famous figures can no longer reasonably expect their personal lives to remain private. For stars, this may be a branding boon or a day-to-day nightmare, depending on the degree to which they aim to seek out and maintain media attention. These developments have also fundamentally affected the nature and form of audience interaction with famous figures. We are not only able to *consume* celebrity culture, but may also take part as active, user-creators *within* that culture. Through social platforms, we can attend to the minutiae of celebrities' lives and judge their words and actions. Finally, and perhaps most critically, we can discuss our experiences, opinions, and beliefs on social media. The ability of the rich and famous to control their public image is now fundamentally challenged by an audience engaged in public social discourse. Online, we have the power to counter, or even condemn, those who we once held up as idols.

Conclusion

Celebrity culture creates highly visible people who are enmeshed in a very elaborate, industrialized production process—they are manufactured cogs—yet are also connected in often deeply meaningful ways to audiences—they are admired as distinct, charismatic individuals. We have seen how, over the years, celebrity has been "machine-made by technology, advertising and public relations."[1] It has been this interplay between the production needs of the ever-expanding, profit-driven entertainment and information industries and the individual and collective hopes, dreams, and fears of fans that has sustained and even engorged this phenomenon.

Celebrity culture has, since the nineteenth century, steadily gained a greater role in and purchase on American culture as communications technologies have proliferated. We have sought to show that while celebrity culture has certainly intensified in the early twenty-first century, it has a long history in our society and has its roots in the urbanization, population growth, rise in leisure time, and multiplying of entertainment and media outlets that began in the 1800s. And certain technologies and media have required and rewarded different traits: physical beauty (film), an appealing voice (radio), musical virtuosity (radio and sound recording), an engaging, reassuring personality (television, YouTube, Instagram).

Each one expanded the realm for celebrity production, and brought celebrities more closely and more intimately into our everyday lives. Radio was the first technology to bring a performer's—or the president's—voice right into your home, a revolutionary shift in the proximity between the famous and everyday people. Television furthered this by adding visual proximity. Today, in the digital age of media convergence—when so many communications technologies are interconnected—celebrity culture is everywhere, on billboards, the sides of buses, on television, in magazines, our computer screens, even (especially) in the phones in our pockets.

We have also sought to trace the persistence of various precedents set, since the nineteenth and early twentieth centuries, in celebrity production and celebrity journalism. P. T. Barnum was the pioneer in showing how to create stars, and while he did so through what was called "hoopla" and "bunkum," he also did so with people who were talented or unusual. He turned unknown people into "must-see" stars. The "just like us" discourse we take for granted has its roots in the "behind-the-scenes" profiles of vaudeville stars, and it was the movie fan magazines of the 1920s that cemented the "at home with" famous stars features. Gossip columns and columnists, with fawning tidbits but also dirt and scandal, became fixtures in our culture. By the 1920s, the template for how sports heroes had to present themselves was set. World War II established the importance of charitable work to a celebrity's profile. Simply put, many of the tropes so familiar to us today have long historical arcs that are testimony both to what we desire from such coverage and to their ongoing durability despite massive changes in our society.

The metastasizing of celebrity culture, its omnipresence, is, as we have seen, the result not only of multiple interlocking technologies but also of various industrial, corporate, economic, and cultural forces. As media outlets, dependent on ratings, clicks, and views, have multiplied, all of them competing for that increasingly exhausted resource—our attention—they have sought to generate more potentially attention-grabbing people. But this visibility must be constantly maintained through all sorts of increasingly technology-dependent strategies. Those who have succeeded in securing the spotlight must maintain their visibility, and their likeability, to avoid losing all the perks—the money, the deference, opportunities for new roles or performance venues—that come with fame. To cite just one example, Doris Roberts, who starred as the mother in the hit TV series *Everyone Loves Raymond*, said that during the height of the show's success she could walk into the incredibly swanky New York restaurant Orso and get a table anytime she wanted. A few years after the show went off the air, she walked in and they told her they were all booked. As she summed it up, "When you're hot, you're hot, and when you're not, you're not."[2] Celebrity, despite all the work and luck that goes into achieving it, can be extremely evanescent and fleeting. This is especially true today when the churn of the news and entertainment cycle seems to operate at breakneck speed.

The digital proliferation of platforms and venues has indeed meant that through a skillful use of YouTube, Instagram, Snapchat, or landing a spot on a reality TV show, those previously unknown can become widely known. The technologies of social media have enabled celebrity to indeed become more democratized. Some have argued that this "obliterates the old distinctions . . . between serious and trivial endeavors."[3] But while Khloe Kardashian may have over sixty-eight million Instagram followers, and Tyler Oakley nearly eight million YouTube subscribers, from which they each profit handsomely, a celebrity hierarchy remains, especially between achieved celebrity (Leonardo DiCaprio, Serena Williams) and attributed celebrity (Snooki of *Jersey Shore*, the latest "housewife" or "bachelor").

At the same time, with a new fluidity among some media, and ongoing competition for our eyeballs and discretionary income among various media industries, the prestige of some outlets is changing. In the 1990s and early 2000s, for example, the hierarchy between being a "movie star," especially an "A-list" star like Denzel Washington, Jane Fonda, Diane Keaton, Jennifer Lawrence, or Tom Hanks, and being a TV star (with the possible exception of TV teen idols) remained rigid. A few, like George Clooney, made the transition from TV to movies. But with the film industry in the early twenty-first century catering increasingly to young people (especially young men), particularly through its summer action or comic-book-inspired blockbusters, opportunities for complex film roles diminished. By the 2010s, television technologies, and content, were once again shifting. In what could be seen as a push back against the flood of reality shows, cable channels, led by HBO and then Showtime and AMC, became much more daring and experimental in their programming, providing actors with the chance to inhabit challenging breakout roles, like *Breaking Bad*'s Walter White, played by Bryan Cranston, who became an A-list actor as a result. Starring in cable and then streaming shows like *Mad Men*, *House of Cards*, *Orange Is the New Black*, or *Grace & Frankie* took on a cachet television actors had not enjoyed prior to the twenty-first century. And production quality dramatically increased.

In some ways, television in the twenty-first century has become more like film, with larger budgets and more expansive and complex scripts. HBO, for example, now spends an estimated $8–$10 million for each episode of some of its juggernauts like *Game of Thrones*, *Westworld*, and *Vinyl*.[4] Plus, the affordability of flat screen Plasma, LCD (liquid crystal display), and LED (light-emitting diode) televisions, coupled with digital, high-resolution production techniques, provide larger screen sizes and enhanced image quality, all of which contribute to a new model of "high quality," prestige television. With these changes has come a shift in the flexibility of the role of television celebrity. "A-listers" now move between film and television—comedians like Aziz Ansari produce stand-up specials, network TV shows, a bestselling book, and a streaming series on Netflix, while A-list movie stars like Anthony Hopkins, Reese Witherspoon, and Nicole Kidman take up roles on made-for-television series.

On top of this, time-shifting technologies, such as DVR (digital video recorder), and streaming services, such as Netflix, Hulu, and Amazon, have also allowed viewers to customize and control their viewing experiences. Indeed, television watching no longer requires a TV. Viewers can tune in on third screens, devices like laptops, tablets, or smartphones that are not primarily or solely intended for television viewing. This flexible, personal nature of television viewing also allows viewers to exert greater control over their exposure to celebrities—we may tune in to less famous folks who we enjoy, or avoid big stars with whom we do not identify. Now that viewers can binge watch the latest season of *Stranger Things* or watch their favorite episode of *My So Called Life* on demand or repeat, the possibilities for viewer immersion, transportation, and parasocial relations increase. With this kind of intensive, concentrated viewing, audiences may feel ever more tied to these worlds, developing deep and meaningful attachments to favorite characters and the stars who play them.

The blurring of the boundaries between news and entertainment, and the celebrification of many politicians, with their exposure on and use of multiple media platforms, seems to have come to its ultimate conclusion with the election of a reality TV star, Donald Trump, to the presidency. By 1992, when Bill Clinton and Al Gore were running for office together, they appeared on talk shows, late night TV (where Clinton played the saxophone on *The Arsenio Hall Show*), and, famously, on MTV, where a high school student felt she could ask the man running for president if he wore boxers or briefs. A new criterion emerged about presidential candidates: Would you want to have a beer with him (and, later, her)?

By the time we got to the 2016 election, one already famous person, Hillary Clinton, who had been in the national spotlight since 1992 as a political celebrity, went up against a reality-TV celebrity (and in New York City, a recurring tabloid fixture) Donald Trump, who had presided over *The Apprentice* from 2004 to 2015. Because he had no political experience to claim as preparing him for the job, and violated so many norms of decorum about what a politician could and could not say, he was extremely newsworthy, especially by television news standards. In addition, he drew throughout his campaign upon the image he had cultivated for himself on reality television, that of a tough-talking and successful businessman. Trump also communicated to his supporters and thus to news outlets via Twitter, unprecedented for a presidential candidate.

Because of its 140-character limit per Tweet, Twitter fit into several established news routines—the use, of course, of headlines and snappy pull quotes, increasingly shorter soundbites given to presidents (and all political candidates), and cable news' reliance on the chyron. Thus his Tweets exploited these preexisting practices, while making them more explosive, because what he said to and about fellow candidates (and celebrities) so violated political conventions they were highly newsworthy. As a highly dramatic media performer who loved the spotlight and sensed that voters were weary of carefully scripted "front stage" personas, Trump took unspeakable comments about race, immigrants, women, and Muslims—as well as about his opponents—out of the back stage and onto the front stage of his rallies. He brought the required performative style of reality TV to which people had become accustomed—bold, declarative, often insulting assertions, dressing down failing contestants—to the political realm. Twitter, which matched his rhetorical style of short words, declarative statements, and incendiary insults, was the perfect medium for him.

Cable channels have to fill the 24/7 news hole, and are always looking for "scoops" or exclusives, especially during a campaign, so when Trump would simply phone in, his calls were of course taken and aired. Not only were most of his rallies broadcast on CNN, they were also plugged with hyped-up chyrons reading "Donald Trump Expected to Speak Any Minute." Because his rallies were filled with drama, vilification, even violence, they were often front-page or leading stories. So in this way,

Trump constantly set the agenda in terms of substance, journalistic practice, and rhetoric, as well as about what most merited coverage—him. He led, and the news media followed. As a result he got approximately $4 billion worth of free media.

Once he came into office, Trump continued to behave like the star of a reality television show rather than like any president before him, and attacked the mainstream media as the promulgators of "fake news." His personal style—flamboyant, unpredictable, combative—and his attacks on the press have made political reporting more like celebrity journalism, with its "what will he do next?" anticipatory frame. Thus, while much of the coverage has been negative, Trump has remained highly visible, even hypervisible, and the nature of his presidency has made following cable news somewhat like following a soap opera. The kind of stories that dominate celebrity journalism—who's in, who's out, who does Trump now like and not like, who's backstabbing whom, who's loyal—now dominate presidential news. CNN, Fox News, and MSNBC reported double-digit ratings growth in the first half of 2017.[5] (His presidency has also, at the same time, revived investigative journalism, at least about Washington and the White House.)

This transformation of the presidency has been a momentous consequence of the penetration of celebrity culture into nearly every realm of our society and our lives. What have been some of the others?

Celebrity culture has made being visible beyond our immediate circle of friends and family a singular and desirable mark of success. Visibility, in so many lines of work—being a chef, an academic, a writer, a CEO—as well as on social media, with the number of followers and "likes," has become the coin of the realm that can be converted into so many privileges and benefits. As the writer George Packer summarizes it, today the "person evolves into a persona, then a brand, then an empire, with the business imperative of grow or die."[6] So celebrity culture invites us to inhabit a particular subject position. It urges us to commodify ourselves, to be other-directed, to value being envied over being respected, and to see fame—being visible on the screens of America—as more important than success. As such, it can make narcissism, self-absorption, and self-branding not just more acceptable, but seemingly required.

Thus it has stoked a hunger for fame in millions of people. This is not surprising. In an age of ongoing automation, bureaucratization, and even dehumanization—voice mail menus where we can't get a human, having to do the same job every day in a tiny cubicle, being herded onto an airplane like cattle as we pass the very lucky few in first class—fantasies of fame continue to offer an irresistible vision of rising above the herd, and being seen as a distinct individual who matters. It fuels consumerism as something of a national religion, as it emphasizes all the enviable things celebrities can buy, and schools us in how to do the same, to be more like them.

So hierarchies of wealth and fame can seem thrilling: look how glamorous and financially insulated it is up there. And don't most of them, because of their talent, beauty, charisma, hard work, deserve it? Thus celebrity culture can legitimize income inequality at a time when the gap between the rich and middle-class Americans is the widest ever recorded: upper-income families are almost seven times wealthier than middle-income ones.[7] At the very same time, it can also breed resentment against those who are "famous for being famous" with seemingly unearned wealth. Celebrities, then, embody the potential of individuals within a system that is capitalist, semidemocratic, and increasingly rigidly class-bound.[8] As the "American dream" seems out of reach to growing numbers of Americans, celebrities, especially the seemingly self-made ones, embody the myth that anyone can become rich and famous.

Celebrity culture also seems to have had an important effect on notions of privacy, on who deserves it and who doesn't, and even how valued it is. With celebrities personifying the importance and value of self-display, and their images more carefully and obviously curated, the ongoing desire to know the "real" celebrity—with outlets eager to provide it—we want to see them unguarded, outside of their managed spaces. So while many may deplore the "stalkerazzi," the images they produce are highly valued. Because people can affectively invest in celebrities through identification or admiration, they want to know if their fandom is merited: Are they decent or arrogant, do they tip well at restaurants, are they good parents, do they cheat on their partners, and, more recently, are they sexual harassers or even predators? And with more cameras in more places—in elevators, hotel lobbies, gas stations, and in anyone's smartphone—the boundaries protecting one's private sphere have shrunk or become more porous. While most everyday people take their own zones of privacy for granted, the cachet of visibility, and the way celebrity culture bolsters the culture of "likes" on social media, has made many much more willing to display what used to be private moments to "friends," as well as to people they don't even know.

The celebrity culture that surrounds us can be both regressive and progressive. It polices women's bodies and behaviors relentlessly, insists with few exceptions that women are nothing without a husband and children, and pits women against each other in "catfights" suggesting that women can rarely get along. It is especially punishing to women as they age. And it pays minimal attention to women's achievements or business acumen. For the most part it excludes people of color from its precincts unless they are caught in a scandal. At the same time, celebrity culture has also helped shatter constraining taboos. Having a child out of wedlock, or being a single mother, was scandalous throughout much of the twentieth century. But by the 1990s, with more celebrities doing both of these things, coverage and attitudes changed. The growing number of openly gay stars—Ellen DeGeneres, Neil Patrick Harris, Sam Smith, Anderson Cooper, to name just a few—has helped further gay acceptance and inspired many everyday people to come out. Bruce Jenner very publicly transitioning to Caitlin and Laverne Cox's star turn on *Orange Is the New Black* opened up visibility and increased sympathy for the transgender community. And Beyoncé, Taylor Swift, Emma Watson, and Samantha Bee embracing feminism helps dismantle negative and erroneous stereotypes about what a feminist is.

Celebrity culture does offer a compelling distraction from other news about politics, public affairs, and the world. It is a primarily feminized public sphere, where relationships, marriage, betrayal, having children, and juggling work and family are at the center. As the inclusive, chatty—and sometime catty—discourse of celebrity gossip hails us to judge celebrity choices, appearance, and behaviors, it does provide social glue through which we can, with others, affirm or challenge morals that matter to us. And our fandom of certain actors or musicians or athletes says something—and *is* meant to say something—about who were are, what our tastes and values are, what our cultural capital is.

Finally, in a culture that is absolutely phobic about aging and death, earning celebrity status, especially if one can maintain it, stokes age-old fantasies about immortality, about being remembered after one is gone.

The mass mourning when Princess Diana, Michael Jackson, Prince, David Bowie, Anthony Bourdain, and Aretha Franklin died, the retrospectives on their lives and impact, the testimonials about what they meant to people, attest to them mattering, and to having an afterlife. Even with "famous for being famous" celebrities, there can be a sense that they have some special quality, some inner gift, a destiny that enables them to rise above the herd, even in death. Because we all carry within us the knowledge that we will, in fact, die, many of us do want our lives to be seen as having had meaning. Becoming a celebrity—but especially an adulated star—offers that fantasy that even after we're gone, our individuality, our meaning to and impact on a culture and its people, will live on, and be admired and even revered. Every iconic poster of Marilyn Monroe, or Audrey Hepburn, or Elvis Presley still on people's walls or public places today speaks to that dominant reverie driving the quest for visibility and fame.

ACKNOWLEDGMENTS

We would like to begin by thanking the editors of this series, Jonathan Gray and Aswin Punathambekar, for their encouragement, enthusiasm, and for providing very important and constructive feedback. Caitlin Lawson was our intrepid research assistant. Two anonymous readers offered very helpful suggestions for revisions. We are particularly grateful to the students in our courses, both at Emmanuel College and the University of Michigan, for the insights they provided us about the impact and ever-evolving role of celebrity culture and journalism in our society. Lisha Nadkarni and Dolma Ombadykow provided essential editorial support. And many thanks to Eric Zinner, for his patience with a manuscript that came in, shall we say, a bit over the word limit he was anticipating. We would especially like to thank our significant others, Scott and T. R., for their ongoing support as we completed the project. Finally, Paddy Scannell has been such an important teacher, mentor, friend, and inspiration to us (and to so many others) in so many aspects of media studies that we dedicate this book to him.

NOTES

INTRODUCTION

1 Driessens, "Celebrity Capital," 543.

2 Braudy, *Frenzy of Renown*, 15.

3 Marshall, *Celebrity and Power*, 6.

4 Giles, *Illusions of Immortality*, 3.

5 Driessens, "Celebrity Capital," 543.

6 Marshall, *Celebrity and Power*, ix.

7 Driessens, "Celebrity Capital," 544.

8 Gabler, "Grand Delusion."

9 Lowenthal, "Biographies in Popular Magazines," 189.

10 Rojek, *Celebrity*, 17–18.

11 Dyer, *Heavenly Bodies*, 17.

12 Sternheimer, *Celebrity Culture and the American Dream*, 10.

13 Ashe, Maltby, and McCutcheon, "Are Celebrity Worshippers More Prone to Narcissism?," 239–46.

14 Kurzman, cited in Driessens, "Celebrity Capital," 545.

15 Schickel, *Intimate Strangers*, 38.

16 Schmid, "Idols of Destruction," 299.

17 Rojek, *Celebrity*, 56–59.

18 Braudy, *Frenzy of Renown*, 32.

19 Dahmen, *Legend of Alexander the Great*.

20 Dahmen, *Legend of Alexander the Great*.

21 Braudy, *Frenzy of Renown*, 103–6.

22 Braudy, *Frenzy of Renown*, 104.

23 West, *Portraiture*, 72.

24 Dahmen, *Legend of Alexander the Great*.

25 Braudy, *Frenzy of Renown*, 198.

26 Braudy, *Frenzy of Renown*, 198.

27 West, *Portraiture*, 72.

28 "Picturing History: A Portrait Set of Early English Kings and Queens," National Portrait Gallery, accessed April 15, 2018. http://www.npg.org.uk.

29 West, *Portraiture*, 93.

30 Braudy, *Frenzy of Renown*, 267.

31 Braudy, *Frenzy of Renown*, 267.

32 Braudy, *Frenzy of Renown*, 266.

33 Braudy, *Frenzy of Renown*, 266–68.

34 Braudy, *Frenzy of Renown*, 334–35.

35 West, *Portraiture*, 81.

36 Ponce de Leon, *Self-Exposure*, 15.

37 Habermas, *Structural Transformation of the Public Sphere*.

38 Leslie Shepard, *The History of Street Literature* (Newton Abbot, UK: David and Charles, 1973), 13.

39 Ponce de Leon, *Self-Exposure*, 16–18.

40 A. R. Williams, "King Tut: The Teen Whose Death Rocked Egypt," *National Geographic News*, November 24, 2015, http://news.nationalgeographic.com/.

41 Jennifer Latson, "The Origins of the 'Pharaoh's Curse' Legend," *Time*, November 26, 2014, http://time.com/3594676/king-tut/.

42 Williams, "King Tut: The Teen Whose Death Rocked Egypt."

43 Latson, "Origins of the 'Pharaoh's Curse' Legend."

44 Tim Masters, "Tutankhamun: How 'Tut-mania' Gripped the World," *BBC News*, July 24, 2014, http://www.bbc.com.

45 McAlister, *Epic Encounters*, 125.

46 E. Meagher, "Museum Tour: King Tut's Road Show Is a Sellout," *Los Angeles Times*, September 8, 1977, A27.

47 "Vendors Strut King Tut Stuff, Even Sour Mash," *New York Times*, December 25, 1978.

48 Braudy, *Frenzy of Renown*, 378.

49 Scannell, *Media and Communication*, 55.

50 Braudy, *Frenzy of Renown*, 3.

CHAPTER 1. THEORIES OF CELEBRITY

1 Marshall, *Celebrity and Power*, 25.

2 Marshall, "Intimately Intertwined in the Most Public Way," 316.

3 Alberoni, "Powerless Elite," 70.

4 Alberoni, "The Powerless Elite," 75–76.

5 Goffman, *Presentation of Self in Everyday Life*.

6 Goffman, *Presentation of Self in Everyday Life*.

7 Goffman, *Presentation of Self in Everyday Life*, 48.

8 Goffman, *Presentation of Self in Everyday Life*, 7.

9 Goffman, *Presentation of Self in Everyday Life*, 59.

10 Marshall, *Celebrity and Power*, 4.

11 "Urbanization of America, Growth of Cities," The USA Online, accessed April 15, 2018. http://www.theusaonline.com.

12 Faragher et al., *Out of Many*, 595.

13 "19th Century American Theater," University of Washington Libraries, accessed April 15, 2018. http://content.lib.washington.edu.

14 Faragher et al., *Out of Many*, 611.

15 Rojek, *Celebrity*, 72.

16 Marshall, "Intimately Intertwined in the Most Public Way."
17 Sternheimer, *Celebrity Culture and the American Dream*, 73.
18 Rojek, *Celebrity*, 48.
19 Rojek, *Celebrity*, 51.
20 Rojek, *Celebrity*, 78.
21 Rojek, *Celebrity*, 52.
22 Rojek, *Celebrity*, 56–59.
23 Rojek, *Celebrity*, 80.
24 Adorno and Horkheimer, "Culture Industries," 131, 133, 126.
25 Adorno and Horkheimer, "Culture Industries," 140.
26 Rojek, *Celebrity*, 97.
27 Lowenthal, "Biographies in Popular Magazines," 189.
28 Lowenthal, "Biographies in Popular Magazines," 191.
29 Lowenthal, "Biographies in Popular Magazines," 193.
30 Lowenthal, "Biographies in Popular Magazines," 195.
31 Lowenthal, "Biographies in Popular Magazines," 194.
32 Lowenthal, "Biographies in Popular Magazines," 196–97.
33 Lowenthal, "Biographies in Popular Magazines," 197–98.
34 Gamson, *Claims to Fame*, 15–16.
35 Gamson, *Claims to Fame*, 41.
36 Schmid, "Idols of Destruction," 298.
37 Sternheimer, *Celebrity Culture and the American Dream*, 214.
38 McDonnell, *Reading Celebrity Gossip Magazines*, 2.
39 McDonald, *Hollywood Stardom*, 3–4.
40 McDonald, *Hollywood Stardom*, 16.
41 "Unemployment Statistics during the Great Depression," United States History, accessed April 15, 2018. http://www.u-s-history.com.
42 David Harvey, *Neoliberalism*, 23.
43 Yvonne Tasker and Diane Negra, *Interrogating Postfeminism* (Durham, NC: Duke University Press, 2007), 21.
44 See Peck, *Age of Oprah*, and Ouellette, "Take Responsibility for Yourself."
45 "The World of Celebrity Giving," Look to the Stars, accessed April 15, 2018, https://www.looktothestars.org.
46 Jensen, "Fandom as Pathology," 9.
47 Jensen, "Fandom as Pathology," 17.
48 Jensen, "Fandom as Pathology," 18.
49 Stuart Hall, 'Encoding and Decoding in the Television Discourse," *Stenciled Paper* 7 (Birmingham: University of Birmingham, CCCS, 1973).
50 Fiske, "Cultural Economy of Fandom," 37–38.
51 Fiske, "Cultural Economy of Fandom," 30.
52 Fiske, "Cultural Economy of Fandom," 37–38.
53 Fiske, "Cultural Economy of Fandom," 40.
54 Fiske, "Cultural Economy of Fandom," 40.

55 Guendouzi, "'You'll Think We're Always Bitching.'"

56 Hermes, "Reading Gossip Magazines," 293–95.

57 Hermes, "Reading Gossip Magazines," 291–93.

58 Hermes, "Reading Gossip Magazines," 293–95.

59 Hermes, "Reading Gossip Magazines," 296.

60 Sternheimer, *Celebrity Culture and the American Dream*.

61 Smith et al., "Envy and Schadenfreude," 158–68.

62 Guendouzi, "You'll Think We're Always Bitching."

63 "Celebrities' Crazy Spending Sprees," *MSN*, October 20, 2016. https://www.msn.com.

64 McDonnell, *Reading Celebrity Gossip Magazines*.

65 Jaggar, "Love and Knowledge," 151–76, 166.

66 Fairclough, "Fame Is a Losing Game."

67 McDonnell, *Reading Celebrity Gossip Magazines*.

68 Schikel, *Intimate Strangers*.

69 Schikel, *Intimate Strangers*, 359–360.

70 This concept was first developed in Horton and Wohl, "Mass Communication and Para-social Interaction," 215–29.

71 Giles, "Parasocial Interaction," 286.

72 Giles, "Parasocial Interaction," 287.

73 Lai, "Glitter and Grain," 215–30.

74 Susan J. Douglas, *The Rise of Enlightened Sexism* (New York: Henry Holt, 2010).

75 Stacey, "Feminine Fascinations," 266–68.

76 Stacey, "Feminine Fascinations," 270–271.

77 Green, Brock, and Kaufman, "Understanding Media Enjoyments," 311–27.

78 Green, Brock, and Kaufman, "Understanding Media Enjoyments," 316.

79 McCutcheon et al., *Celebrity Worshippers*, 120, 136.

80 John B. Thompson, *The Media and Modernity* (Stanford: Stanford University Press, 1995), 223–24.

81 McDonnell, *Reading Celebrity Gossip Magazines*, 8.

82 McDonnell, *Reading Celebrity Gossip Magazines*, 30–31.

83 Douglas, *Rise of Enlightened Sexism*.

84 Douglas, *Rise of Enlightened Sexism*.

85 McDonnell, *Reading Celebrity Gossip Magazines*, 48.

86 Holmes and Negra, *In the Limelight and under the Microscope*, 2.

87 *In Touch*, December 19, 2005, 58–61.

88 "Bare Bones!," *Star*, August 12, 2006, 34–35.

89 Douglas, *Rise of Enlightened Sexism*.

90 Ad, "Hollywood Summer Trends," in *Life & Style*, June 20, 2016.

91 "Money I$ No Object," *Life & Style*, June 20, 2016.

92 "Finally, a Baby for Khloe," *Life & Style*, June 20, 2016, 29.

93 "Scarlett's Hubby Playing Mr. Mom," *OK!*, June 20, 2016, 33.

94 "A Baby for George and Amal," *Life & Style*, June 13, 2016, 26–29.

95 "Boyfriend Report Card," *Life & Style*, June 13, 2016, 41.

96 Lindsay Kimble, "Scott Disick Is 'Dating a New Girl Every Week,' Source Says," People.com, June 27, 2016, http://www.people.com.

97 Carrie Battan, "Money for Nothing: The Lucrative World of Club Appearances," *GQ*, April 4, 2016, http://www.gq.com.

98 "Another Kardashian Boob Job," *Life & Style*, 7.

99 "Celebrity Man Boobs," *TV Guide*, accessed April 15, 2018, http://www.tvguide .com.

100 Douglas, *Rise of Enlightened Sexism*.

101 Douglas, *Rise of Enlightened Sexism*.

102 "Who Wore It Better?," *In Touch*, December 19, 2005, 96–97.

103 "Hot or Not?," *In Touch*, July 10, 2006, 52–53.

104 Fairclough, "Fame Is a Losing Game."

105 Holmes and Negra, *In the Limelight and under the Microscope*, 7.

106 Holmes and Negra, *In the Limelight and under the Microscope*, 6–7; one can also see the performance on YouTube, where it has been viewed tens of millions of times, see "Susan Boyle's First Audition: Britain's Got Talent–'I Dreamed a Dream,'" posted by "Chris Smith," July 25, 2010, accessed April 15, 2018, https:// www.youtube.com/watch?v=aRiJNS8Oz6E.

107 Natalie Robehmed, "The World's Highest-Paid Actresses 2016: Jennifer Lawrence Banks $46 Million Payday Ahead of Melissa McCarthy," *Forbes*, August 23, 2016, https://www.forbes.com.

108 Tadena, "For *Vanity Fair*."

109 Benjamin Snyder, "There's a Huge Pay Disparity between Male and Female Super-models," *Fortune*, July 15, 2015, http://fortune.com.

CHAPTER 2. THE RISE OF MASS CULTURE AND THE PRODUCTION
OF CELEBRITIES

1 Much of this discussion of the Astor Place riots draws from Neal Gabler's excellent account in *Life: The Movie*, 32–37.

2 Levine, "William Shakespeare and the American People," 34–66.

3 "19th Century American Theater," University of Washington Libraries, accessed April 15, 2018, http://content.lib.washington.edu.

4 Nasaw, *Going Out*, 10–11.

5 Nasaw, *Going Out*, 12.

6 Gabler, *Life*, 33–37; for amount her concerts grossed, see Ohmann, *Selling Culture*, 19.

7 Mroczka, "Broadway Disasters."

8 Gabler, *Life: The Movie*, 34.

9 Mroczka, 'Broadway Disasters."

10 Letter to the editor, *New York Courier and Enquirer*, May 9, 1849.

11 Gabler, *Life: The Movie*, 34.

12 "Forrest and Macready," citing the *Express*, May 9, 1849.

13 Paul Mroczka, "Broadway Disasters."

14 Letter to the editor, *New York Courier and Enquirer*, May 9, 1849.

15 Gabler, *Life: The Movie*, 35.

16 Thomas W. Pittman, "Three Old-Times Theatres," *New York Times*, June 22, 1902, 7.

17 Wallace, *Fabulous Showman*, 53.

18 Allen, *Horrible Prettiness*, 62–64.

19 Wallace, *Fabulous Showman*, 11.

20 Burgeson, "P. T. Barnum."

21 Harris, *Humbug*, 119.

22 Allen, *Horrible Prettiness*, 66–70.

23 Shrumm, "Meet Jenny Lind."

24 These crucial points from Ohmann, *Selling Culture*, 19.

25 Siegel, *Galleries of Friendship and Fame*.

26 Hamilton and Hargreaves, *Beautiful and the Damned*, 44.

27 Volpe, "Cartes de Visite Craze."

28 Siegel, *Galleries of Friendship and Fame*, 60.

29 Volpe, "Cartes de Visite Craze."

30 Siegel, *Galleries of Friendship and Fame*, 52–53.

31 Volpe, "Cartes de Visite Craze."

32 Hamilton and Hargreaves, *Beautiful and the Damned*, 45.

33 Hamilton and Hargreaves, *Beautiful and the Damned*, 45.

34 Hamilton and Hargreaves, *Beautiful and the Damned*, 46.

35 Emery and Emery, *Press and America*, 186–88.

36 Emery and Emery, *Press and America*, 210.

37 Henderson, "Media and the Rise of Celebrity Culture," 50.

38 Lewis, *From Traveling Show to Vaudeville*, 4–5.

39 Lewis, *From Traveling Show to Vaudeville*, 9.

40 Nasaw, *Going Out*, 20–21.

41 Henderson, "Media and the Rise of Celebrity Culture," 50.

42 Ponce de Leon, *Self-Exposure*, 208.

43 Ponce de Leon, *Self-Exposure*, 41.

44 "William Randolph Hearst," Biography, accessed April 15, 2018, http://www.biography.com.

45 Nasaw, *Going Out*, 22–23.

46 Nasaw, *Going Out*, 23.

47 Camille Forbes, *Introducing Bert Williams: Burnt Cork, Broadway, and the Story of America's First Black Star* (New York: Basic Books, 2008), 178–79.

48 Forbes, *Introducing Bert Williams*, 34–35.

49 Huggins, *Harlem Renaissance*, 283.

50 Forbes, *Introducing Bert Williams*, 227–28.

51 Forbes, *Introducing Bert Williams*, 91.

52 Ponce de Leon, *Self-Exposure*, 210–11.

53 Ponce de Leon, *Self-Exposure*, 48.

54 This summary draws from an interview with Professor Paula Uruburu for the American Experience broadcast "Murder of the Century," at http://www.pbs.org, and from her book *American Eve*; also from Baker, "Evelyn Nesbit."

55 Ohmann, Selling Culture, 29.

56 Uruburu, *American Eve*, 307, 308, 384, 301, 319.

57 Uruburu, *American Eve*, 311.

58 Cited in Uruburu, *American Eve*, 317.

59 "Evelyn Nesbit: Vaudeville and Performance," *Ragtime*, Sept. 11, 2012, http://zach ragtime.blogspot.com.

60 Nasaw, *Going Out*, 28.

61 Ponce de Leon, *Self-Exposure*, 31.

62 Henderson, "Media and the Rise of Celebrity Culture," 51.

63 Ponce de Leon, *Self-Exposure*, 13.

64 Ponce de Leon, *Self-Exposure*, 38.

65 Lears, *Fables of Abundance*, 138.

66 Boorstin, *Image*, 13.

CHAPTER 3. SILVER SCREENS AND THEIR STARS

1   Hellmuth Karasek, "Lokomotive der Gefühle," *Spiegel* 52 (1994): 154.

2   Loiperdinger and Elzer, "Lumiere's Arrival of the Train."

3   Merritt, "Nickelodeon Theaters, 1905–1914," 81.

4   Merritt, "Nickelodeon Theaters," 86.

5   Czitrom, *Media and the American Mind*, 44–47.

6   deCordova, *Picture Personalities*, 103.

7   McDonald, *Star System*, 15.

8   Basinger, *Star Machine*, 18.

9   Staiger, "Seeing Stars," 11.

10 McDonald, *Star System*, 29.

11 McDonald, *Star System*.

12 Basinger, *Star Machine*, 18–19.

13 Basinger, *Star Machine*, 36–56.

14 Basinger, *Star Machine*, 36–56.

15 Schikel, *Intimate Strangers*, 14.

16 Katz, *Film Encyclopedia*, 225.

17 Katz, *Film Encyclopedia*, 76.

18 Cochrane, "If Looks Could Kill."

19 Nicholas Barber, "Clara Bow: The Original 'It Girl,'" http://www.bbc.com; Katz, *The Film Encyclopedia*, 147.

20 deCordova, *Picture Personalities*, 52.

21 deCordova, *Picture Personalities*, 51

22 deCordova, *Picture Personalities*, 113.

23 deCordova, *Picture Personalities*, 98.

24 Ponce de Leon, *Self-Exposure*, 215.

25 "The Unknown Hollywood I Know" was a headline on the October 1931 issue of *Photoplay*.

26 Slide, *Inside the Hollywood Fan Magazine*, 13.

27 Slide, *Inside the Hollywood Fan Magazine*, 122.

28 Gamson, *Claims to Fame*, 29.

29 Cited in Ponce de Leon, *Self-Exposure*, 226.

30 Cited in Ponce de Leon, *Self-Exposure*, 230.

31 Lowenthal, "Biographies in Popular Magazines," 196–98.

32 Ponce de Leon, *Self-Exposure*, 232, 235–36.

33 Slide, *Inside the Hollywood Fan Magazine*, 6.

34 Rojek, *Celebrity*, 97.

35 *Photoplay*, January 1933.

36 Laurel and Hardy for Old Gold, 1937; Bing Crosby for Chesterfield, 1944.

37 Spencer Tracy for Lucky Strike, 1938.

38 Joe Lewis for Chesterfield, 1944; Joe DiMaggio for Camel, 1941.

39 Elmer Sunfield, "She Won in a Walk," *Hollywood*, January 1938, 50.

40 Wes D. Gehring, *Carole Lombard: The Hoosier Tornado* (Indianapolis: Indiana Historical Society Press, 2003).

41 Lowenthal, "Biographies in Popular Magazines," 197–98.

42 Collins, "Powerful Rivalry between Hedda Hopper and Louella Parsons."

43 Uruburu, *American Eve*, 313.

44 Emery and Emery, *Press and America*, 325–26.

45 Ellis and Ellis, *Mammoth Book of Celebrity Murder*, 448.

46 Katz, *Film Encyclopedia*, 598; "The Mysterious Death of Newport Movie Mogul Thomas Ince," New England Historical Society, accessed April 15, 2018, http://www.newenglandhistoricalsociety.com; also see Danny Buckland, "Death in Hollywood: The Seedy Side of the American Dream (1920s-1930s)," *Sunday Express*, February 9, 2014, http://www.express.co.uk.

47 McDonald, *Hollywood Stardom*, 90.

48 Taylor, Pinguelo, and Cedrone, "Reverse-Morals Clause," 65, 75–76.

49 Collins, "Powerful Rivalry between Hedda Hopper and Louella Parsons."

50 Schickel, *Intimate Strangers*, 98.

51 Schickel, *Intimate Strangers*, 99.

52 Faraci, "Talkie Terror."

53 "Mary Pickford: The Long Decline," *PBS: American Experience*, accessed April 15, 2018, http://www.pbs.org.

54 Basinger, *Star Machine*, 518.

55 Sternheimer, *Celebrity Culture and the American Dream*, 73.

56 Rojek, *Celebrity*, 72.

57 Marshall, "Intimately Intertwined in the Most Public Way."

58 Basinger, *Star Machine*.

59 Adorno and Horkheimer, "Culture Industries," 126, 131, 133.

60 Witheridge, "'I'd Rather Make $700 a Week Playing a Maid Than Working as One.'"

61 Pautz, "Decline in Average Weekly Cinema Attendance, 1930–2000," 11.

62 "US Supreme Court Decides Paramount Anti-Trust Case," in "History: This Day in History," accessed April 15, 2018, http://www.history.com.

63 Bomboy, "Day the Supreme Court Killed Hollywood's Studio System."

64 Sternheimer, *Celebrity Culture and the American Dream*, 190–91.

65 Desjardins, "Systematizing Scandal," 208.

66 Desjardins, "Systematizing Scandal," 208.

67 Slide, *Inside the Hollywood Fan Magazine*, 179–83.

68 Howe, *Paparazzi*.

69 Blasberg, "Ron Galella on the Paparazzi's Golden Era."

70 Cashmore, *Elizabeth Taylor*, 135–44.

71 Cashmore, *Elizabeth Taylor*, 20.

72 Slide, *Inside the Hollywood Fan Magazine*, 188–89, 219.

73 McDonald, *Hollywood Stardom*, 196–98.

74 McDonald, *Hollywood Stardom*, 181.

75 McDonald, *Hollywood Stardom*, 184–89.

76 Marshall, *Celebrity and Power*, 105–7, 111–13.

77 McDonald, *Hollywood Stardom*, 284.

78 McDonald, *Hollywood Stardom*, 215.

CHAPTER 4. RADIO

 1 Marshall, *Celebrity and Power*, 154.

 2 Pitts and Hoffmann, *Rise of the Crooners*, 13–14.

 3 Douglas, *Terrible Honesty*, 365.

 4 Marshall, *Celebrity and Power*, 150–51.

 5 Peretti, *Creation of Jazz*, 152; Leonard, *Jazz and the White Americans*, 91.

 6 Marshall, *Celebrity and Power*, 151.

 7 Potter, "Almost as Good as Presley."

 8 Douglas, *Early Days of Radio Broadcasting*, 158.

 9 Kenney, *Phonograph*, 7.

10 Millard, *America on Record*, 11.

11 Barnouw, *Tower in Babel*, 125; "The Long Arm of Radio Is Reaching Everywhere," *Current Opinion*, May 1922, 685.

12 "'Listening In,' Our New National Pastime," *Review of Reviews*, January 1923, 52; Waldemar Kaempffert, "Radio Broadcasting," *Review of Reviews*, April 1922, 399.

13 *New York Times*, March 2, 1922, 20, cited in Susan J. Douglas, *Inventing American Broadcasting, 1899-1922* (Baltimore: Johns Hopkins University Press, 1987), 303.

14 Smith, "Radio."

15 Leonard, "Impact of Mechanization," 48.

16 For a more detailed discussion of music and the inner life, see Storr, *Music and the Mind*.

17 Douglas, Early Days of Radio Broadcasting, 168.

18 Leonard, *Jazz and the White Americans*, 95–99.

19 Baraka, *Blues People*, 100; Douglas, *Terrible Honesty*, 391.

20 Millard, *America on Record*, 66–67.

21 Ogren, *Jazz Revolution*, 91.

22 Sidran, *Black Talk*, 69.

23 Douglas, Early Days of Radio Broadcasting, 173–74.

24 "Jazz," *Outlook*, March 5, 1924, 381.

25 Douglas, *Terrible Honesty*, 336.

26 Eberly, *Music in the Air*, 43.

27 Chris Albertson, *Bessie* (New York: Stein and Day, 1972), 48, 52, 68–69.

28 Dave Peyton, "The Musical Bunch," *Chicago Defender*, October 31, 1925, 6.

29 Eberly, *Music in the Air*, 86, 93.

30 Eberly, *Music in the Air*, 45.

31 Eberly, *Music in the Air*, 44.

32 Collier, *Duke Ellington*, 54, 96.

33 Douglas, *Terrible Honesty*, 420.

34 Peyton, "Musical Bunch," 6.

35 For the debates about crossover in the later part of the century, see Perry, "Ain't No Mountain High Enough."

36 Hilmes, *Radio Voices*, 79.

37 Sidran, *Black Talk*.

38 For the definitive discussion on the critical importance of African American music to the prestige enjoyed by American culture in the 1920s, see Douglas, *Terrible Honesty*.

39 Thomas DeLong, cited in Dempsey, "Singers on the Radio," 1273.

40 Millard, America on Record, 11.

41 Marshall, *Celebrity and Power*, 155.

42 McCracken, "'God's Gift to Us Girls,'" 365.

43 Pitts and Hoffmann, *Rise of the Crooners*, 7.

44 McCracken, "Rudy Vallee," 1449.

45 Excerpts from McCracken, *Real Men Don't Sing*, posted on http://www.popmat ters.com.

46 Excerpts from McCracken, *Real Men Don't Sing*, posted on http://www.popmat ters.com.

47 Dempsey, "Singers on the Radio," 1273.

48 Wertheim, *Radio Comedy*, 48.

49 Watkins, *On the Real Side*, 278.

50 Ely, *Adventures of* Amos'n'Andy, 4–5.

51 Ely, *Adventures of* Amos'n'Andy, 117.

52 Gilbert Seldes, "Some Radio Entertainers," *New Republic*, May 20, 1931, 19.

53 Ely, *Adventures of* Amos'n'Andy, 120.

54 Allen, *Horrible Prettiness*, 173. See also Zanger, "The Minstrel Show as Theater of Misrule," 33–38; and Saxton, "Blackface Minstrelsy and Jacksonian Ideology."

55 See Huggins's brilliant discussion in *Harlem Renaissance*, especially chapter 6.

56 Watkins, *On the Real Side*.

57 Wertheim, *Radio Comedy*, 87.

58 "Will Rodgers," The Official Website of Will Rodgers, accessed April 16, 2018. http://www.cmgww.com.

59 "Will Rodgers," The Official Website of Will Rodgers, accessed April 16, 2018. http://www.cmgww.com.

60 Chorba, "Will Rogers," 1221.

61 Chorba, "Will Rogers," 1222.

62 Cantril and Allport, *Psychology of Radio*, 223.

63 Cantril and Allport, *Psychology of Radio*, 222–23.

64 Goodwin, *No Ordinary Time*, 59.

65 *Life*, December 2, 1937, 49–50.

66 "Special Features," *Radio Mirror*, May 1934, November 1934, accessed April 16, 2018. http://archive.org.

67 This material on Winchell is from Gabler, *Winchell*, and from Douglas, *Listening In*, 168–72.

68 Museum of Broadcast Communications, RA 292, "Jergens Journal," May 18, 1941; Winchell quotation from Gabler, *Winchell*, 162.

69 Gabler, *Winchell*, xii, 162.

70 Gabler, *Winchell*, 15.

71 Ponce de Leon, *Self-Exposure*, 1.

72 "An American Aviator," Charles Lindbergh, accessed April 16, 2018, http://www .charleslindbergh.com.

73 Ponce de Leon, *Self-Exposure*, 3.

74 Halper, "Talent Shows," 1366–67.

75 Ponce de Leon, *Self-Exposure*, 242–45.

76 Ponce de Leon, *Self-Exposure*, 241–73.

77 Ponce de Leon, *Self-Exposure*, 254.

78 Taylor, "Sports."

79 Ponce de Leon, *Self-Exposure*, 261.

80 Ponce de Leon, *Self-Exposure*, 273.

81 "Princeton-Chicago Football Game Is Broadcast across the Country," History: This Day in History, accessed April 16, 2018, http://www.history.com.

82 Eastman, "Sportscasters," 1313.

83 "World at Ringside by Proxy," *Literary Digest*, October 5, 1935, 32–33.

84 Douglas, *Listening In*, 208.

85 Erenberg, *Greatest Fight of Our Generation*, 157.

86 Douglas, *Listening In*, 206–8.

87 Bradlee, "Feud with Writers Helped Ted Williams Hit Harder."

88 "Babe Ruth," National Baseball Hall of Fame, accessed April 16, 2018, http://base ballhall.org.

89 "Babe Ruth," Biography, accessed April 16, 2018, http://www.baberuth.com/biog raphy/.

90 "Babe Ruth," National Baseball Hall of Fame, accessed April 16, 2018. http://base ballhall.org.

91 Ponce de Leon, *Self-Exposure*, 269.

92 Bradlee, "Feud with Writers Helped Ted Williams Hit Harder."

93 Erenberg, *Greatest Fight of Our Generation*, 180.

94 "USO Shows in Prose: Entertainment during WWII," https://www.uso.org; Pratte, "Bob Hope," 726.

95 Merton, Lowenthal, and Curtis, *Mass Persuasion*, 2.

96 Merton, Lowenthal, and Curtis, *Mass Persuasion*, 90.

97 Merton, Lowenthal, and Curtis, *Mass Persuasion*, 38.

98 Anderson, *Imagined Communities*; Michele Hilmes also felt obliged to cite Anderson in *Radio Voices*, 11–13.

99 Anderson, *Imagined Communities*, 6–7.

100 "Radio's New Voice Is Golden," *Business Week*, March 5, 1960, 94–99.

101 Ennis, *Seventh Stream*, 132.

102 Faragher et al., *Out of Many*, 807.

103 Fornatale and Mills, *Radio in the Television Age*, 44.

104 Ennis, *Seventh Stream*, 136.

105 Lipsitz, *Rainbow at Midnight*, 315.

106 For an analytical assessment of this phenomenon, see Lott, "White Like Me," 475.

107 "Elvis Presley Bio," *Rolling Stone*, accessed April 16, 2018, http://www.rollingstone .com.

108 "Elvis Presley Bio," *Rolling Stone*, accessed April 16, 2018, http://www.rollingstone .com.

109 "Elvis on the Ed Sullivan Show," Elvis Presley Photos, accessed April 16, 2018, http://www.elvispresleymusic.com.

110 Marshall, *Celebrity and Power*, 162.

111 Jackson, *Big Beat Heat*, 95.

112 Fornatale and Mills, Radio in the Television Age, 43.

113 Cited in Jackson, Big Beat Heat, 96.

114 Ward, Stokes, and Tucker, *Rock of Ages*, 272.

CHAPTER 5. TV AND THE NEED FOR FAMILIARITY

1 Cashmore, *Celebrity Culture*, 30.

2 Schickel, *Intimate Strangers*, 13.

3 Marshall, *Celebrity and Power*, 119.

4 Prior, *Post-Broadcast Democracy*, 68.

5 Gathman, "Elgin's Madman Muntz Lived Up to His Name."

6 Coombs and Batchelor, *We Are What We Sell*, 197.

7 Edgerton, *Columbia History of American Television*, 105.

8 Lambert, "At 50, Levittown Contends with Its Legacy of Bias."

9 Marshall, *Celebrity and Power*, 119.

10 Tichi, *Electronic Hearth*, 50.

11 Marshall, *Celebrity and Power*, 119.

12 Langer, "Television's 'Personality System,'" 183.

13 Langer, "Television's 'Personality System,'" 193.

14 Langer, "Television's 'Personality System,'" 185.

15 Marshall, *Celebrity and Power*, 121.

16 Murray, *Hitch Your Antenna to the Stars*, 1.

17 Murray, *Hitch Your Antenna to the Stars*, 72.

18 Murray, *Hitch Your Antenna to the Stars*, xi.

19 Murray, *Hitch Your Antenna to the Stars*, xi.

20 Murray, *Hitch Your Antenna to the Stars*, xi.

21 Murray, *Hitch Your Antenna to the Stars*, 65.

22 Murray, *Hitch Your Antenna to the Stars*, 67.

23 Goodman, "Milton Berle 1908–2002."

24 "Growth Strategies: Desi Arnaz and Lucille Ball," *Entrepreneur*, accessed April 16, 2018, https://www.entrepreneur.com.

25 Coyne and Gilbert, *Desilu*, 33.

26 "The Oscars," *Time* 61, no. 13 (1953): 86.

27 "The Academy Awards through the Years," *Los Angeles Times*, February 26, 2017, http://timelines.latimes.com/academy-awards/.

28 Miller, "Evolution of Hollywood's Red Carpet."

29 Dayan and Katz, *Media Events*, 1.

30 Fastenberg, "Top Ten Presidential Pop Culture Moments."

31 "The Kennedy-Nixon Debates," *History*, accessed April 16, 2018, http://www.history.com.

32 Sneed, "How John F. Kennedy's Assassination Changed Television Forever."

33 "Sputnik and the Dawn of the Space Age," NASA, accessed April 16, 2018, https://history.nasa.gov.

34 "Profile of John Glenn," NASA, accessed April 16, 2018, https://www.nasa.gov.

35 "Space Program and Television," *Museum*, accessed April 16, 2018, http://www.museum.tv.

36 Teitel, "How NASA Broadcast Neil Armstrong from the Moon."

37 Street, *Mass Media, Politics, and Democracy*.

38 Larson, "Johnny Carson's Best 'Tonight Show' Interviews."

39 Marshall, *Celebrity and Power*, 130–36.

40 Hinkle, "Summer of '61."

41 Kahn, "Pursuit of No. 60."

42 Smart, *Sport Star*, 87.

43 Meserole, "Arledge Created Monday Night Football."

44 Sarmento, "NBA on Network Television."

45 Bloom, *There You Have It*, 69–74.

46 "Billie Jean King," *Biography*, accessed April 16, 2018, https://www.biography
.com.

47 Sarmento, "NBA on Network Television," 23–25.

48 Sarmento, "NBA on Network Television," 49–50.

49 Sarmento, "NBA on Network Television," 66.

50 Sarmento, "NBA on Network Television," 67.

51 Smart, *Sport Star*, 111.

52 C. L. Cole and David L. Andrews, "America's New Son: Tiger Woods and America's Multiculturalism," in *The Celebrity Culture Reader*, ed. P. David Marshall (New York: Routledge, 2006), 356.

53 "*People*'s Premiere," *Time*, March 4, 1974, 54.

54 Gregory and Gregory, *When Elvis Died*, 27–30.

55 "The Public Interest Standard in Television Broadcasting," *Benton: Public Interest Voices for the Digital Age*, accessed April 16, 2018, https://www.benton.org.

56 "The Policy and Regulatory Landscape," FCC, accessed April 16, 2018, https://transition.fcc.gov.

CHAPTER 6. MUSICAL CELEBRITY

1 Frith, *Sound Effects*, 217.

2 Marshall, *Celebrity and Power*, 193.

3 Frith, *Sound Effects*, 35.

4 Frith, *Sound Effects*, 38.

5 Goodwin and Frith, *On Record*, 426.

6 Douglas, *Listening In*, 32.

7 Marshall, *Celebrity and Power*, 154.

8 Marshall, *Celebrity and Power*, 193.

9 Ilson, *Sundays with Sullivan*, 57.

10 Susan J. Douglas, *Where the Girls Are: Growing Up with the Mass Media* (New York: Times Books, 1994), 113–21.

11 Marshall, "Celebrity Legacy of the Beatles," 506.

12 Ward, Stokes, and Tucker, *Rock of Ages*, 265.

13 Ward, Stokes, and Tucker, *Rock of Ages*, 266.

14 Ward, Stokes, and Tucker, *Rock of Ages*, 166.

15 Ward, Stokes, and Tucker, *Rock of Ages*, 255.

16 Marshall, *Celebrity and Power*, 171.

17 Frith, *Sound Effects*, quoting music critic and producer Jon Landau, 49.

18 Matos, "1966 vs. 1971."

19 "The FM Boom," *Newsweek*, May 22, 1972, 57; Christopher H. Sterling and John M. Kittross, *Stay Tuned*, 2nd ed. (Belmont, CA: Wadsworth, 1990), 379.

20 *Broadcasting*, September 24, 1973, 31.

21 Douglas, *Listening In*, 37.

22 Everrett, *Beatles as Musicians*, 307.
23 Dave Lewis and Simon Pallett, *Led Zeppelin: The Concert File* (New York: Omnibus Press, 2005), 90.
24 Frith, *Popular Music*, 39.
25 Marshall, *Celebrity and Power*, 165.
26 Marshall, *Celebrity and Power*, 173.
27 Frith, *Sound Effects*, 226–28.
28 Frith, *Sound Effects*, 228.
29 Marshall, *Celebrity and Power*, 168–70.
30 Marshall, *Celebrity and Power*, 166.
31 Marshall, *Celebrity and Power*, 170.
32 Gamson, *Claims to Fame*, 67.
33 Caulfield, "Rewinding the Charts."
34 Ward, Stokes, and Tucker, *Rock of Ages*, 524.
35 Weber, "Robert Isabell."
36 Charlton, "Bill Bernstein's Exuberant Images of New York City's Disco Days."
37 Ward, Stokes, and Tucker, *Rock of Ages*, 532.
38 Ward, Stokes, and Tucker, *Rock of Ages,* 521.
39 Clerk, *Madonnastyle*.
40 "Best-Selling Female Recording Artist," *Guinness World Records*, http://www.guinnessworldrecords.com; Gary Trust, "Greatest of All-Time Charts," *Billboard*, November 30, 2017, https://www.billboard.com.
41 Izadi, "This Is How David Bowie Confronted MTV."
42 Nittle, "How MTV Handled Accusations of Racism and Became More Inclusive."
43 Rose, *Black Noise*, 100.
44 Freydkin, "Lilith Fair."
45 Travers, "Spice World."
46 "Timeline," Spice Girls, accessed April 16, 2018, http://www.thespicegirls.com.
47 Gowan, "Requiem for Napster."
48 Goldman, "Music's Lost Decade."
49 Crum, "ITunes Sales May Be Down."
50 Greenburg, "Justin Bieber on the Business of Social Media."
51 Ben Sisaro, "With a Tap of Taylor Swift's Fingers, Apple Retreated," *New York Times*, June 22, 2015, https://www.nytimes.com.
52 Lyndsey Havens, "Chance the Rapper's 'Coloring Book' Is First Streaming-Only Album to Win a Grammy," *Billboard*, 2/13/2017, https://www.billboard.com.
53 Pallotta and Stelter, "Super Bowl 50 Audience Is Third Largest in TV History."
54 Coscarelli, "Beyoncé's Lemonade Debuts at No. 1."
55 Duboff, "Examining Beyoncé's Social Media Mastery."

CHAPTER 7. EVERYONE'S A STAR
1 *American Idol*, FOX, 2002–16.
2 Rowe, "Full 2010–11."

3 Graser, "Coke Builds 'Harmony' with 'Idol.'"
4 Murray and Ouellette, *Reality TV*, 9–10.
5 Mifflin, "Media Business."
6 Schmid, "Idols of Destruction," 300.
7 Kissell, "An Eye-Land Paradise."
8 *Big Brother*, CBS, 2001–present.
9 *The Amazing Race*, CBS, 2002–present.
10 *Newlyweds: Nick and Jessica*, MTV, 2003–5.
11 *Laguna Beach: The Real Orange County*, MTV, 2004–6.
12 *The Hills*, MTV, 2006–10.
13 *America's Next Top Model*, UPN/CW/VH1, 2003–present.
14 *Project Runway*, Bravo/Lifetime, 2004–present.
15 *The Apprentice*, NBC, 2004–present.
16 *Top Chef*, Bravo, 2006–present.
17 *Queer Eye for the Straight Guy*, Bravo, 2003–7.
18 *What Not to Wear*, TLC, 2003–13.
19 *The Bachelor*, ABC 2002–present.
20 *Joe Millionaire*, Fox, 2003.
21 *The Simple Life*, FOX/E!, 2003–7.
22 *The Osbournes*, MTV, 2003–5.
23 *Jersey Shore*, MTV, 2009–12.
24 *My Super Sweet 16*, MTV, 2005–8.
25 *Here Comes Honey Boo Boo*, TLC, 2012–14.
26 Murray and Ouellette, *Reality TV*, 3.
27 Glynn, *Tabloid Culture*, 9.
28 "How Angelina Stole Brad," *Us Weekly*, May 23, 2005.
29 Hermes, *Reading Women's Magazines*.
30 Jonas-Hain, "Starstruck Fight It Out with 'Team' T-shirts."
31 Dumenco, "Media Guy," 24.
32 As reported in publication media kits, see https://www.usmagazine.com/mediakits-print-rates-specs/.
33 Ives, "Guess Who's Not Getting Any Fatter," 1.
34 Pérez-Peña, "In Deepening Ad Decline, Sales Fall 8% at Magazines," 131–32.
35 Kelly, "Celebrity Magazines Aren't Dead Yet."
36 Kaufman, "'Britney Spears Economy' Brings in Millions."
37 Lai, "Glitter and Grain," 219.
38 "FOX's 'The Simple Life' Premiere Draws 13 Million Viewers and the Night's Highest Adults 18–49 Rating," *Reality TV World*, December 3, 2003, http://www.realitytvworld.com/news/.
39 Djansezian, "Get the Scoop on Paris Hilton's Prison Release Outfit."
40 Fairclough, "Fame Is a Losing Game."
41 Burns, *Celeb 2.0*, 1.

42 Shafrir, "Truth about Perez Hilton's Traffic."
43 Redmond, "Intimate Fame Everywhere," 35.
44 Meyrowitz, *No Sense of Place*, 2–3, 7.
45 Meyrowitz, *No Sense of Place*, 47–48.
46 Meyrowitz, *No Sense of Place*, 48.
47 Goffman, *Presentation of Self in Everyday Life*, 7.
48 Burns, *Celeb 2.0*, 50.
49 Kim Kardashian West (@KimKardashian), post to Twitter, 12:41 PM-11 July 2017. Accessed April 25, 2018.
50 Mi-Anne Chan, "You HAVE to Try These Alternatives to Kylie Jenner's Sold-Out Lip Kits," *Refinery29*, November 13, 2017, http://www.refinery29.com.
51 McClean, *Keeping Up the Kardashian Brand*, 75.
52 Robehmed, "No, Kim Kardashian Probably Didn't Make $80 Million."
53 Khamis, Ang, and Welling, "Self-Branding, 'Micro-Celebrity,' and the Rise of Social Media Influencers," 194.
54 Marwick and boyd, "I Tweet Honestly, I Tweet Passionately," 122.
55 Marwick, *Status Update*, 115, 119.
56 Robehmed, "How Michelle Phan Built a $500 Million Company."
57 Craig, "Mapping the Future of Entertainment: Social Media."
58 Khamis, Ang, and Welling, "Self-Branding, 'Micro-Celebrity,' and the Rise of Social Media Influencers," 195.
59 Khamis, Ang, and Welling, "Self-Branding, 'Micro-Celebrity,' and the Rise of Social Media Influencers," 197.
60 Monllos, "Why More Brands Are Adding Young Influencers"; Kirkpatrick, "Social Media Star James Charles Is Named First Male CoverGirl!"
61 Petski, "'TRL.'"
62 Turner, *Understanding Celebrity*, 83.
63 Schmid, *Natural Born Celebrities*, 262.
64 Saltz, "Art at Arm's Length."
65 Krämer and Winter, "Impression Management 2.0."
66 Fairclough, "Fame Is a Losing Game."
67 Lai, "Glitter and Grain," 215–30.
68 Klam, *Stars in Our Eyes*, 10.
69 Klam, *Stars in Our Eyes*, 50–51.
70 Solove, "Should Celebrities Have Privacy?"
71 Lee, "Strict Liability and the Anti-Paparazzi Act."
72 Solove, "Should Celebrities Have Privacy?"
73 Stone, "California Passes New Paparazzi Drone Law."
74 Lee, "Strict Liability and the Anti-Paparazzi Act," 8.
75 Lee, "Strict Liability and the Anti-Paparazzi Act," 8.
76 Petit, "#MeToo."
77 Almukhtar, Gold, and Buchanan, "After Weinstein."

CONCLUSION

1 Packer, "Celebrating Inequality."
2 Klam, *Stars in Our Eyes*, 13.
3 Packer, "Celebrating Inequality."
4 Goldberg, "HBO's 'Westworld.'"
5 Otterson, "Cable News Ratings."
6 Packer, "Celebrating Inequality."
7 Fry and Kochhar, "America's Wealth Gap."
8 Marshall, "Introduction," 4.

SELECTED BIBLIOGRAPHY

Adorno, Theodor, and Max Horkheimer. "The Culture Industries: Enlightenment as Mass Deception." In *Dialectic of Enlightenment*. New York: Herder and Herder, 1972.

Alberoni, Francesco. "The Powerless Elite: Theory and Sociological Research on the Phenomenon of the Stars." In *Sociology of Mass Communication*, edited by Dennis McQuail. Harmondsworth, UK: Penguin, 1972.

Allen, Robert C. *Horrible Prettiness: Burlesque and American Culture*. Chapel Hill: University of North Carolina Press, 1991.

Almukhtar, Sarah, Michael Gold, and Larry Buchanan. "After Weinstein: 71 Men Accused of Sexual Misconduct and Their Fall from Power." *New York Times*, February 8, 2018. https://www.nytimes.com/.

Anderson, Benedict. *Imagined Communities: Reflections on the Origins and Spread of Nationalism*. New York: Verso, 1983.

Ashe, Diane D., John Maltby, and Lynn E. McCutcheon. "Are Celebrity Worshippers More Prone to Narcissism? A Brief Report." *North American Journal of Psychology* 7 (2005): 239–46.

Baker, Lindsay. "Evelyn Nesbit: The World's First Supermodel." BBC.com, January 4, 2014. http://www.bbc.com.

Baraka, Amiri. *Blues People*. New York: Morrow Quill Paperbacks, 1963.

Barnouw, Erik. *A Tower in Babel*. New York: Oxford University Press, 1966.

Basinger, Jeanine. *The Star Machine*. New York: Vintage Books, 2009.

Berlant, Lauren. *The Female Complaint: The Unfinished Business of Sentimentality in American Culture*. Durham, NC: Duke University Press, 2008.

Biressi, Anita, and Heather Nunn. *The Tabloid Culture Reader*. London: Open University Press, 2007.

Blasberg, Derek. "Ron Galella on the Paparazzi's Golden Era and Why Marlon Brando Broke His Jaw." *Vanity Fair*, November 19, 2015.

Bloom, John. *There You Have It: The Life, Legacy, and Legend of Howard Cosell*. Amherst: University of Massachusetts Press, 2010.

Bomboy, Scott. "The Day the Supreme Court Killed Hollywood's Studio System." *Constitution Daily*, May 4, 2017. https://constitutioncenter.org.

Boorstin, Daniel. *The Image: A Guide to Pseudo-Events in America*. New York: Vintage, 1992.

Bradlee, Ben, Jr. "Feud with Writers Helped Ted Williams Hit Harder." *Boston Globe*, December 2, 2013. https://www.bostonglobe.com.

Braudy, Leo. *The Frenzy of Renown: Fame and Its History*. New York: Oxford University Press, 1986.

Burgeson, John. "P. T. Barnum: Master of Advertising and Promotion." *CT Post*, July 4, 2010. http://www.ctpost.com.

Burns, Kelli S. *Celeb 2.0: How Social Media Foster Our Fascination with Popular Culture*. Santa Barbara: Praeger, 2009.

Cantril, Hadley, and Gordon Allport. *The Psychology of Radio*. New York: Harper & Brothers. 1935.

Cashmore, Ellis. *Celebrity/Culture*. 2nd ed. London: Routledge, 2014.

———. *Elizabeth Taylor: A Private Life for Public Consumption*. New York: Bloomsbury Academic, 2016.

Caulfield, Keith. "Rewinding the Charts: In 1978, the Bee Gees Sparked Disco Fever." *Billboard*, May 13, 2014. http://www.billboard.com.

Charlton, Lauretta. "Bill Bernstein's Exuberant Images of New York City's Disco Days." *New Yorker*, January 4, 2017. http://www.newyorker.com.

Chorba, Frank J. "Will Rogers." In *The Encyclopedia of Radio*, edited by Christopher Sterling. New York: Fitzroy Dearborn, 2004.

Clerk, Carol. *Madonnastyle*. London: Omnibus Press, 2009.

Cochrane, Kira. "If Looks Could Kill." *Guardian*, January 10, 2008. https://www.theguardian.com.

Collier, James. *Duke Ellington*. Oxford: Oxford University Press, 1987.

Collins, Amy Fine. "The Powerful Rivalry between Hedda Hopper and Louella Parsons." *Vanity Fair*, April 1997.

Connell, Ian. "Personalities in the Popular Media." In *Journalism and Popular Culture*, edited by P. Dahlgren and C. Sparks, 64–83. London: Sage, 1992.

Coombs, Danielle Sarver, and Bob Batchelor. *We Are What We Sell: How Advertising Shapes American Life . . . and Always Has*. Santa Barbara: Praeger, 2014.

Coscarelli, Joe. "Beyoncé's Lemonade Debuts at No. 1 with Huge Streaming Numbers." *New York Times*, May 2, 2016. https://www.nytimes.com/.

Coyne, Steven, and Tom Sanders Gilbert. *Desilu: The Story of Lucille Ball and Desi Arnaz*. New York: William Morrow and Co., 1993.

Craig, David. "Mapping the Future of Entertainment: Social Media." USC-US China Institute, accessed April 16, 2018. https://www.youtube.com/watch?v=TqY-JA_zJzM.

Crum, Rex. "ITunes Sales May Be Down, but Apple Says Music Sales Are Not on the Way Out." *Silicon Beat*, May 12, 2016. http://www.siliconbeat.com.

Czitrom, Daniel J. *Media and the American Mind: From Morse to McLuhan*. Chapel Hill: University of North Carolina Press, 1982.

Dahmen, Karsten. *The Legend of Alexander the Great on Greek and Roman Coins*. New York: Routledge, 2006.

Dayan, Daniel, and Elihu Katz. *Media Events: The Live Broadcasting of History*. Cambridge: Harvard University Press, 1994.

deCordova, Richard. *Picture Personalities: The Emergence of the Star System in America*. Chicago: University of Illinois Press, 1990.

Dempsey, J. M. "Singers on the Radio." In *The Encyclopedia of Radio*, edited by Christopher Sterling. New York: Fitzroy Dearborn, 2004.

Desjardins, Mary R. "Systematizing Scandal: *Confidential* magazine, Stardom, and the State of California." In *Headline Hollywood: A Century of Film Scandal*, edited by A. L. McLean and D. A. Cook. New Brunswick, NJ: Rutgers University Press, 2001.

Djansezian, Kevork. "Get the Scoop on Paris Hilton's Prison Release Outfit." *PeopleStyle*, June 26, 2007. http://stylenews.people.com/.

Douglas, Ann. *Terrible Honesty: Mongrel Manhattan in the 1920s*. New York: Farrar, Straus and Giroux, 1995.

Douglas, George H. *The Early Days of Radio Broadcasting*. Jefferson, NC: McFarland & Company, 1987.

Douglas, Susan J. *Enlightened Sexism: The Seductive Message That Feminism's Work Is Done*. New York: Henry Holt, 2010.

———. "*Jersey Shore*: Ironic Viewing." In *How to Watch Television*, edited by Evan Thompson and Jason Mittell. New York: New York University Press, 2013.

———. *Listening In: Radio and the American Imagination*. New York: Times Books, 1999.

Douglas, Susan J., and Meredith W. Michaels. *The Mommy Myth: The Idealization of Motherhood and How It Has Undermined All Women*. New York: Free Press, 2005.

Driessens, Olivier. "Celebrity Capital: Redefining Celebrity Using Field Theory." *Theoretical Sociology* 42 (August 2013).

Duboff, Josh. "Examining Beyoncé's Social Media Mastery: Less Is Always More." *Vanity Fair*, September 16, 2016. https://www.vanityfair.com.

Dumenco, Simon. "The Media Guy: In the Celeb-azine Universe, Subtle Shades of Stupidity." *Advertising Age*, September 5, 2005.

Dyer, Richard. *Heavenly Bodies: Film Stars and Society*. 2nd ed. London: Routledge, 2003.

———. *Stars*. London: BFI Publishing, 1998.

Eastman, Susan Tyler. "Sportscasters." In *The Encyclopedia of Radio*, edited by Christopher Sterling, New York: Fitzroy Dearborn, 2004.

Eberly, Philip K. *Music in the Air: America's Changing Tastes in Popular Music, 1920–1980*. New York: Hastings House, 1982.

Edgerton, Gary. *The Columbia History of American Television*. New York: Columbia University Press, 2009.

Ellis, Chris, and Julie Ellis. *The Mammoth Book of Celebrity Murder*. New York: Carroll and Graf, 2005.

Ely, Melvin Patrick. *The Adventures of* Amos'n'Andy: *A Social History of an American Phenomenon*. Charlottesville: University of Virginia Press, 2001.

Emery, Michael, and Edwin Emery. *The Press and America: An Interpretive History of the Mass Media*. Englewood Cliffs, NJ: Prentice Hall, 1988.

Ennis, Philip. *The Seventh Stream: The Emergence of RocknRoll in American Popular Music*. Hanover, NH: Wesleyan University Pres, 1992.

Erenberg, Lewis. *The Greatest Fight of Our Generation: Louis vs. Schmeling*. New York: Oxford University Press, 2006.

Everrett, Walter. *The Beatles as Musicians: The Quarry Men through Rubber Soul*. Oxford: Oxford University Press, 2001.

Fairclough, Kirsty. "Fame Is a Losing Game: Gossip Blogging, Bitch Culture, and Postfeminism." *Genders* 48 (2008).

Faraci, Devin. "Talkie Terror: The Transition from Silents to Sound." Birth. Movies. Death, August 31, 2014. http://birthmoviesdeath.com.

Faragher, John Mack, Mari Jo Buhle, Daniel Czitrom, and Susan H. Armitage. *Out of Many: A History of the American People*. 2nd ed. Upper Saddle River, NJ: Prentice Hall, 1997.

Fastenberg, Dan. "Top Ten Presidential Pop Culture Moments." *Time*, July 29, 2010. http://content.time.com/.

Feasey, R. "Reading *Heat*: The Meanings and Pleasures of Star Fashions and Celebrity Gossip." *Continuum: Journal of Media & Cultural Studies* 22 (2008): 687–99.

Fiske, John. "The Cultural Economy of Fandom." In *The Adoring Audience: Fan Culture and Popular Media*, edited by Lisa A. Lewis. New York: Routledge, 1992.

Fornatale, Pete, and Josh Mills. *Radio in the Television Age*. New York: Overlook Books, 1980.

Freydkin, Donna. "Lilith Fair: Lovely, Lively, and Long Overdue." *CNN*, July 28, 1998. http://www.cnn.com.

Frith, Simon. "Popular Music: Critical Concepts in Media and Cultural Studies." *Music and Identity* 4 (2004).

———. *Sound Effects: Youth, Leisure, and the Politics of Rock 'n' Roll*. New York: Pantheon, 1981.

Fry, Richard, and Rakesh Kochhar. "America's Wealth Gap between Middle-Income and Upper-Income Families Is Widest on Record." *Pew Research*, December 17, 2014. http://www.pewresearch.org.

Gabler, Neal. "Grand Delusion, Being Famous vs. Being a Celebrity." *Los Angeles Times*, July 25, 1999.

———. *Life: The Movie*. New York: Vintage Books, 1998.

———. *Winchell: Gossip, Power and the Culture of Celebrity*. New York: Alfred A. Knopf, 1994.

Gamson, Joshua. *Claims to Fame: Celebrity in Contemporary America*. Berkeley: University of California Press, 1994.

Gathman, Dave. "Elgin's Madman Muntz Lived Up to His Name." *Chicago Tribune*, October 31, 2015. http://www.chicagotribune.com.

Giles, David C. *Illusions of Immortality*. New York: St. Martin's Press, 2000.

———. "Parasocial Interaction: A Review of the Literature and a Model for Future Research." *Media Psychology* 4 (2002): 279–305.

Gledhill, C. *Stardom: Industry of Desire*. New York: Routledge, 1991.

Glynn, Kevin. *Tabloid Culture: Trash Taste, Popular Power, and the Transformation of American Television*. Durham, NC: Duke University Press, 2000.

Goffman, Erving. *The Presentation of Self in Everyday Life*. Garden City, NY: Doubleday, 1959.

Goldberg, Lesley. "HBO's 'Westworld,' with $100 Million Price Tag, Faces Huge Expectations." *Hollywood Reporter*, October 1, 2016.

Goldman, David. "Music's Lost Decade." *CNN Money*, February 3, 2010. http://money .cnn.com.

Goodman, Tim. "Milton Berle, 1908–2002. 'Mr. Television' Dies at 93." *SFGate*, March 28, 2002. http://www.sfgate.com.

Goodwin, Andrew, and Simon Frith. *On Record: Rock, Pop, and the Written Word*. New York: Pantheon, 1990.

Goodwin, Doris Kearns. *No Ordinary Time: Franklin and Eleanor Roosevelt: The Home Front in World War II*. New York: Simon & Schuster, 1994.

Gowan, Michael. "Requiem for Napster." *PC World*, May 18, 2002. https://www.pcworld .idg.com.

Graser, Marc. "Coke Builds 'Harmony' with 'Idol.'" *Variety*, May 12, 2011. http://variety .com.

Green, Melanie C., Timothy C. Brock, and Geoff F. Kaufman. "Understanding Media Enjoyment: The Role of Transportation into Narrative Worlds." *Communication Theory* 14 (2004): 311–27.

Greenburg, Zach O'Malley. "Justin Bieber on the Business of Social Media." *Forbes*, June 22, 2012. https://www.forbes.com.

Gregory, Neal, and Janice Gregory. *When Elvis Died*. New York: Scripps, 1992.

Guendouzi, Jacqueline. "'You'll Think We're Always Bitching': The Functions of Cooperativity and Competition in Women's Gossip." *Discourse Studies* 3 (2001).

Habermas, Jürgen. *The Structural Transformation of the Public Sphere*. 6th ed. Cambridge, MA: MIT Press, 1991.

Hall, Stuart. "Encoding, Decoding." In *The Cultural Studies Reader*, edited by Simon During, 90–103. New York: Routledge, 1993.

Halper, Donna L. "Talent Shows." In *Encyclopedia of Radio*, edited by Christopher Sterling. New York: Fitzroy Dearborn, 2004.

Halpern, Jake. *Fame Junkies: The Hidden Truth behind America's Favorite Addiction*. New York: Houghton Mifflin. 2008.

Hamilton, Peter, and Roger Hargreaves. *The Beautiful and the Damned: The Creation of Identity in Nineteenth Century Photography*. Hampshire, UK: Lund Humphries, 2001.

Harris, Neil. *Humbug: The Art of P. T. Barnum*. Chicago: University of Chicago Press, 1981.

Harvey, David. *A Brief History of Neoliberalism*. New York: Oxford University Press, 2005.

Henderson, Amy. "Media and the Rise of Celebrity Culture." *OAH Magazine of History* 6 (1992).

Hermes, Joke. "Reading Gossip Magazines: The Imagined Communities of 'Gossip' and 'Camp.'" In *The Celebrity Culture Reader*, edited by P. David Marshall. New York: Routledge, 2006.

———. *Reading Women's Magazines: An Analysis of Everyday Media Use*. Cambridge: Polity Press, 1995.

Herwitz, Daniel. *The Star as Icon: Celebrity in the Age of Mass Consumption*. New York: Columbia University Press, 2006.

Hilmes, Michele. *Radio Voices*. Minneapolis: University of Minnesota Press, 1997.

Hinkle, Annette. "Summer of '61: Biography's Fresh Take on Roger Maris." *Sag Harbor Express*, June 9, 2010. http://sagharborexpress.com.

Holmes, Su, and Diane Negra, eds. *In the Limelight and under the Microscope: Forms and Functions of Female Celebrity*. New York: Continuum, 2011.

Holmes, Su, and Sean Redmond. *Framing Celebrity: New Directions in Celebrity Culture*. New York: Routledge. 2006.

Horton, Donald, and R. Richard Wohl. "Mass Communication and Para-social Interaction." *Psychiatry* 19 (1956): 215–29.

Howe, Pete. *Paparazzi: And Our Obsession with Celebrity*. New York: Artisan Books, 2005.

Huggins, Nathan Irvin. *Harlem Renaissance*. New York: Oxford University Press, 1971.

Ilson, Bernie. *Sundays with Sullivan: How* The Ed Sullivan Show *Brought Elvis, the Beatles, and Culture to America*. Lanham, MD: Taylor Trade Publishing, 2008.

Ives, Nat. "Guess Who's Not Getting Any Fatter! Celeb Mags Max Out." *Advertising Age*, April 9, 2007.

Izadi, Elahe. "This Is How David Bowie Confronted MTV When It Was Still Ignoring Black Artists." *Washington Post*, January 11, 2016. https://www.washingtonpost.com.

Jackson, John A. *Big Beat Heat: Alan Freed and the Early Years of Rock and Roll*. New York: Schirmer Books, 1995.

Jaggar, Alison. "Love and Knowledge: Emotion in Feminist Epistemology." *Inquiry* 32 (1989): 151–76.

Jensen, Joli. "Fandom as Pathology: The Consequences of Characterization." In *The Adoring Audience: Fan Culture and Popular Media*, edited by Lisa A. Lewis. New York: Routledge, 1992.

Johansson, Sofia. "'They Just Make Sense': Tabloid Newspapers as an Alternative Public Sphere." In *Media and Public Spheres*, edited by R. Butsch, 83–95. New York: Palgrave, 2007.

Jonas-Hain, Samantha. "Starstruck Fight It Out with 'Team' T-shirts." *Fox*, June 29, 2006. http://www.foxnews.com.

Kahn, Roger. "Pursuit of No. 60: The Ordeal of Roger Maris." *Sports Illustrated*, October 2, 1961. https://www.si.com.

Katz, Ephraim. *The Film Encyclopedia*. New York: Perigree Books, 1979.

Kaufman, Gil. "'Britney Spears Economy' Brings in Millions for Magazines, Label, Paparazzi." MTV, January 24, 2008. http://www.mtv.com/news/.

Kelly, Keith J. "Celebrity Magazines Aren't Dead Yet." *New York Post*, February 16, 2016. https://nypost.com.

Kenney, William. *The Phonograph and Recorded Music in American Life, 1870–1945*. New York: Oxford University Press, 1999.

Khamis, Susie, Lawrence Ang, and Raymond Welling. "Self-Branding, 'Micro-Celebrity' and the Rise of Social Media Influencers." *Celebrity Studies* 8 (2017): 194.

Kirkpatrick, Emily. "Social Media Star James Charles Is Named First Male CoverGirl!" *PeopleStyle*, October 11, 2016. http://people.com.

Kissell, Rick. "An Eye-Land Paradise: CBS Sets Summer Record with Socko 'Survivor.'" *Variety*, August 25, 2000.

Klam, Julie. *The Stars in Our Eyes: The Famous, the Infamous, and Why We Care Way Too Much about Them*. New York: Riverhead Books, 2017.

Krämer, Nicole, and Stephan Winter. "Impression Management 2.0: The Relationship of Self-Esteem, Extraversion, Self-Efficacy, and Self-Presentation within Social Networking Sites." *Journal of Media Psychology* 20 (2008): 106–16.

Lai, Adrienne. "Glitter and Grain: Aura and Authenticity in the Celebrity Photographs of Juergen Teller." In *Framing Celebrity: New Directions in Celebrity Culture*, edited by Su Holmes and Sean Redmond, 215–30. New York: Routledge, 2006.

Lambert, Bruce. "At 50, Levittown Contends with Its Legacy of Bias." *New York Times*, September 28, 1997. http://www.nytimes.com.

Langer, John. "Television's 'Personality System.'" In *The Celebrity Culture Reader*, edited by P. David Marshall. London: Routledge, 2006.

Larson, Peter. "Johnny Carson's Best 'Tonight Show' Interviews Get New Life on TCM." *Orange County Register*, March 3, 2014.

Lears, T. J. Jackson. *Fables of Abundance: A Cultural History of Advertising in America*. New York: Basic Books, 1994.

Lee, Matthew. "Strict Liability and the Anti-Paparazzi Act: The Best Solution to Protect Children of Celebrities." *Hastings Law Journal Online* 66. http://www.hastingslaw-journal.org.

Leonard, Neil. "The Impact of Mechanization." In *American Music: From Storyville to Woodstock*, edited by Charles Nanry. New Brunswick: Transaction Books, 1972.

———. *Jazz and the White Americans: The Acceptance of a New Art Form*. Chicago: University of Chicago Press, 1962.

Levine, Lawrence W. "William Shakespeare and the American People: A Study in Cultural Transformation." *American Historical Review* 89 (1984): 34–66.

Lewis, Robert M. *From Traveling Show to Vaudeville: Theatrical Spectacle in America, 1830–1910*. Baltimore: John Hopkins University Press, 2003.

Lipsitz, George. *Rainbow at Midnight: Labor and Culture in the 1940s*. Urbana: University of Illinois Press, 1994.

Loiperdinger, M., and B. Elzer. "Lumiere's Arrival of the Train: Cinema's Founding Myth." *Moving Image* 4 (2004): 89–118. Retrieved January 20, 2017, from Project MUSE database.

Lott, Eric. "White Like Me: Racial Cross-Dressing and the Construction of American Whiteness." In *Cultures of United States Imperialism*, edited by Amy Kaplan and Donald E. Pease. Durham, NC: Duke University Press, 1993.

Lowenthal, Leo. "Biographies in Popular Magazines." In *Radio Research, 1942–43*, edited by Paul Lazarsfeld and Frank Stanton. New York: Duell, Sloan, and Pearce, 1944.

Marshall, P. David. *Celebrity and Power: Fame in Contemporary Culture*. Minneapolis: University of Minnesota Press, 1997.

———. "The Celebrity Legacy of the Beatles." In *The Celebrity Culture Reader*, edited by P. David Marshall. New York: Routledge, 2006.

———. "Intimately Intertwined in the Most Public Way: Celebrity and Journalism." In *The Celebrity Culture Reader*, edited by P. David Marshall. New York: Routledge, 2006.

———. Introduction to *The Celebrity Culture Reader*, edited by P. David Marshall. New York: Routledge, 2006.

Marwick, Alice E. *Status Update: Celebrity, Publicity and Branding in the Social Media Age*. New Haven: Yale University Press, 2013.

Marwick, Alice E., and danah boyd. "I Tweet Honestly, I Tweet Passionately: Twitter Users, Context Collapse, and the Imagined Audience." *New Media & Society* 13 (2010): 122.

Matos, Michaelangelo. "1966 vs. 1971: When 'Rock 'n' Roll' Became 'Rock' and What We Lost." September 22, 2016. http://www.npr.org.

McAlister, Melanie. *Epic Encounters: Culture, Media, and U.S. Interests in the Middle East, 1945–2000*. Berkeley: University of California Press, 2001.

McClean, Amanda Scheiner. *Keeping Up the Kardashian Brand: Celebrity, Materialism, and Sexuality*. Lanham, MD: Lexington Books, 2014.

McCracken, Allison. "'God's Gift to Us Girls': Crooning, Gender, and the Re-Creation of American Popular Song, 1928–1933." *American Music* 17 (1999).

———. *Real Men Don't Sing: Crooning in American Culture*. Chapel Hill, NC: Duke University Press, 2015.

———. "Rudy Vallee." In *The Encyclopedia of Radio*, edited by Christopher Sterling. New York: Fitzroy Dearborn, 2004.

McCutcheon, Lynn E., John Maltby, James Houran, and Diane D. Ashe. *Celebrity Worshippers: Inside the Minds of Stargazers*. Baltimore: Publish America, 2004.

McDonald, Paul. *Hollywood Stardom*. Malden, MA: Wiley Blackwell, 2013.

———. *The Star System: Hollywood's Production of Popular Identities*. London: Wallflower Press, 2000.

McDonnell, Andrea. *Reading Celebrity Gossip Magazines*. London: Polity Press, 2014.

———. "Stars in Space: Celebrity Gossip Magazines, Guilt, and the Liminoid Airport." *Critical Studies in Media Communication* (2015). doi:10.1080/15295036.2015.1033730.

McDonnell, Andrea, and Clare M. Mehta. "We Could Never Be Friends: Representing Cross-Sex Friendship on Celebrity Gossip Websites." *Psychology of Popular Media Culture* (2014). doi:10.1037/ppm0000032.

McRobbie, Angela. *Feminism and Youth Culture: From 'Jackie' to 'Just Seventeen'*. Houndmills, Basingstoke, Hampshire: Macmillan, 1991.

Merritt, Russel. "Nickelodeon Theaters, 1905–1914: Building an Audience for the Movies." In *The American Film Industry*, edited by Tim Balio, 83–102. Madison: University of Wisconsin Press, 1985.

Merton, Robert K., Marjorie Fiske Lowenthal, and Alberta Curtis. *Mass Persuasion: The Social Psychology of a War Bond Drive.* New York: Harper & Brothers. 1946.

Meserole, Mike. "Arledge Created Monday Night Football." ESPN.com, December 6, 2002. http://www.espn.com.

Meyrowitz, Joshua. *No Sense of Place: The Impact of Electronic Media on Social Behavior.* New York: Oxford University Press, 1985.

Mifflin, Lawrie. "The Media Business: Simpson Case Gives Cable an Edge on the Networks." *New York Times,* February 20, 1995. https://www.nytimes.com/.

Millard, Andre. *America on Record: A History of Recorded Sound.* Cambridge: Cambridge University Press, 1995.

Miller, Julie. "The Evolution of Hollywood's Red Carpet, from the Golden Age to the GlamCam360." *Vanity Fair,* August 11, 2014.

Monllos, Kristina. "Why More Brands Are Adding Young Influencers to Their Marketing and Creative Teams." *Adweek,* September 18, 2017. http://www.adweek.com/.

Mroczka, Paul. "Broadway Disasters: The Astor Place Riot." In "Broadway Disasters, Broadway Theatre History," June 21, 2013. http://broadwayscene.com.

Murray, Susan. *Hitch Your Antenna to the Stars: Early Television and Broadcast Stardom.* New York: Routledge, 2005.

Murray, Susan, and Laurie Ouellette. *Reality TV: Remaking Television Culture.* New York: New York University Press, 2004.

Nasaw, David. *Going Out: The Rise and Fall of Public Amusements.* New York: Basic Books, 1993.

Nittle, Nadra Kareem. "How MTV Handled Accusations of Racism and Became More Inclusive." *ThoughtCo.,* February 27, 2018. https://www.thoughtco.com.

Ogren, Kathy J. *The Jazz Revolution: Twenties America and the Meaning of Jazz.* New York: Oxford University Press, 1992.

Ohmann, Richard. *Selling Culture: Magazines, Markets, and Class at the Turn of the Century.* New York: Verso, 1996.

Otterson, Joe. "Cable News Ratings: MSNBC, CNN, and Fox News Post Double-Digit Growth in Q-2." *Variety,* June 27, 2017. http://variety.com/.

Ouellette, Laurie. "Take Responsibility for Yourself: *Judge Judy* and the Neoliberal Citizen." In *Reality TV: Remaking Television Culture,* edited by Susan Murray and Laurie Ouellette, 231–50. New York: New York University Press, 2004.

Packer, George. "Celebrating Inequality." *New York Times,* May 19, 2013. http://www.nytimes.com/.

Pallotta, Frank, and Brian Stelter. "Super Bowl 50 Audience Is Third Largest in TV History." *CNN Media,* February 8, 2016. http://money.cnn.com.

Pautz, M. C. "The Decline in Average Weekly Cinema Attendance, 1930–2000." *Issues in Political Economy* 11 (2002). Retrieved from https://works.bepress.com.

Peck, Janice. *The Age of Oprah: Cultural Icon for the Neoliberal Era.* New York: Routledge, 2008.

Peretti, Burton W. *The Creation of Jazz.* Urbana: University of Illinois Press, 1992.

Pérez-Peña, Richard. "In Deepening Ad Decline, Sales Fall 8% at Magazines." *New York Times*, July 11, 2008. http://www.nytimes.com/.

Perry, Steve. "Ain't No Mountain High Enough: The Politics of Crossover." In *Facing the Music*, edited by Simon Frith. New York: Pantheon, 1988.

Petit, Stephanie. "#MeToo: Sexual Harassment and Assault Movement Tweeted over 500,000 Times as Celebs Share Stories." *People*, October 16, 2017. http://people .com/.

Petski, Denise. "'TRL': Eva Gutowski, Gabbie Hanna, and Gigi Gorgeous Tapped as Social Media Correspondents for MTV Show." *Deadline*, August 23, 2017. http:// deadline.com/.

Pitts, Michael, and Frank Hoffmann. *The Rise of the Crooners: Gene Austin, Russ Columbo, Bing Crosby, Nick Lucas, Jonny Marvin, and Rudy Vallee*. Lanham, MD: Scarecrow Press, 2002.

Ponce de Leon, Charles. *Self-Exposure: Human-Interest Journalism and the Emergence of Celebrity in America, 1890–1940*. Chapel Hill: University of North Carolina Press, 2002.

Potter, John. "Almost as Good as Presley: Caruso the Pop Idol." *Public Domain Review*, February 13, 2012. https://publicdomainreview.org/.

Pratte, Alf. "Bob Hope." In *The Encyclopedia of Radio*, edited by Christopher Sterling. New York: Fitzroy Dearborn, 2004.

Prior, Markus. *Post-Broadcast Democracy: How Media Choice Increases Inequality in Political Involvement and Polarizes Elections*. New York: Cambridge University Press, 2007.

Redmond, Sean. "Intimate Fame Everywhere." In *Framing Celebrity: New Directions in Celebrity Culture*, edited by Su Holmes and Sean Redmond. London: Taylor and Francis, 2006.

Robehmed, Natalie. "How Michelle Phan Built a $500 Million Company." *Forbes*, October 5, 2015. https://www.forbes.com/.

———. "No, Kim Kardashian Probably Didn't Make $80 Million from Her iPhone Game." *Forbes*, March 8, 2016. http://www.forbes.com/.

Rojek, Chris. *Celebrity*. London: Reaktion Books, 2001.

Rose, Tricia. *Black Noise: Rap Music and Black Culture in Contemporary America*. Hanover, NH: Wesleyan University Press, 1994.

Rowe, Douglas. "Full 2010–11: CBS Tops Viewership, Fox is No. 1 in Demo and Idol Remains Most-Watched." *TV Guide*, June 1, 2011. http://www.tvguide.com/.

Saltz, Jerry. "Art at Arm's Length: A History of the Selfie." *New York Magazine* 47 (2014): 71–75.

Sarmento, Mario. "The NBA on Network Television: A Historical Analysis." PhD diss., University of Florida, 1998.

Saxton, Alexander. "Blackface Minstrelsy and Jacksonian Ideology." *American Quarterly* 27 (1975): 3–28.

Scannell, Gerald R. *Media and Communication*. Thousand Oaks, CA: Sage, 2007.

Schickel, Richard. *Intimate Strangers: The Culture of Celebrity*. New York: Doubleday, 1986.

Schmid, David. "Idols of Destruction: Celebrity and the Serial Killer." In *Framing Celebrity: New Directions in Celebrity Culture*, edited by Su Holmes and Sean Redmond. London: Taylor and Francis, 2006.

———. *Natural Born Celebrities: Serial Killers in American Culture*. Chicago: University of Chicago Press, 2006.

Shafrir, Doree. "The Truth about Perez Hilton's Traffic." *Gawker*, July 10, 2007. http://gawker.com.

Shrumm, Regan. "Meet Jenny Lind, One of America's First Female Celebrities." National Museum of American History. http://americanhistory.si.edu.

Sidran, Ben. *Black Talk*. New York: Da Capo Press, 1971.

Siegel, Elizabeth. *Galleries of Friendship and Fame: A History of Nineteenth-Century Photograph Albums*. New Haven: Yale University Press, 2010.

Sisaro, Ben. "With a Tap of Taylor Swift's Fingers, Apple Retreated." *New York Times*, June 22, 2015. https://www.nytimes.com.

Slide, Anthony. *Inside the Hollywood Fan Magazine: A History of Star Makers, Fabricators, and Gossip Mongers*. Jackson: University Press of Mississippi, 2010.

Smart, Barry. *The Sport Star: Modern Sport and the Cultural Economy of Sporting Celebrity*. London: Sage, 2005.

Smith, Richard H., Terence J. Turner, Ron Garonzik, Colin W. Leach, Vannesa Urch-Druskat, and Christine M. Weston. "Envy and Schadenfreude." *Personality and Social Psychology Bulletin* 22 (1996): 158–68.

Smith, Stephen. "Radio: The Internet of the 1930s." American RadioWorks, November 10, 2014. http://www.americanradioworks.org.

Sneed, Tierney. "How John F Kennedy's Assassination Changed Television Forever." *US News and World Report*, November 14, 2013. https://www.usnews.com.

Solove, Daniel. "Should Celebrities Have Privacy? A Response to Jennifer Lawrence." *Teach Privacy*, November 24, 2014. https://teachprivacy.com.

Stacey, Jackie. "Feminine Fascinations: A Question of Identification?" In *The Celebrity Culture Reader*, edited by P. David Marshall, 266–68. New York: Routledge, 2006.

Staiger, Janet. "Seeing Stars." In *Stardom: Industry of Desire*, edited by Christine Gledhill. New York: Routledge, 1991.

Sternheimer, Karen. *Celebrity Culture and the American Dream: Stardom and Social Mobility*. London: Routledge, 2011.

Stone, Jeff. "California Passes New Paparazzi Drone Law to Protect Celebrity Children." *International Business Times*, October 1, 2014. http://www.ibtimes.com.

Storr, Anthony. *Music and the Mind*. New York: Free Press, 1993.

Street, John. *Mass Media, Politics, and Democracy*. 2nd ed. Basingstoke: Palgrave Macmillan, 2010.

Tadena, Nathalie. "For *Vanity Fair*, Online Buzz on Caitlyn Jenner Issue Drove Print Consumption." *Wall Street Journal*, October 7, 2015.

Taylor, Jim. "Sports: What Makes the Great Ones Great." *Psychology Today*, December 2, 2009. https://www.psychologytoday.com.

Taylor, Porcher R., Fernando M. Pinguelo, and Timothy D. Cedrone. "The Reverse-Morals Clause: The Unique Way to Save Talent's Reputation and Money in a New Era of Corporate Crimes and Scandals." *Cardozo Arts and Entertainment Law Journal* 28 (2010): 65–113.

Teitel, Amy Shira. "How NASA Broadcast Neil Armstrong from the Moon." *Popular Science*, February 6, 2016. http://www.popsci.com.

Thompson, John B. *The Media and Modernity*. Stanford: Stanford University Press, 1995.

Tichi, Cecelia. *Electronic Hearth: Creating an American Television Culture*. Oxford: Oxford University Press, 1992.

Travers, Peter. "Spice World." *Rolling Stone*, January 23, 1998. http://www.rollingstone.com.

Turner, Graeme. *Ordinary People and the Media: The Demotic Turn*. Los Angeles: Sage, 2010.

———. *Understanding Celebrity*. Los Angeles: Sage, 2004.

Uruburu, Paula. *American Eve: Evelyn Nesbit, Stanford White, the Birth of the "It" Girl, and the Crime of the Century*. New York: Riverhead Books, 2008.

Volpe, Andrea L. "The Cartes de Visite Craze." *New York Times*, August 6, 2013. https://opinionator.blogs.nytimes.com.

Wallace, Irving. *The Fabulous Showman: The Life and Times of P.T. Barnum*. New York: Knopf, 1959.

Ward, Ed, Geoffrey Stokes, and Ken Tucker. *Rock of Ages: The Rolling Stone History of Rock & Roll*. New York: Summit Books, 1986.

Watkins, Mel. *On the Real Side*. New York: Touchstone Books, 1994.

Weber, Bruce. "Robert Isabell, Who Turned Events into Wondrous Occasions, Dies at 57." *New York Times*, July 10, 2009, A17.

Wertheim, Arthur Frank. *Radio Comedy*. New York: Oxford University Press, 1979.

West, Shearer. *Portraiture*. New York: Oxford University Press. 2004.

Wheeler, Mark. *Celebrity Politics*. London: Polity, 2013.

Witheridge, Annette. "'I'd Rather Make $700 a Week Playing a Maid Than Working as One': How the FIRST Black Oscar Winner Dealt with Being Segregated from White *Gone with the Wind* Co-stars at Academy Awards." *Daily Mail*, February 25, 2016. http://www.dailymail.co.uk.

Zanger, Jules. "The Minstrel Show as Theater of Misrule." *Quarterly Journal of Speech* 60 (1974): 33–38.

INDEX

Murrow, Edward R., 160, *161*; back stage and, 162; in World War II, 161

music: authenticity and, 200; celebrity fanatic and, 207; concert of, 196–97, 203–4; disco, 211–12; fandom and, 123–24, 195; fan magazines for, 203, 207; films and, 210; folk, 201–2; gender norms and, 215–16; hyper-regimented celebrity culture in 1990s, 209–10; jazz, 128, 129–30, 158; *The Partridge Family*, 205–7; power of, 122; punk movement and, 213; race music, 129, 130; rhythm and blues, 158; rock, 202, 204–5, 216–17; rock 'n' roll, 9, 156–59, *157*, 191–92, 197–204; *Rolling Stone* on, 203; symbolic significance of, 195–96; teenybopper culture and, 181, 205–10, *206*, 222, 224. *See also* radio

music stars: associative identification of, 195–96; Beatles as, 197–201, *198*, 203–4; Beyoncé as, 62, 225–26, 246; Bieber as, 47, 224; Boy George as, 215–16; Cher as, 210–11; cross-platform promotion of, 210–13; Cyrus as, 70; Jackson as, 216–17, *217*, 218; Madonna as, 45, 214–15, *216*, 218; movies and, 210; Sinatra as, 144–45, *145*; social media and, 226–27; twenty-first century, 222–27; World War II and, 150. *See also* radio stars

music technology and distribution, 196; Caruso and, 126, 133; CDs as, 222–23; gramophone and, 125; in-car stereos as, 203; iTunes platform and, 223; microphone and, 127, 132–33; Napster and, 222–23; phonograph and, 123–26, 128–29; records as, 202; Spotify and, 223–24; stereo as, 202–3; streaming-only albums and, 225. *See also* radio

music video. *See* MTV

Namath, Joe, 185
narcissism, 5, 264

Nasaw, David, 66, 80
Negra, Diane, 55, 61
neoliberalism: celebrity culture and, 39–41; individualism and, 40; self-actualization and, 40–41; Trump and, 39
Nesbit, Evelyn, *84*, 89, 106; Gibson, C., and, 83; Thaw and, 83–84; vaudeville and, 85; White raping, 83, 84
New Deal, 39, 138
New Kids on the Block, 208–9
newspaper gossip columns, 144; back stage and, 140; destructive stories of, 109; Hopper as, 105, 106, 108–9; Lindbergh in, 143; Parsons as, 105–6, 108; Winchell starting, 141–42
newspapers: artist drawings in, 75; Cochran as journalist for, 78, 89; *Daily News* as, 106; "dramatic paragraphers" in, 79; Hearst owning, 80; jazz journalism in, 106, 108, 116–17; Keith and, 80; mass-circulation of, 77, 79, 83, 88; muckrakers for, 86–87; penny press and, 67; photography in, 75; post–Civil War period and, 77; Progressive movement and, 86–87; transportation systems and, 88
New York World, 78
nickelodeons, 92, 94
Nixon, Richard, *175*, 175–76, *179*, *191*
Normand, Mabel, 108
notoriety, 37

Oakley, Tyler, 250–51, 261
Obama, Barack, 138, 179
Odom, Lamar, 58
Onassis, Jacqueline Kennedy, 118, 119, 176–77
outlaw emotions, 48

Paltrow, Gwyneth, 257; Facebook page of, 244–45; front stage of, 245
paparazzi, 254; burden of celebrity and, 255; California laws on,

TRL. See *Total Request Live*
Trollope, Frances, 68–69
Trump, Donald, 37, 138, 262; neoliberalism and, 39; news coverage of, 263–64; reality television and, 2, 179, 263
Turner, Graeme, 252
Turner, Lana, 104
Tutankhamun (King), 15–16; immortality and, 17

ungovernable acts, 24–25, 175–76; public and, 245
urbanization: first impression and, 33; immigration and, 27–28, 42; leisure time and, 42, 257; World War II and African American, 155
U.S. v. Paramount et al, 115–16

Valentino, Rudolph, 42–43
Vallee, Rudy, *133, 134*
Van Doren, Charles, 171–72
vaudeville, 28; behind-the-scenes and, 260; Berle and, 168; celebrity production and, 78, 85; celebrity scandal and, 82, 85; films and, 93; Keith and, 79; morality and, 82; Nesbit and, 85; race and, 80–81; radio and, 136–37; television and, 167; Walker and, 81, *82*; Williams, B., in, 80–81, *82*

vlogging: beauty, on YouTube, 250; celebrity gossip and, 243; intimacy of, 251

Walker, George, 81, *82*
Walters, Barbara, 192
Warhol, Andy, 6
Waters, Ethel, 130
Weber, Max, 29
Weinstein, Harvey, 3, 47, 257
White, Stanford: Nesbit raped by, 83, 84; Thaw murdering, 83–85
Whiteman, Paul, 130
Williams, Bert, 80–81, *82*
Williams, Robin, 121
Williams, Ted, 150
Winchell, Walter, 141–43
Winfrey, Oprah, 182, *182*
Woods, Tiger, 190
"The Work of Art in the Age of Mechanical Reproduction" (Benjamin), 17–19
World War II: African American urbanization in, 155; Murrow in, 161; music stars and, 150; radio and, 151

Yo! MTV Raps, 218
YouTube, 252, 261; Bieber and, 224; LGBTQ audience and, 62, 250; viral, 250

Zamora, Pedro, 230

ABOUT THE AUTHORS

Susan J. Douglas is the Catherine Neafie Kellogg Professor of Communication Studies at the University of Michigan. She is the author of five books, including *The Rise of Enlightened Sexism* (2010), *Listening In: Radio and the American Imagination* (1999), and *Where the Girls Are: Growing Up Female with the Mass Media* (1994).

Andrea McDonnell is Associate Professor of Communication and Media Studies at Emmanuel College. She is the author of *Reading Celebrity Gossip Magazines* (Polity, 2014), and her work has appeared in *Critical Studies in Media Communication*, *Body Image*, and *Psychology of Popular Media Culture*.